BY CARRIE HARRIS

ON THE WALL

ILLUSTRATED BY STIPE KALAJŽIĆ

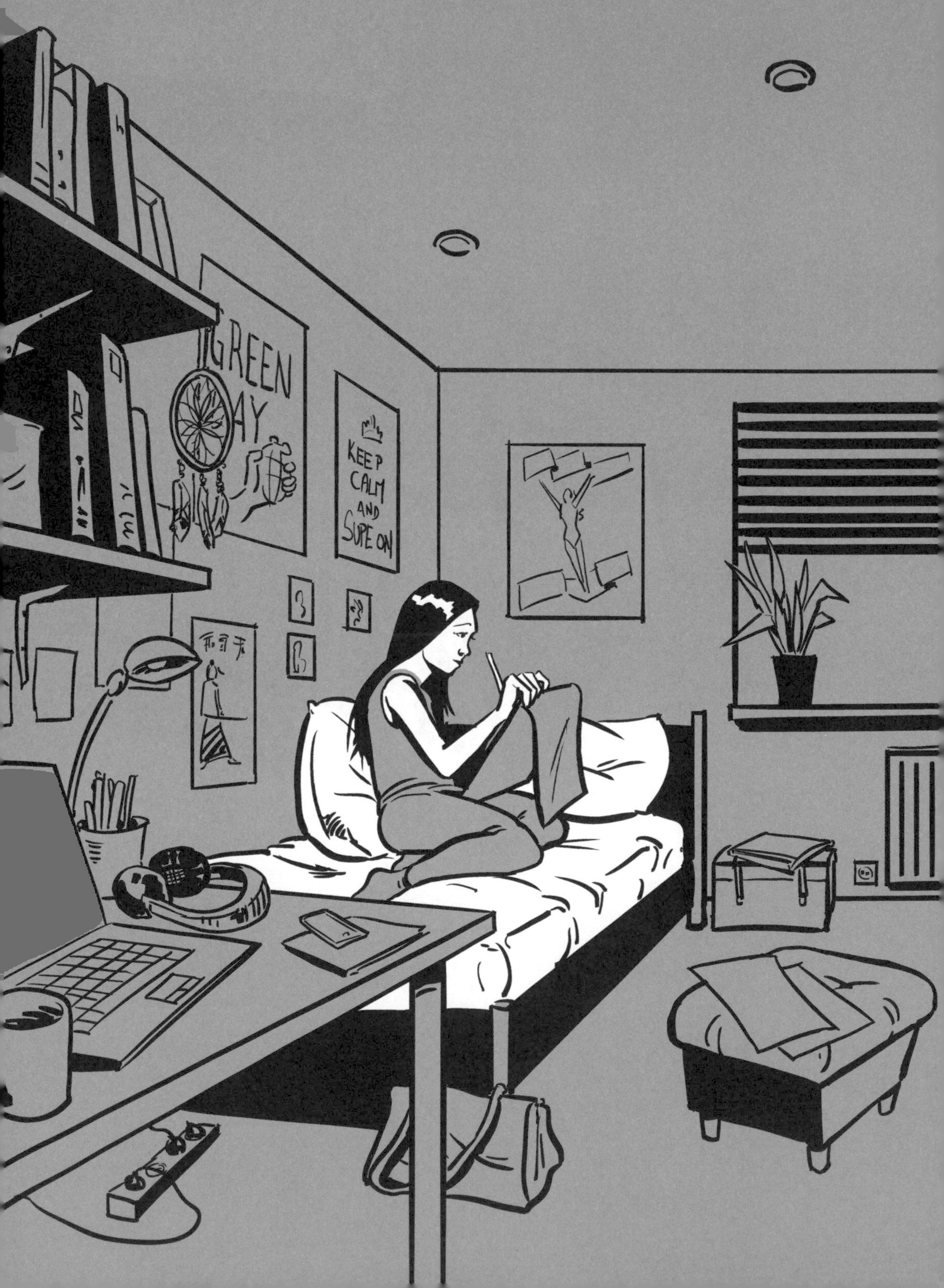
GREEN
AY
KEEP CALM AND SUPE ON

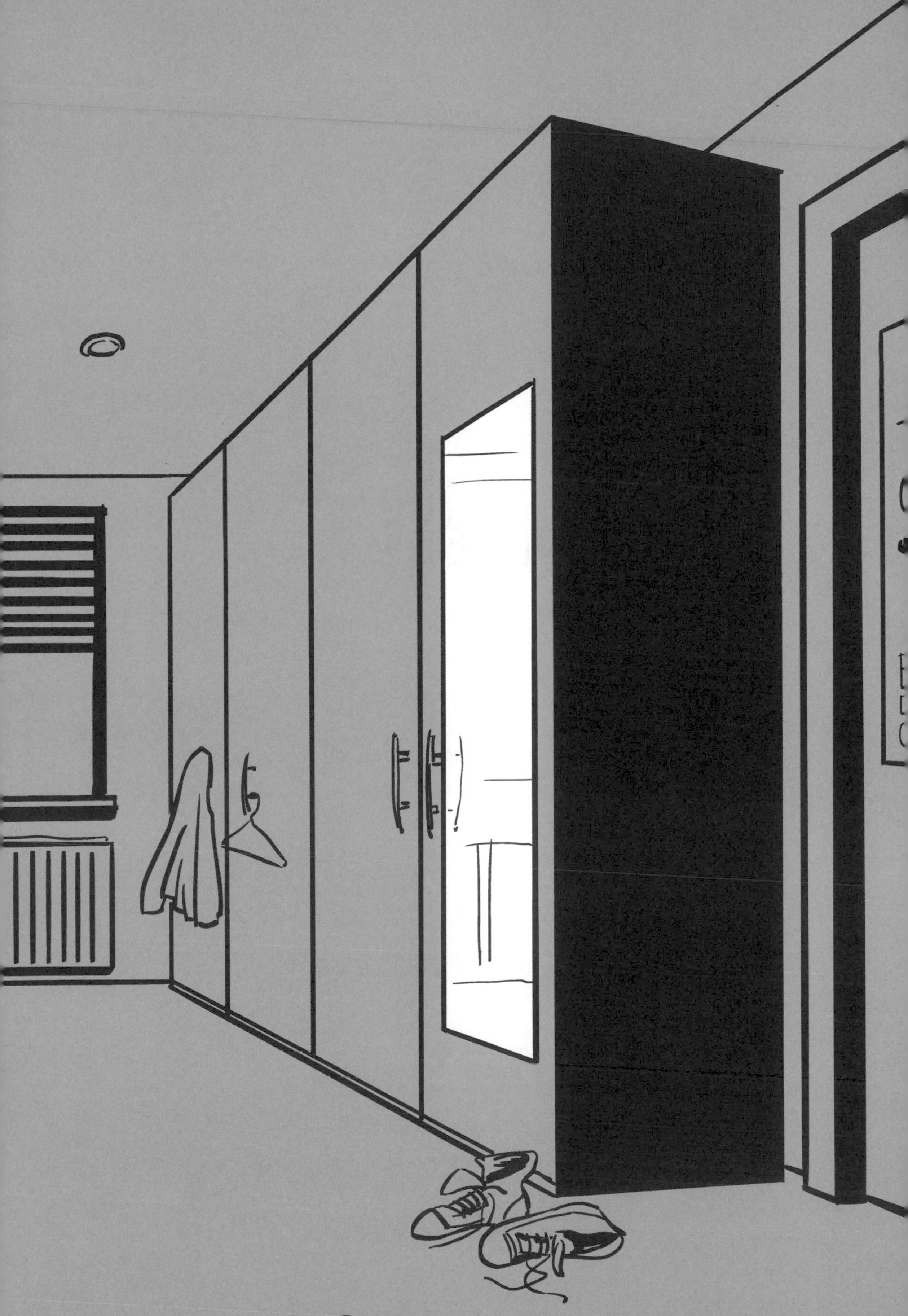

ON THE WALL

TEXT © 2017 CARRIE HARRIS
ILLUSTRATIONS © 2017 STIPE KALAJZIC

ISBN: 978-1-944937-15-7

WRITTEN BY CARRIE HARRIS
ILLUSTRATED BY STIPE KALAJZIC
PUBLISHED BY ONE PEACE BOOKS 2017

PRINTED IN CANADA

1 2 3 4 5 6 7 8 9 10

ONE PEACE BOOKS
43-32 22ND STREET STE 204 LONG ISLAND CITY NEW YORK 11101
WWW.ONEPEACEBOOKS.COM

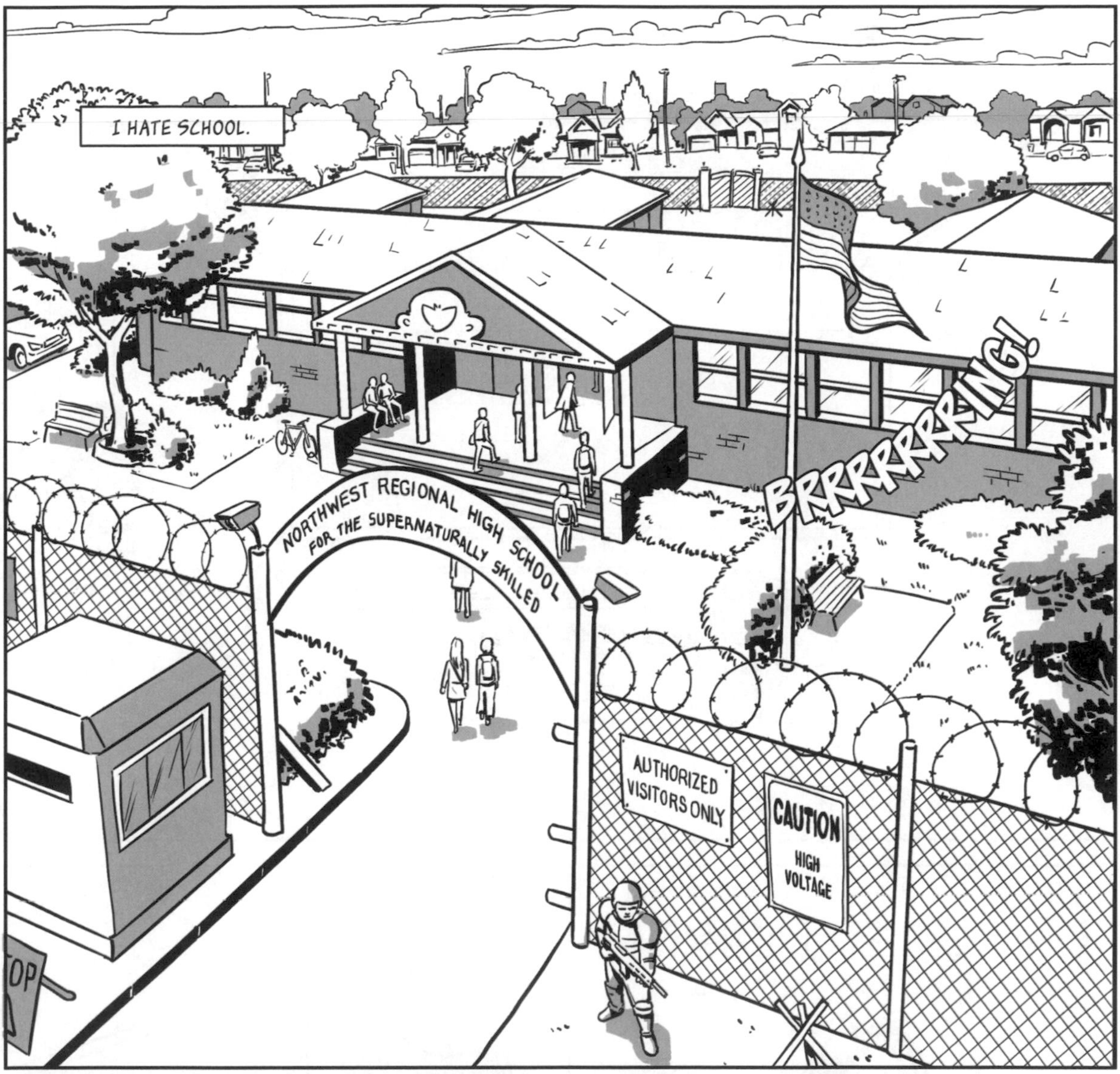
I HATE SCHOOL.
NORTHWEST REGIONAL HIGH SCHOOL
FOR THE SUPERNATURALLY SKILLED
BRRRRRRRING!
AUTHORIZED VISITORS ONLY
CAUTION
HIGH VOLTAGE

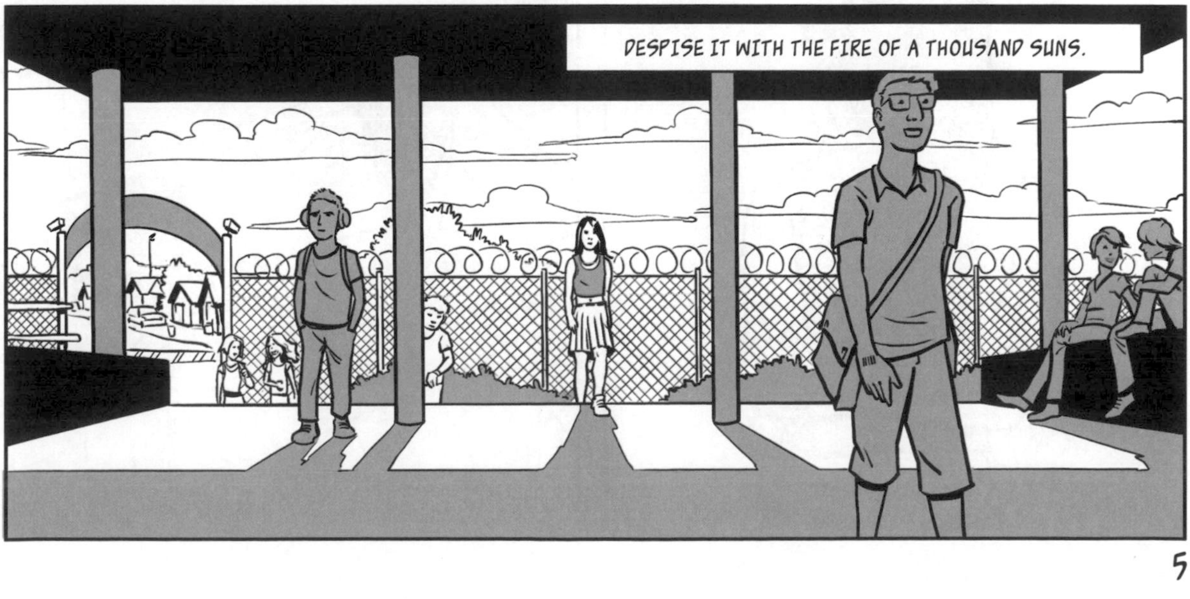
DESPISE IT WITH THE FIRE OF A THOUSAND SUNS.

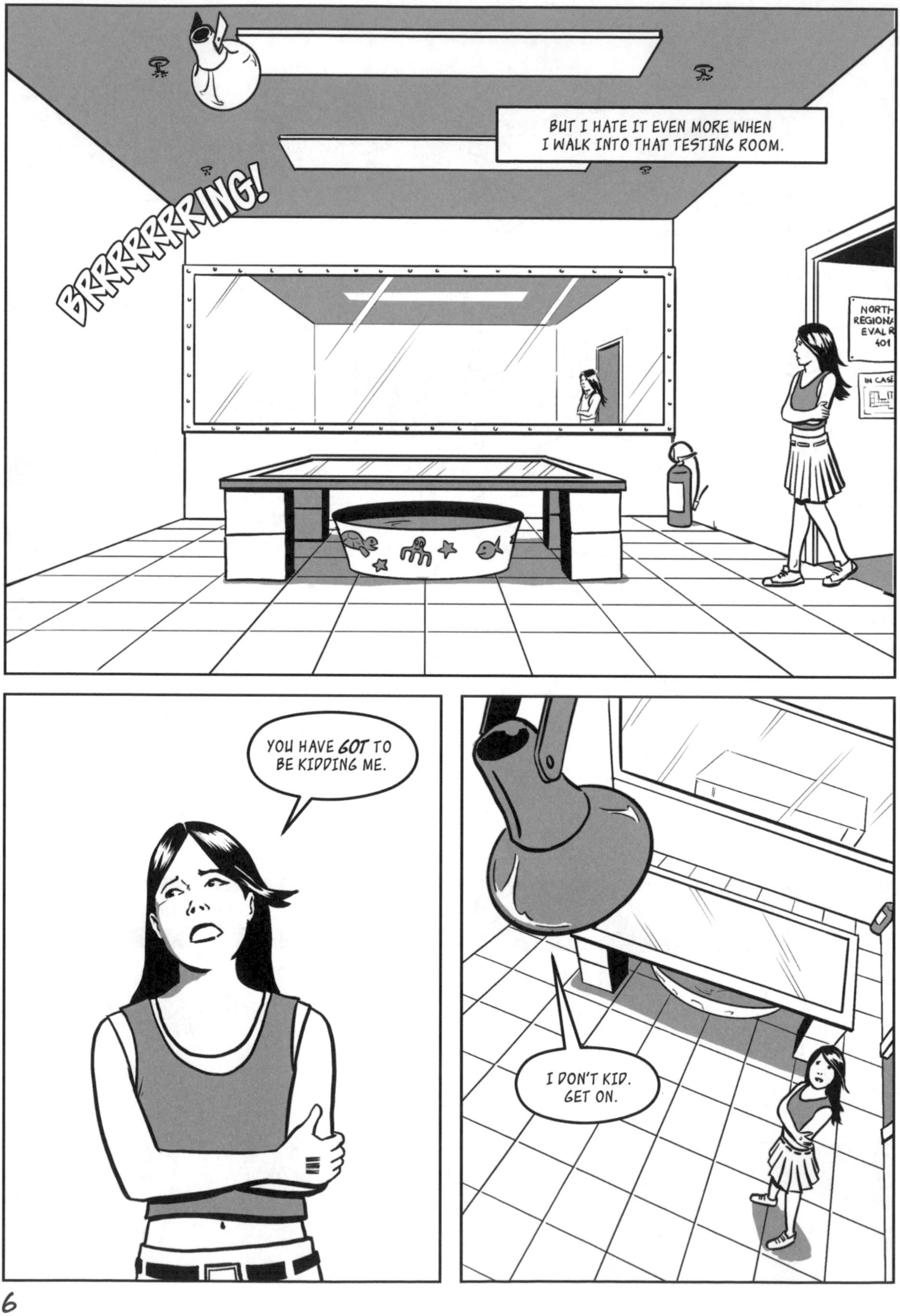
BUT I HATE IT EVEN MORE WHEN I WALK INTO THAT TESTING ROOM.
BRRRRRRRING!
NORTH
REGIONA
EVAL R
401
IN CAS
YOU HAVE *GOT* TO BE KIDDING ME.
I DON'T KID. GET ON.

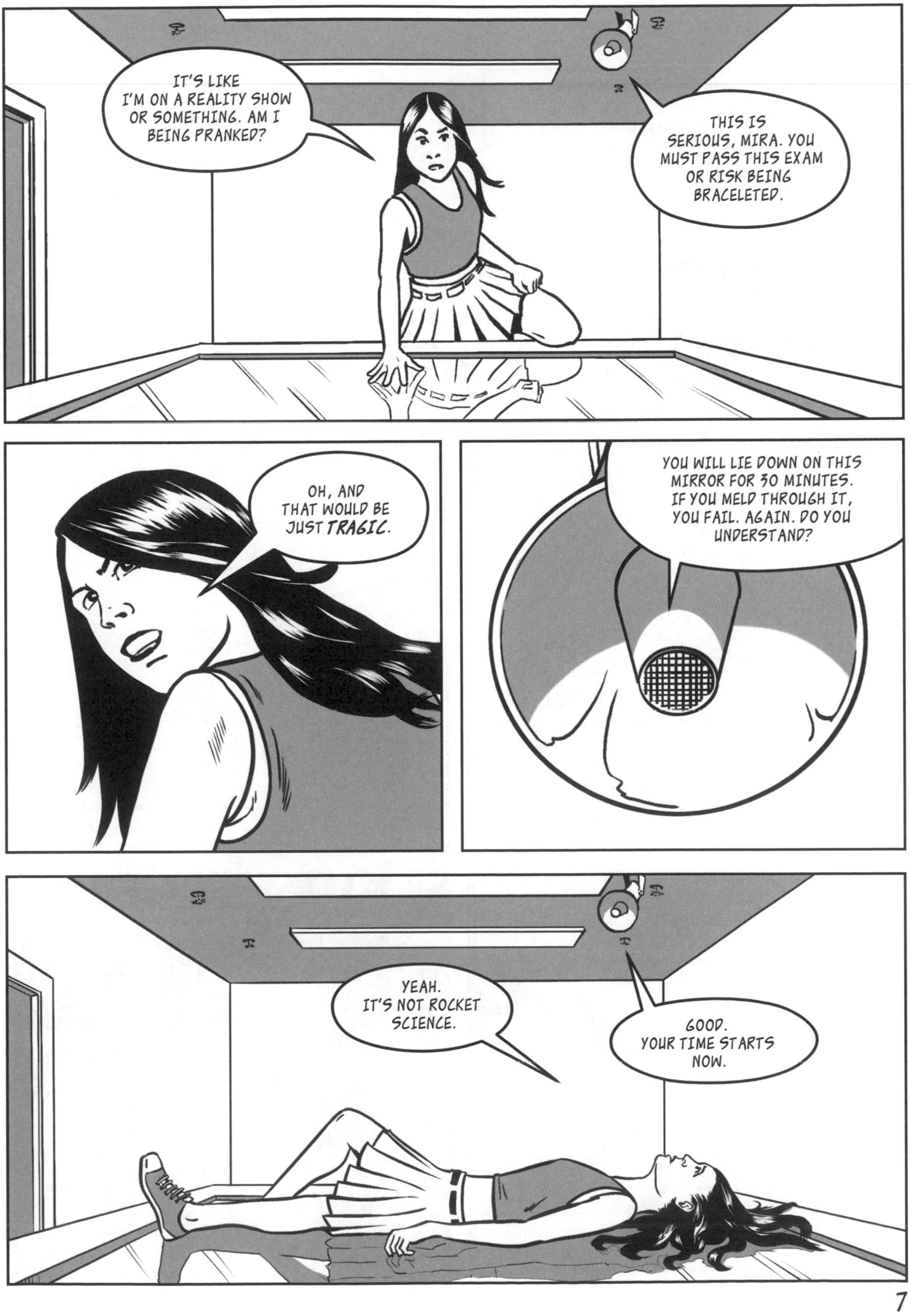
IT'S LIKE I'M ON A REALITY SHOW OR SOMETHING. AM I BEING PRANKED?
THIS IS SERIOUS, MIRA. YOU MUST PASS THIS EXAM OR RISK BEING BRACELETED.
OH, AND THAT WOULD BE JUST TRAGIC.
YOU WILL LIE DOWN ON THIS MIRROR FOR 30 MINUTES. IF YOU MELD THROUGH IT, YOU FAIL. AGAIN. DO YOU UNDERSTAND?
YEAH. IT'S NOT ROCKET SCIENCE.
GOOD. YOUR TIME STARTS NOW.

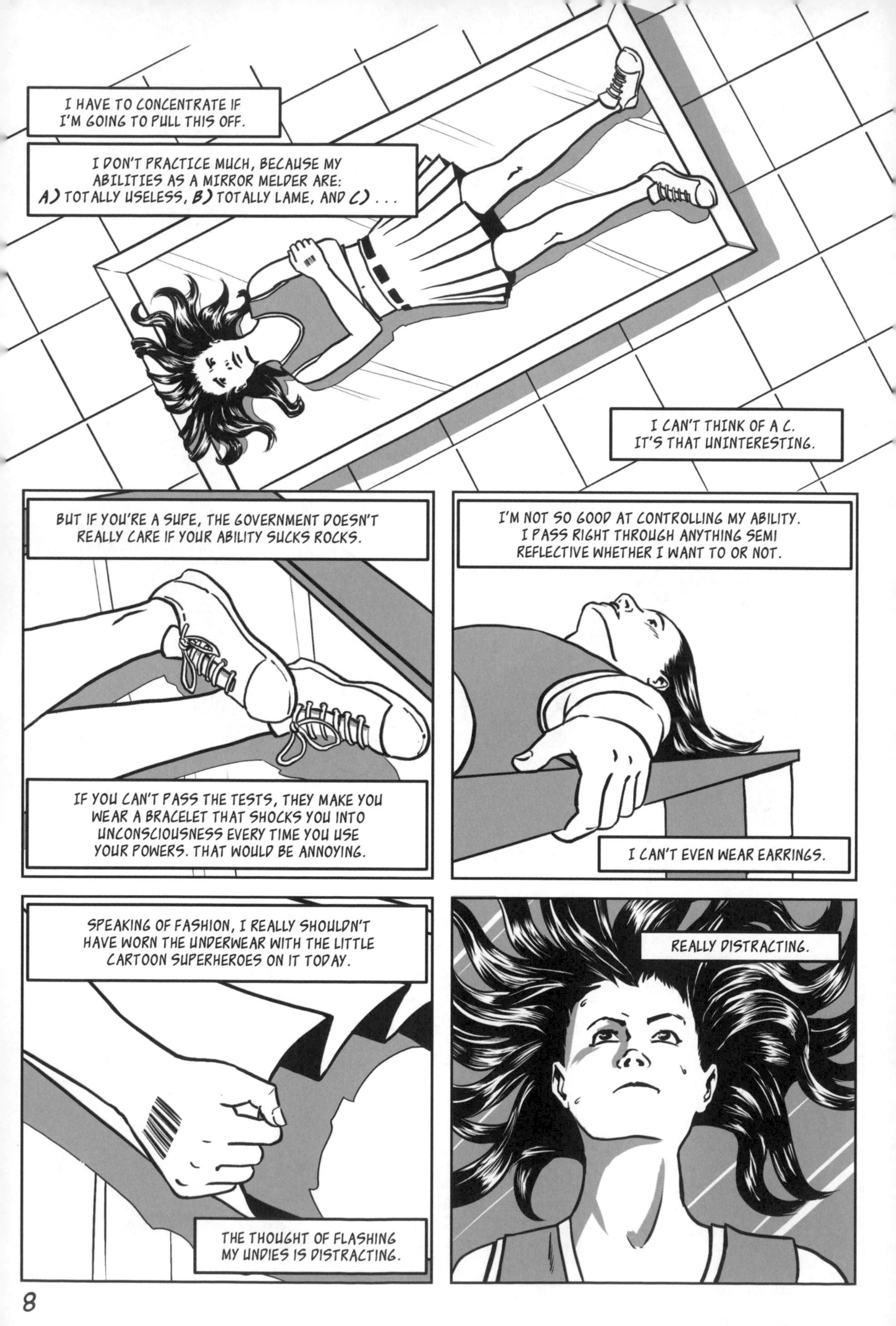
I HAVE TO CONCENTRATE IF I'M GOING TO PULL THIS OFF.
I DON'T PRACTICE MUCH, BECAUSE MY ABILITIES AS A MIRROR MELDER ARE: A) TOTALLY USELESS, B) TOTALLY LAME, AND C) . . .
I CAN'T THINK OF A C. IT'S THAT UNINTERESTING.
BUT IF YOU'RE A SUPE, THE GOVERNMENT DOESN'T REALLY CARE IF YOUR ABILITY SUCKS ROCKS.
IF YOU CAN'T PASS THE TESTS, THEY MAKE YOU WEAR A BRACELET THAT SHOCKS YOU INTO UNCONSCIOUSNESS EVERY TIME YOU USE YOUR POWERS. THAT WOULD BE ANNOYING.
I'M NOT SO GOOD AT CONTROLLING MY ABILITY. I PASS RIGHT THROUGH ANYTHING SEMI REFLECTIVE WHETHER I WANT TO OR NOT.
I CAN'T EVEN WEAR EARRINGS.
SPEAKING OF FASHION, I REALLY SHOULDN'T HAVE WORN THE UNDERWEAR WITH THE LITTLE CARTOON SUPERHEROES ON IT TODAY.
THE THOUGHT OF FLASHING MY UNDIES IS DISTRACTING.
REALLY DISTRACTING.

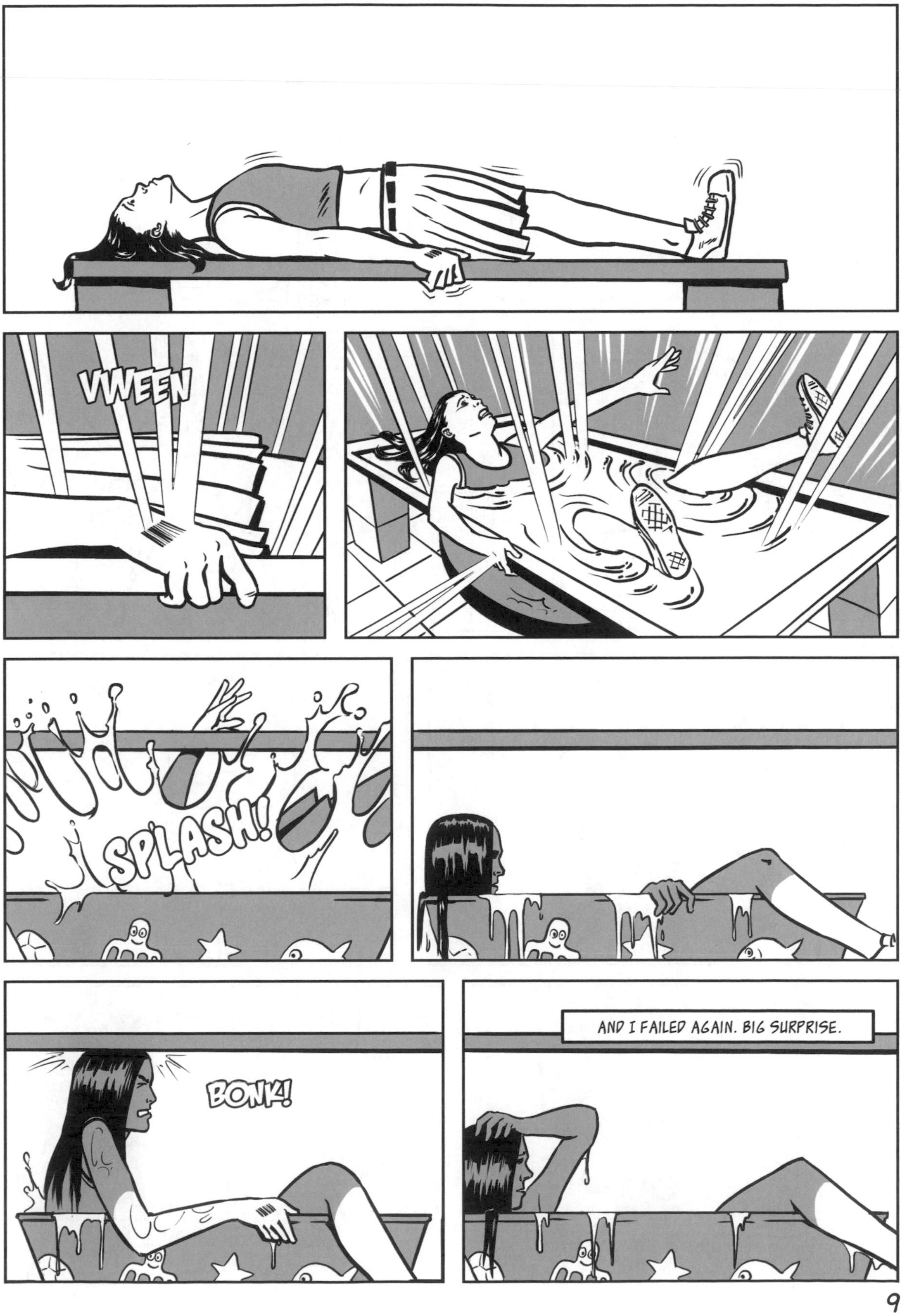
VWEEN
SPLASH!
BONK!
AND I FAILED AGAIN. BIG SURPRISE.

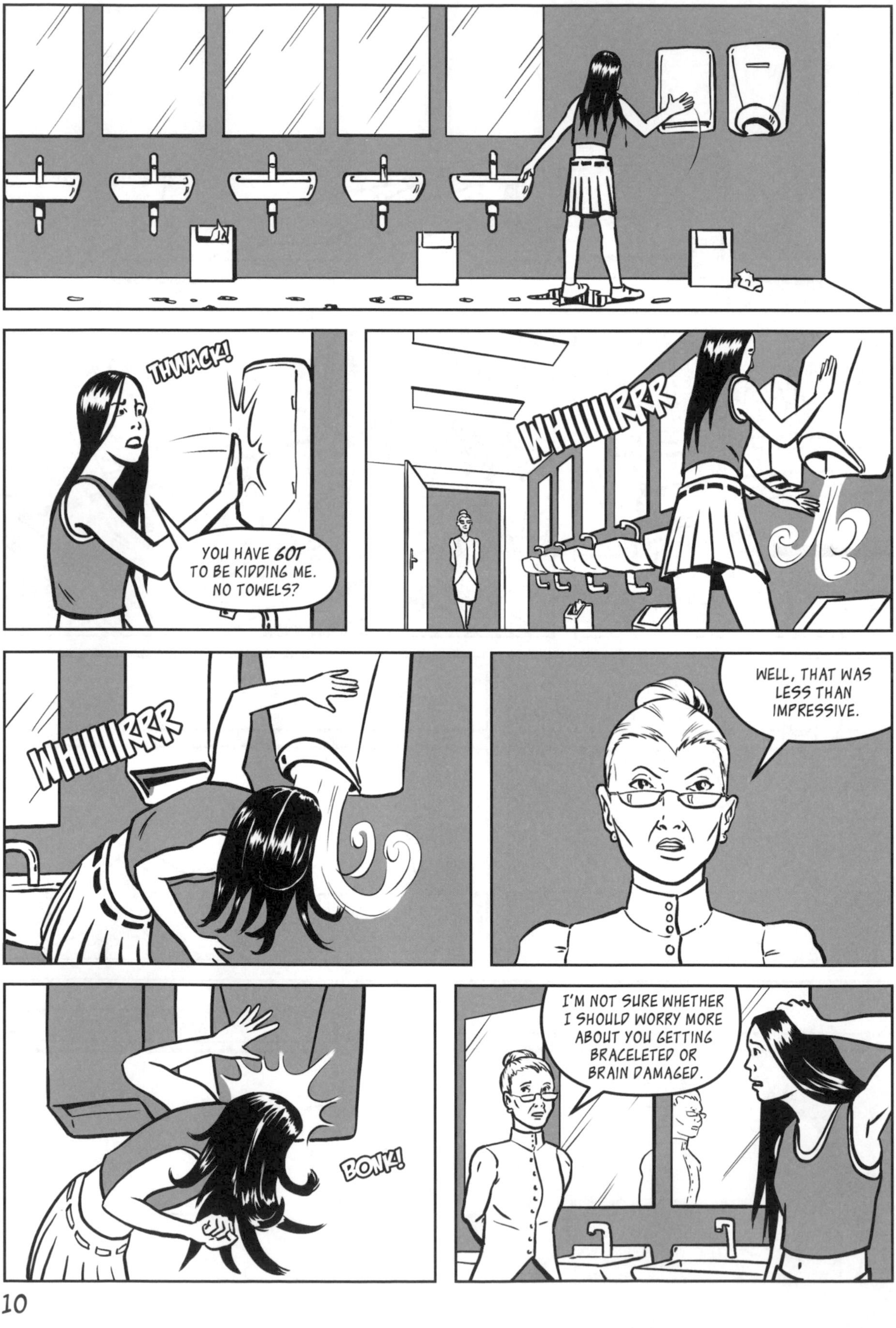
THWACK!
YOU HAVE GOT TO BE KIDDING ME. NO TOWELS?
WHIIIIIRRR
WHIIIIIRRR
WELL, THAT WAS LESS THAN IMPRESSIVE.
BONK!
I'M NOT SURE WHETHER I SHOULD WORRY MORE ABOUT YOU GETTING BRACELETED OR BRAIN DAMAGED.

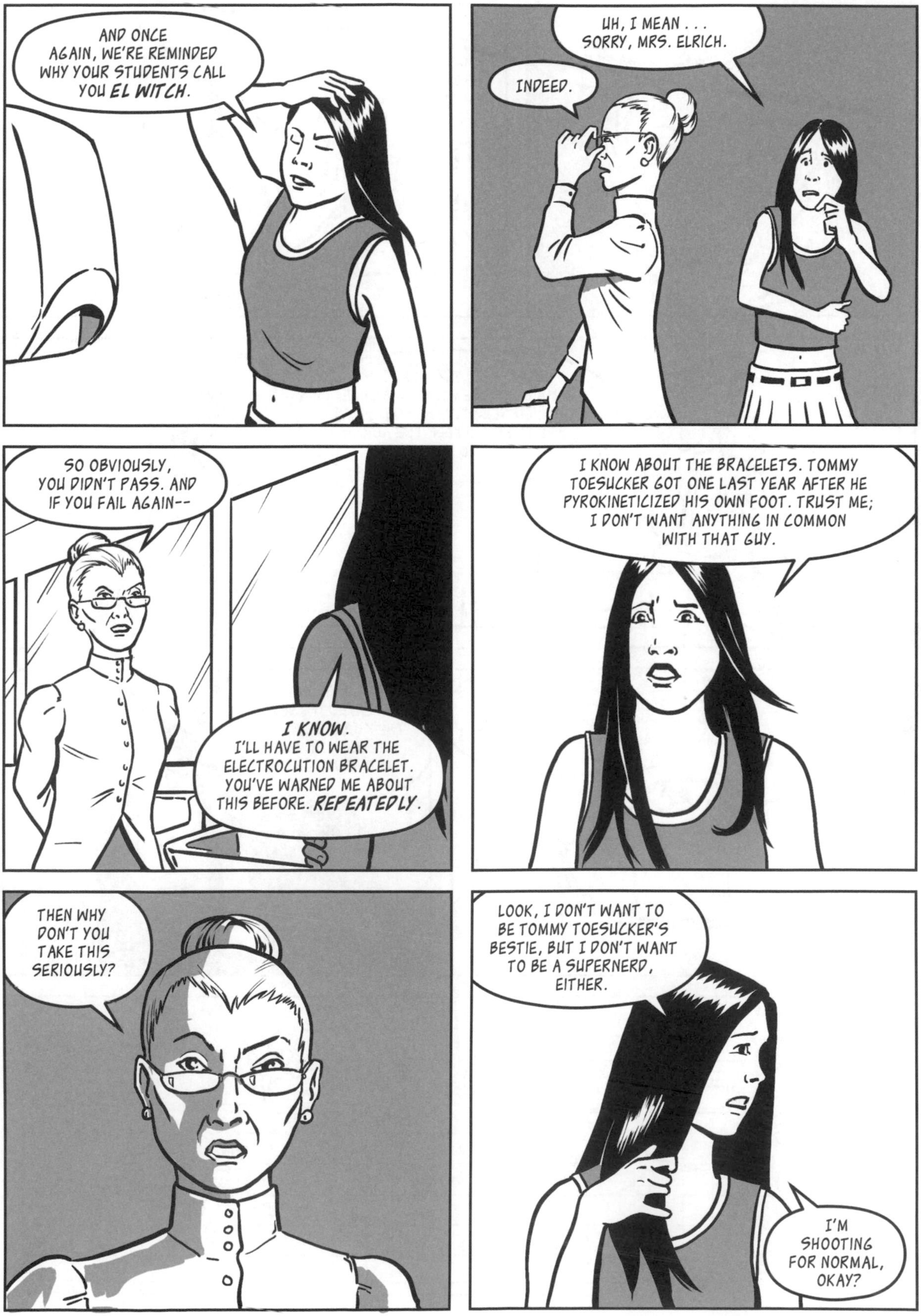
AND ONCE AGAIN, WE'RE REMINDED WHY YOUR STUDENTS CALL YOU **EL WITCH**.
UH, I MEAN . . . SORRY, MRS. ELRICH.
INDEED.
SO OBVIOUSLY, YOU DIDN'T PASS. AND IF YOU FAIL AGAIN--
I KNOW. I'LL HAVE TO WEAR THE ELECTROCUTION BRACELET. YOU'VE WARNED ME ABOUT THIS BEFORE. **REPEATEDLY**.
I KNOW ABOUT THE BRACELETS. TOMMY TOESUCKER GOT ONE LAST YEAR AFTER HE PYROKINETICIZED HIS OWN FOOT. TRUST ME; I DON'T WANT ANYTHING IN COMMON WITH THAT GUY.
THEN WHY DON'T YOU TAKE THIS SERIOUSLY?
LOOK, I DON'T WANT TO BE TOMMY TOESUCKER'S BESTIE, BUT I DON'T WANT TO BE A SUPERNERD, EITHER.
I'M SHOOTING FOR NORMAL, OKAY?

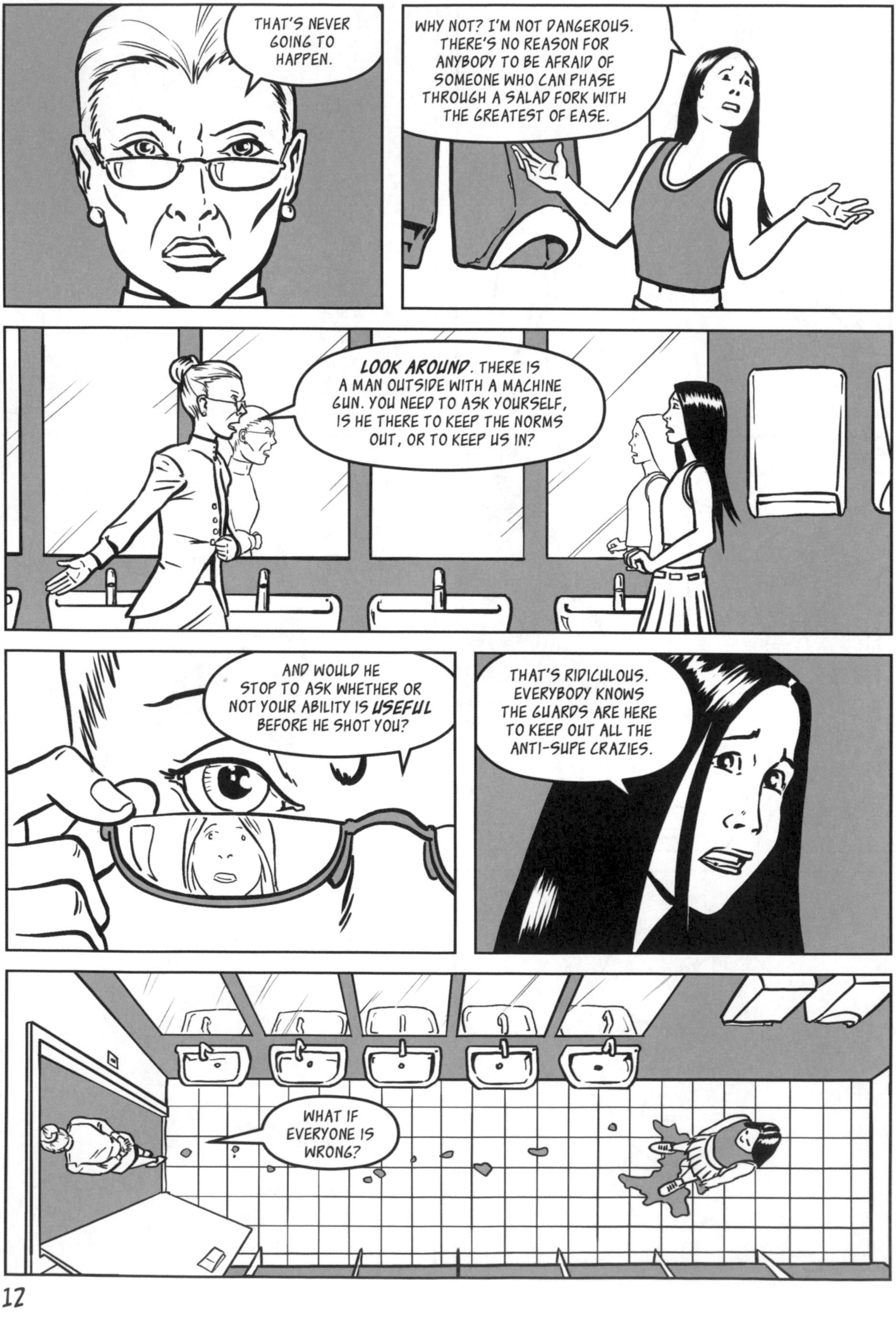
THAT'S NEVER GOING TO HAPPEN.
WHY NOT? I'M NOT DANGEROUS. THERE'S NO REASON FOR ANYBODY TO BE AFRAID OF SOMEONE WHO CAN PHASE THROUGH A SALAD FORK WITH THE GREATEST OF EASE.
LOOK AROUND. THERE IS A MAN OUTSIDE WITH A MACHINE GUN. YOU NEED TO ASK YOURSELF, IS HE THERE TO KEEP THE NORMS OUT, OR TO KEEP US IN?
AND WOULD HE STOP TO ASK WHETHER OR NOT YOUR ABILITY IS *USEFUL* BEFORE HE SHOT YOU?
THAT'S RIDICULOUS. EVERYBODY KNOWS THE GUARDS ARE HERE TO KEEP OUT ALL THE ANTI-SUPE CRAZIES.
WHAT IF EVERYONE IS WRONG?

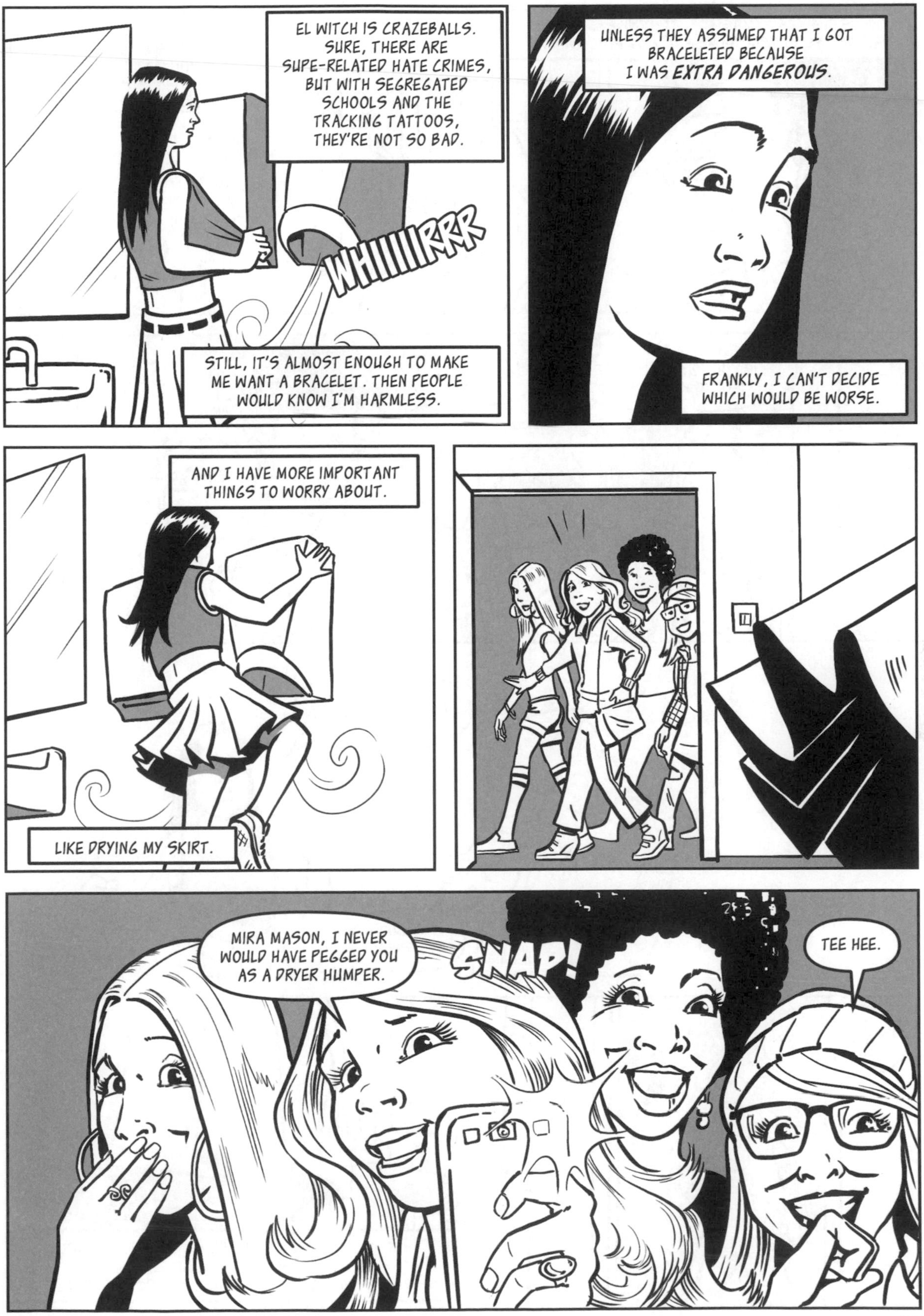
EL WITCH IS CRAZEBALLS. SURE, THERE ARE SUPE-RELATED HATE CRIMES, BUT WITH SEGREGATED SCHOOLS AND THE TRACKING TATTOOS, THEY'RE NOT SO BAD.
WHIIIIIRRR
STILL, IT'S ALMOST ENOUGH TO MAKE ME WANT A BRACELET. THEN PEOPLE WOULD KNOW I'M HARMLESS.
UNLESS THEY ASSUMED THAT I GOT BRACELETED BECAUSE I WAS *EXTRA DANGEROUS*.
FRANKLY, I CAN'T DECIDE WHICH WOULD BE WORSE.
AND I HAVE MORE IMPORTANT THINGS TO WORRY ABOUT.
LIKE DRYING MY SKIRT.
MIRA MASON, I NEVER WOULD HAVE PEGGED YOU AS A DRYER HUMPER.
SNAP!
TEE HEE.

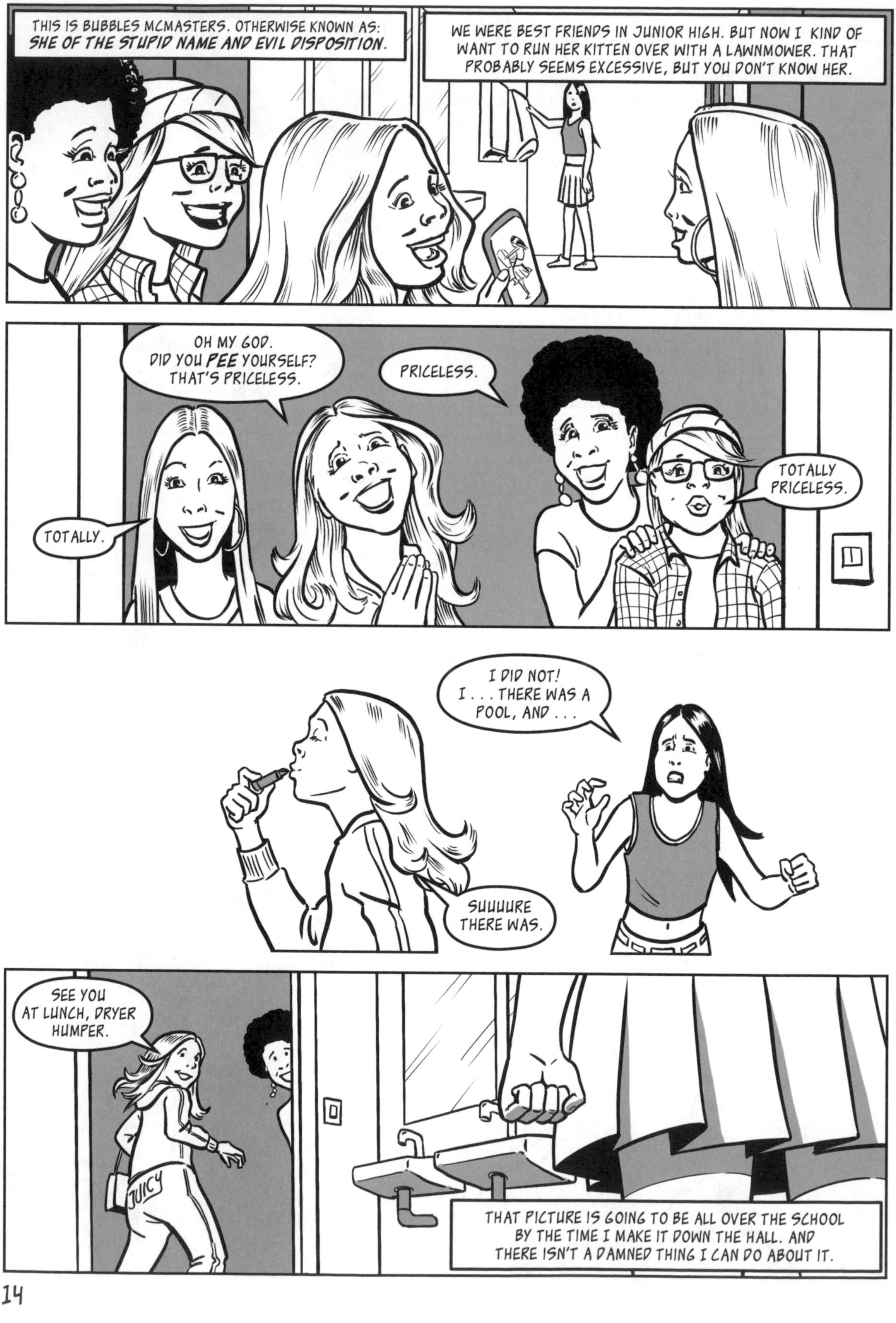
THIS IS BUBBLES MCMASTERS. OTHERWISE KNOWN AS: *SHE OF THE STUPID NAME AND EVIL DISPOSITION*.
WE WERE BEST FRIENDS IN JUNIOR HIGH. BUT NOW I KIND OF WANT TO RUN HER KITTEN OVER WITH A LAWNMOWER. THAT PROBABLY SEEMS EXCESSIVE, BUT YOU DON'T KNOW HER.
OH MY GOD. DID YOU *PEE* YOURSELF? THAT'S PRICELESS.
PRICELESS.
TOTALLY.
TOTALLY PRICELESS.
I DID NOT! I . . . THERE WAS A POOL, AND . . .
SUUUURE THERE WAS.
SEE YOU AT LUNCH, DRYER HUMPER.
JUICY
THAT PICTURE IS GOING TO BE ALL OVER THE SCHOOL BY THE TIME I MAKE IT DOWN THE HALL. AND THERE ISN'T A DAMNED THING I CAN DO ABOUT IT.

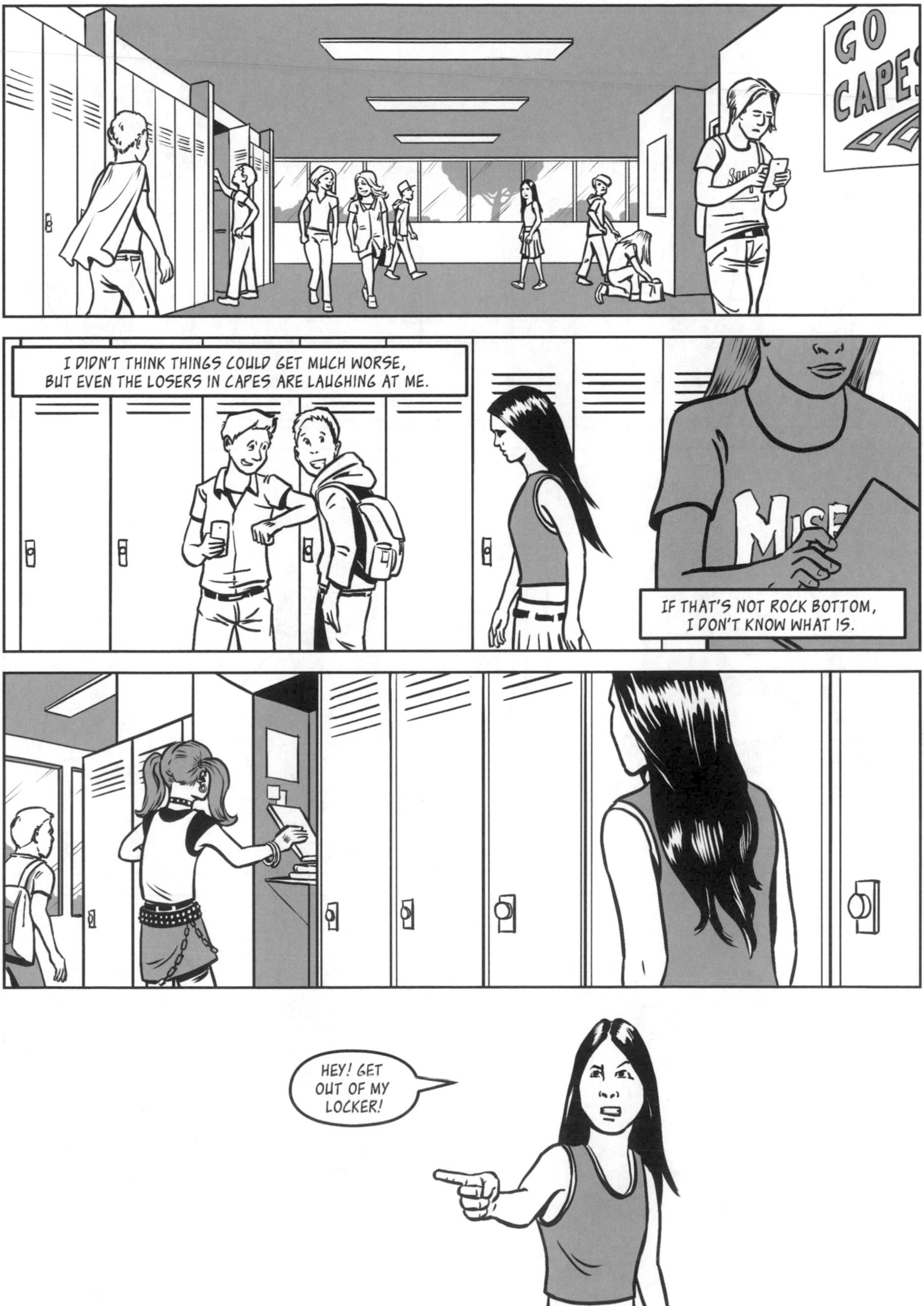
GO CAPES
I DIDN'T THINK THINGS COULD GET MUCH WORSE, BUT EVEN THE LOSERS IN CAPES ARE LAUGHING AT ME.
IF THAT'S NOT ROCK BOTTOM, I DON'T KNOW WHAT IS.
HEY! GET OUT OF MY LOCKER!

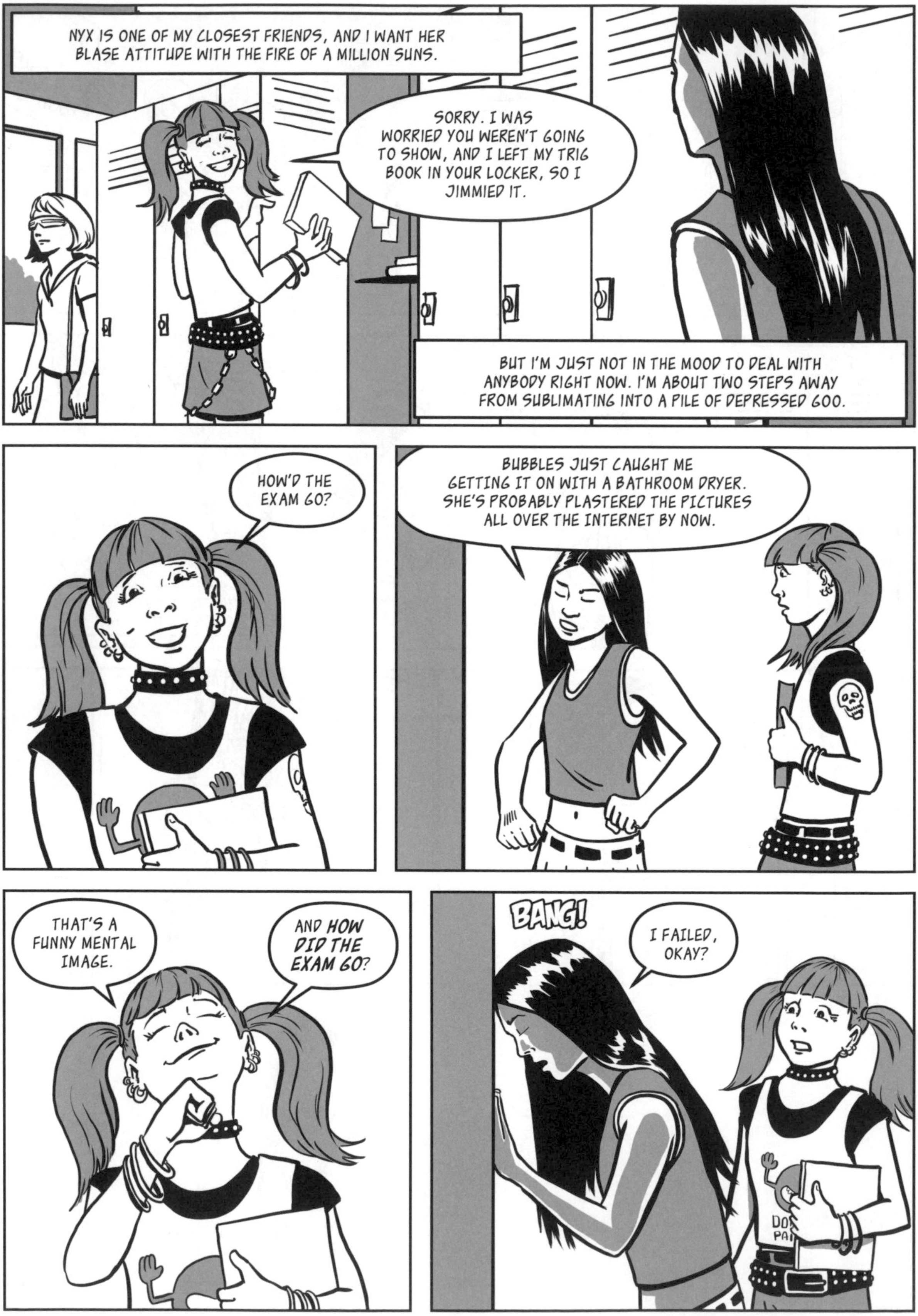
NYX IS ONE OF MY CLOSEST FRIENDS, AND I WANT HER BLASE ATTITUDE WITH THE FIRE OF A MILLION SUNS.
SORRY. I WAS WORRIED YOU WEREN'T GOING TO SHOW, AND I LEFT MY TRIG BOOK IN YOUR LOCKER, SO I JIMMIED IT.
BUT I'M JUST NOT IN THE MOOD TO DEAL WITH ANYBODY RIGHT NOW. I'M ABOUT TWO STEPS AWAY FROM SUBLIMATING INTO A PILE OF DEPRESSED GOO.
HOW'D THE EXAM GO?
BUBBLES JUST CAUGHT ME GETTING IT ON WITH A BATHROOM DRYER. SHE'S PROBABLY PLASTERED THE PICTURES ALL OVER THE INTERNET BY NOW.
THAT'S A FUNNY MENTAL IMAGE.
AND *HOW DID THE EXAM GO*?
BANG!
I FAILED, OKAY?

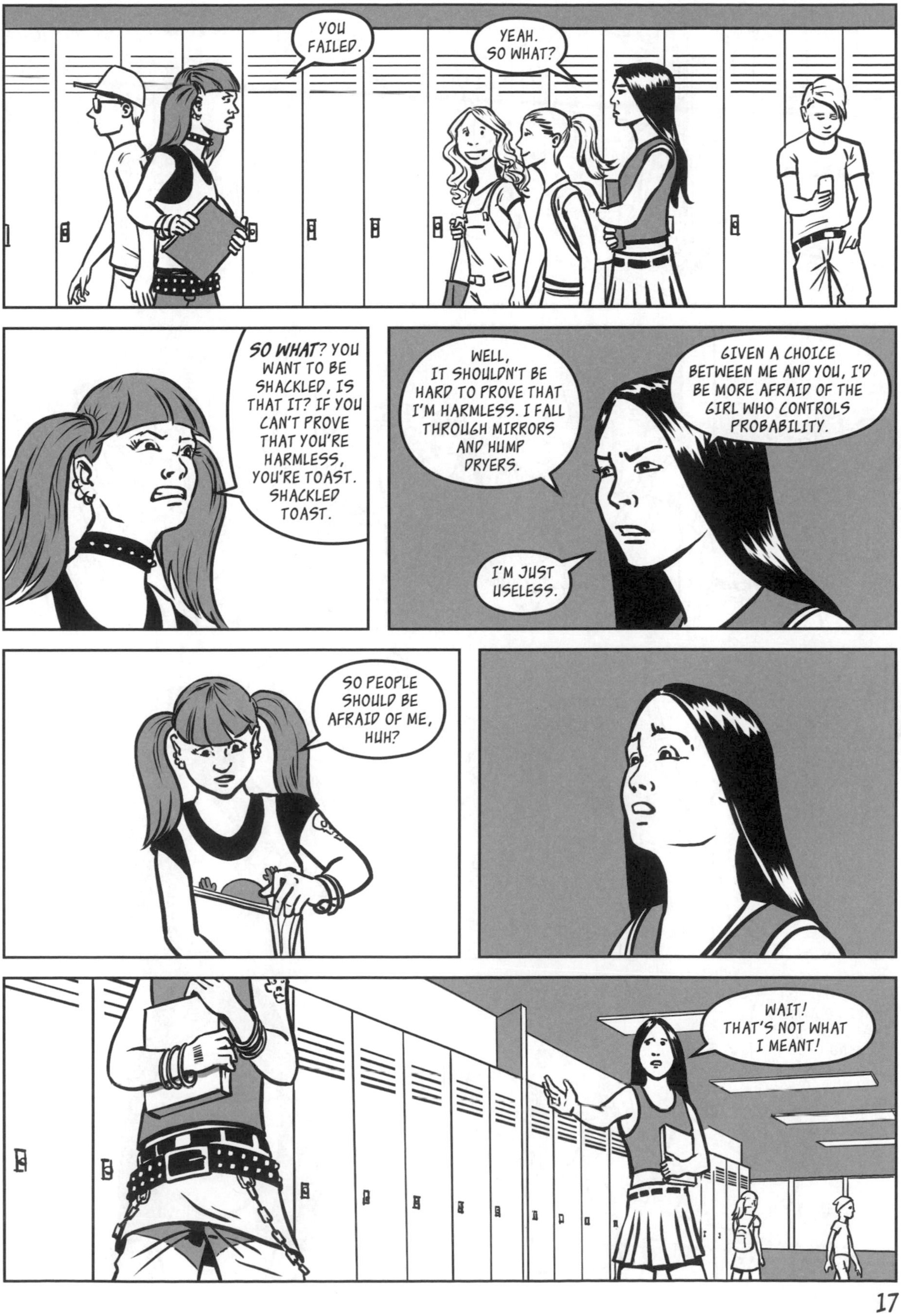
YOU FAILED.
YEAH. SO WHAT?
SO WHAT? YOU WANT TO BE SHACKLED, IS THAT IT? IF YOU CAN'T PROVE THAT YOU'RE HARMLESS, YOU'RE TOAST. SHACKLED TOAST.
WELL, IT SHOULDN'T BE HARD TO PROVE THAT I'M HARMLESS. I FALL THROUGH MIRRORS AND HUMP DRYERS.
GIVEN A CHOICE BETWEEN ME AND YOU, I'D BE MORE AFRAID OF THE GIRL WHO CONTROLS PROBABILITY.
I'M JUST USELESS.
SO PEOPLE SHOULD BE AFRAID OF ME, HUH?
WAIT! THAT'S NOT WHAT I MEANT!

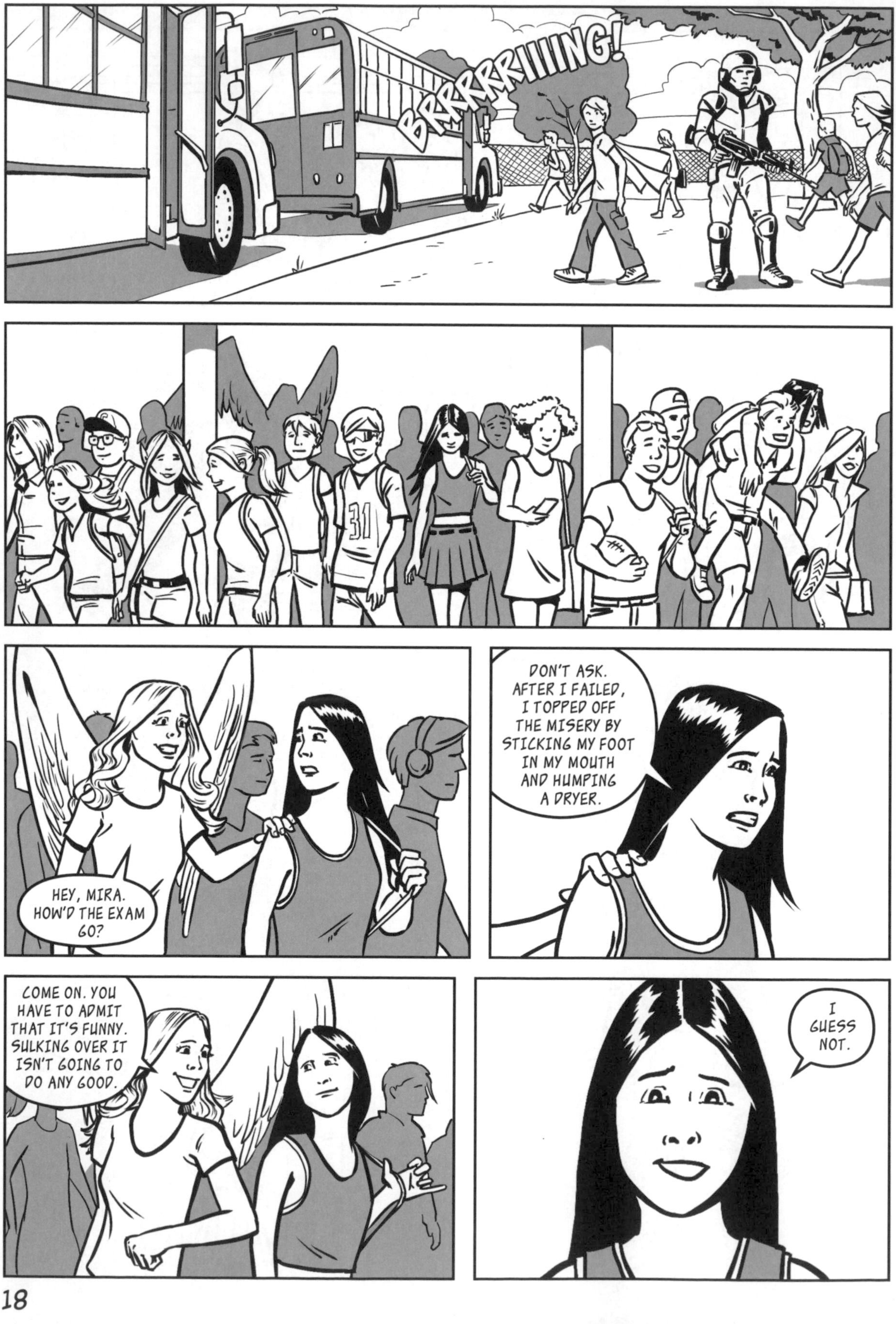
BRRRRRIIIING!
HEY, MIRA. HOW'D THE EXAM GO?
DON'T ASK. AFTER I FAILED, I TOPPED OFF THE MISERY BY STICKING MY FOOT IN MY MOUTH AND HUMPING A DRYER.
COME ON. YOU HAVE TO ADMIT THAT IT'S FUNNY. SULKING OVER IT ISN'T GOING TO DO ANY GOOD.
I GUESS NOT.

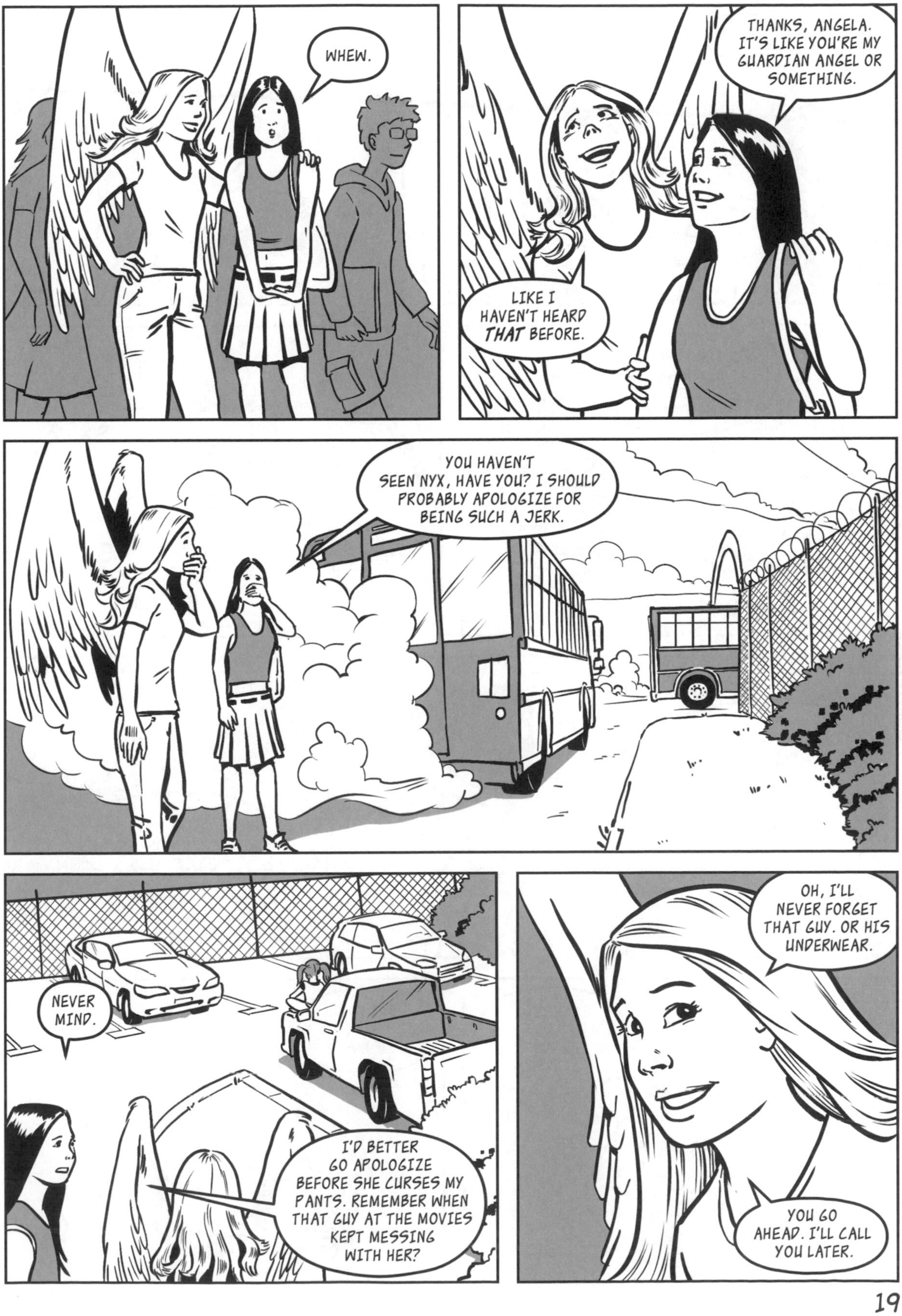
WHEW.
THANKS, ANGELA. IT'S LIKE YOU'RE MY GUARDIAN ANGEL OR SOMETHING.
LIKE I HAVEN'T HEARD THAT BEFORE.
YOU HAVEN'T SEEN NYX, HAVE YOU? I SHOULD PROBABLY APOLOGIZE FOR BEING SUCH A JERK.
NEVER MIND.
I'D BETTER GO APOLOGIZE BEFORE SHE CURSES MY PANTS. REMEMBER WHEN THAT GUY AT THE MOVIES KEPT MESSING WITH HER?
OH, I'LL NEVER FORGET THAT GUY. OR HIS UNDERWEAR.
YOU GO AHEAD. I'LL CALL YOU LATER.

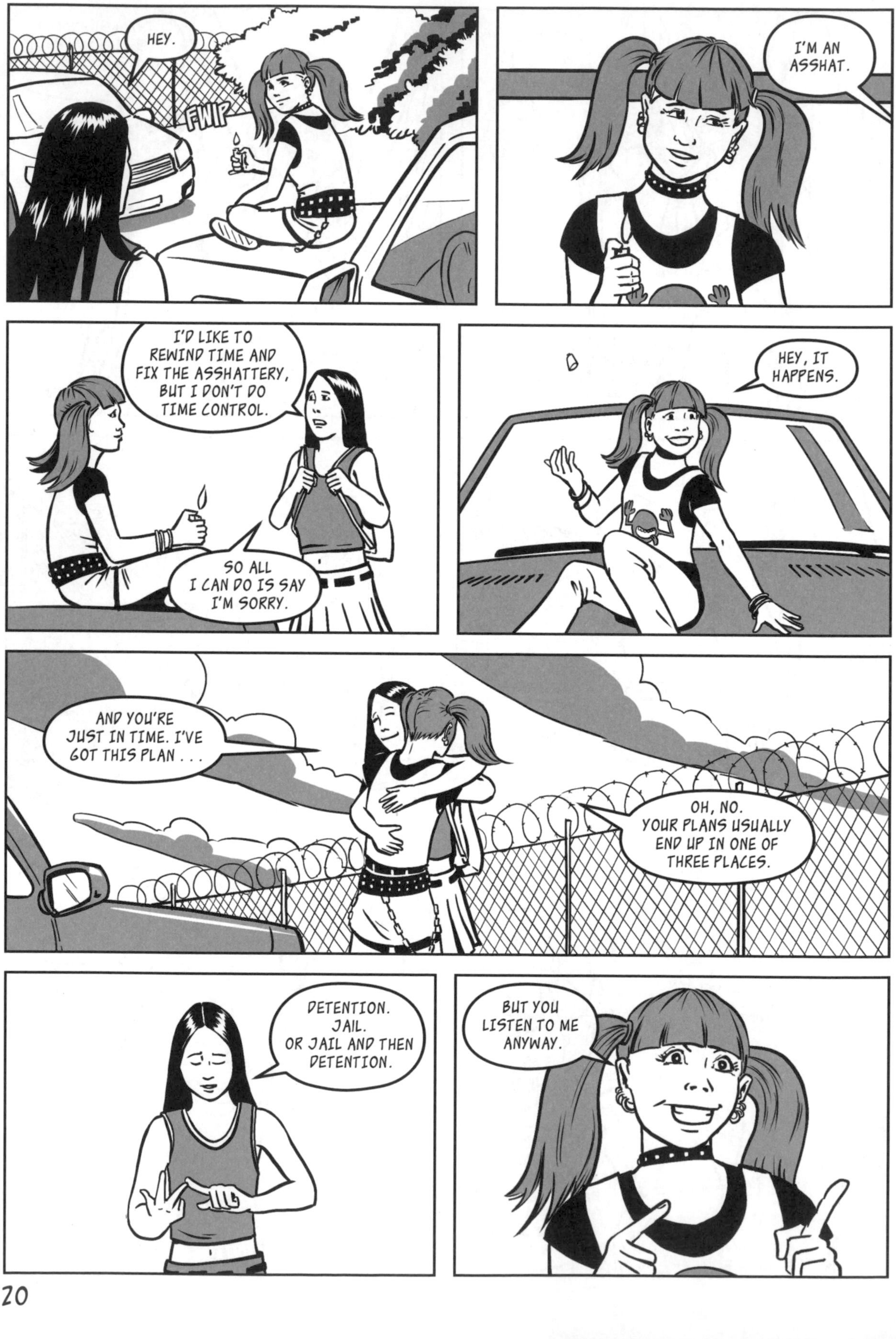
HEY.
FWIP
I'M AN ASSHAT.
I'D LIKE TO REWIND TIME AND FIX THE ASSHATTERY, BUT I DON'T DO TIME CONTROL.
SO ALL I CAN DO IS SAY I'M SORRY.
HEY, IT HAPPENS.
AND YOU'RE JUST IN TIME. I'VE GOT THIS PLAN . . .
OH, NO. YOUR PLANS USUALLY END UP IN ONE OF THREE PLACES.
DETENTION. JAIL. OR JAIL AND THEN DETENTION.
BUT YOU LISTEN TO ME ANYWAY.

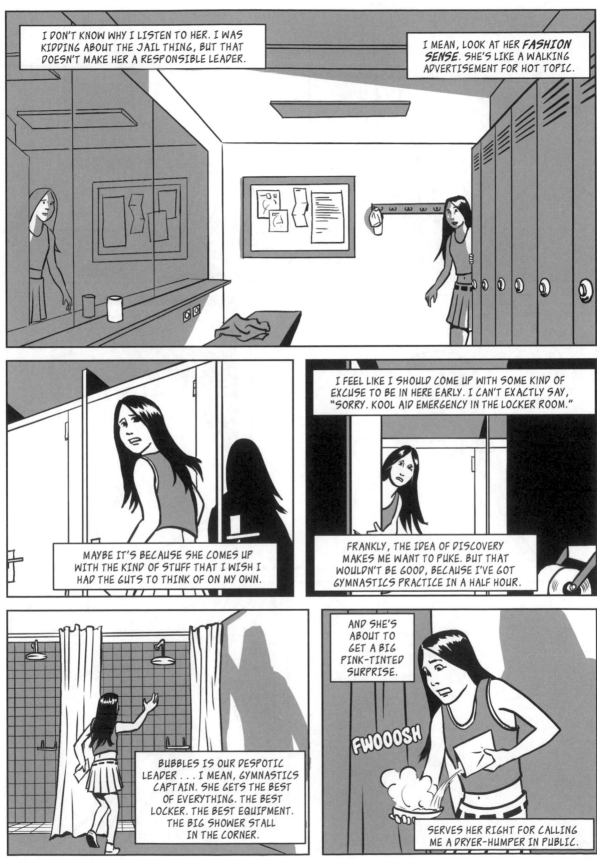

I DON'T KNOW WHY I LISTEN TO HER. I WAS KIDDING ABOUT THE JAIL THING, BUT THAT DOESN'T MAKE HER A RESPONSIBLE LEADER.

I MEAN, LOOK AT HER *FASHION SENSE*. SHE'S LIKE A WALKING ADVERTISEMENT FOR HOT TOPIC.

MAYBE IT'S BECAUSE SHE COMES UP WITH THE KIND OF STUFF THAT I WISH I HAD THE GUTS TO THINK OF ON MY OWN.

I FEEL LIKE I SHOULD COME UP WITH SOME KIND OF EXCUSE TO BE IN HERE EARLY. I CAN'T EXACTLY SAY, "SORRY. KOOL AID EMERGENCY IN THE LOCKER ROOM."

FRANKLY, THE IDEA OF DISCOVERY MAKES ME WANT TO PUKE. BUT THAT WOULDN'T BE GOOD, BECAUSE I'VE GOT GYMNASTICS PRACTICE IN A HALF HOUR.

BUBBLES IS OUR DESPOTIC LEADER . . . I MEAN, GYMNASTICS CAPTAIN. SHE GETS THE BEST OF EVERYTHING. THE BEST LOCKER. THE BEST EQUIPMENT. THE BIG SHOWER STALL IN THE CORNER.

AND SHE'S ABOUT TO GET A BIG PINK-TINTED SURPRISE.

FWOOOSH

SERVES HER RIGHT FOR CALLING ME A DRYER-HUMPER IN PUBLIC.

21

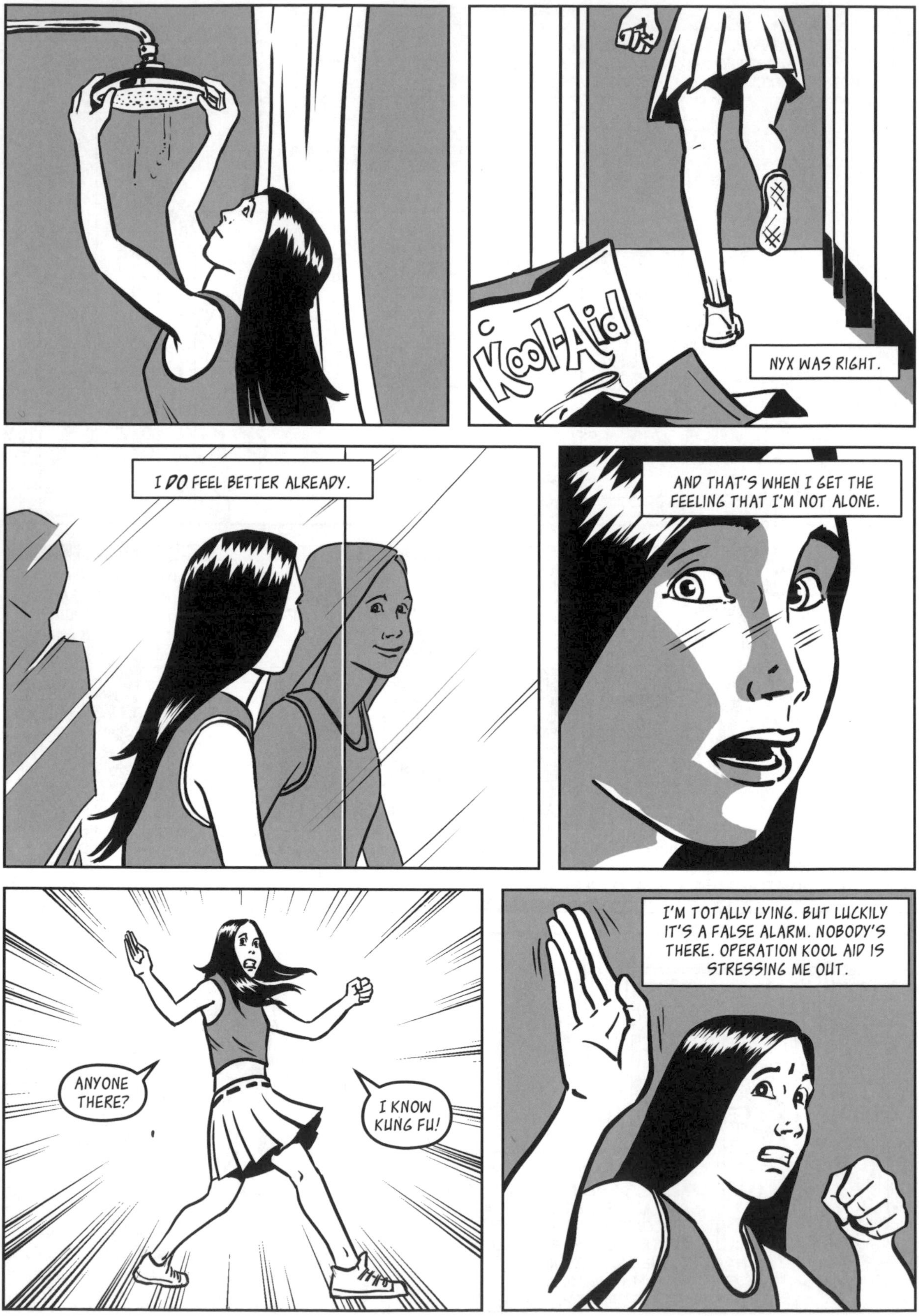
Kool-Aid
NYX WAS RIGHT.
I DO FEEL BETTER ALREADY.
AND THAT'S WHEN I GET THE FEELING THAT I'M NOT ALONE.
ANYONE THERE?
I KNOW KUNG FU!
I'M TOTALLY LYING. BUT LUCKILY IT'S A FALSE ALARM. NOBODY'S THERE. OPERATION KOOL AID IS STRESSING ME OUT.

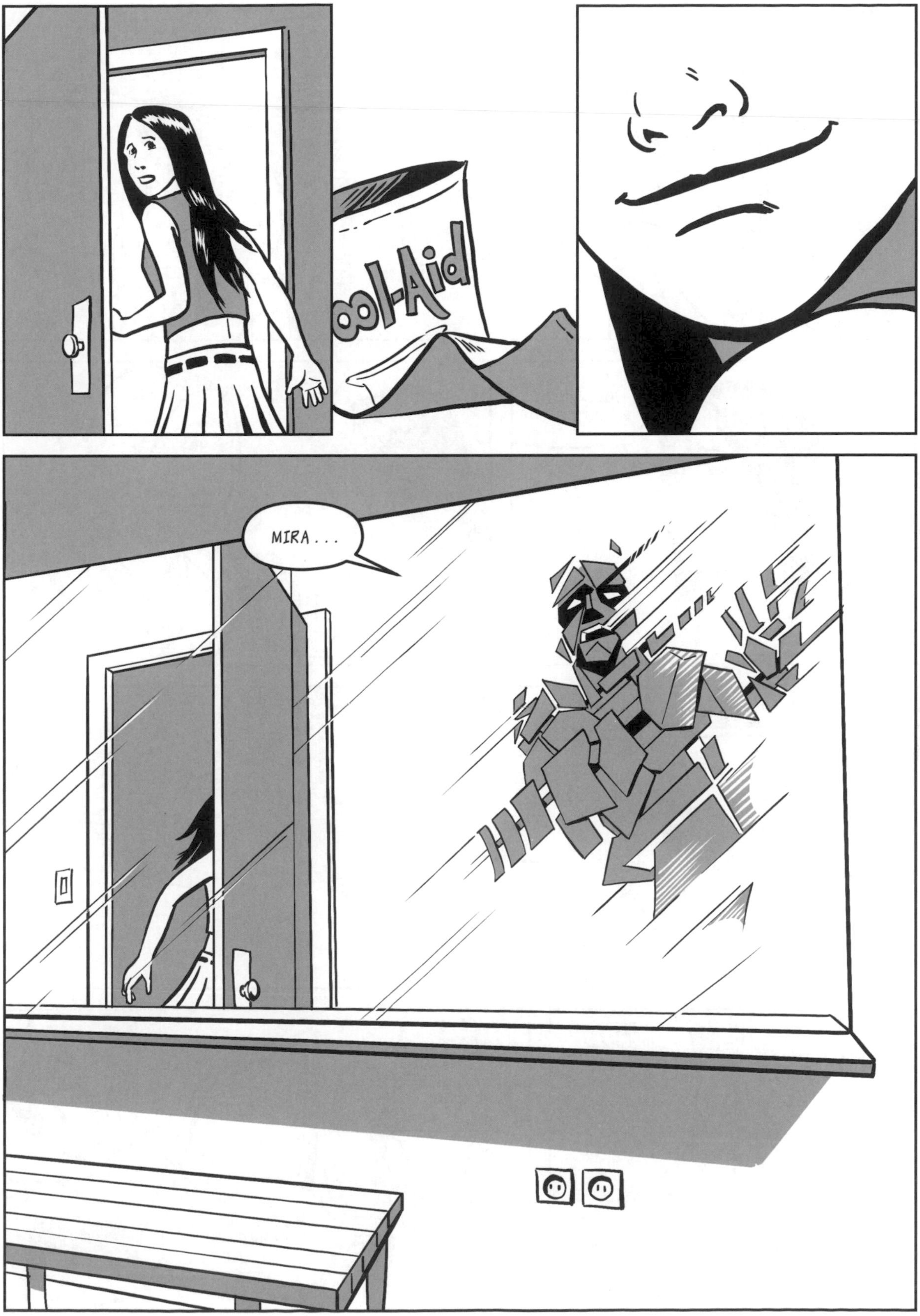
ool-Aid
MIRA . . .

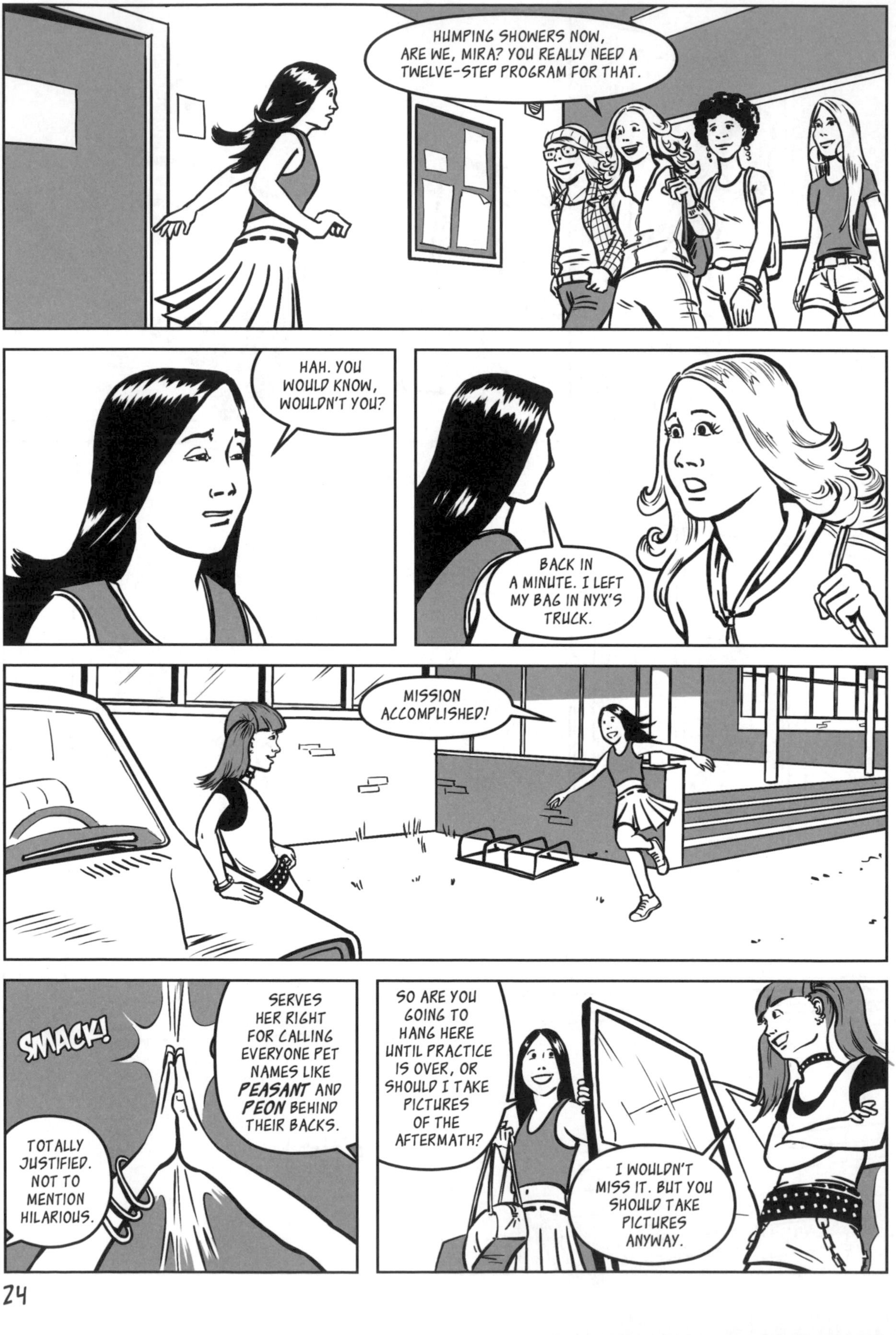
HUMPING SHOWERS NOW, ARE WE, MIRA? YOU REALLY NEED A TWELVE-STEP PROGRAM FOR THAT.
HAH. YOU WOULD KNOW, WOULDN'T YOU?
BACK IN A MINUTE. I LEFT MY BAG IN NYX'S TRUCK.
MISSION ACCOMPLISHED!
SMACK!
SERVES HER RIGHT FOR CALLING EVERYONE PET NAMES LIKE *PEASANT* AND *PEON* BEHIND THEIR BACKS.
TOTALLY JUSTIFIED. NOT TO MENTION HILARIOUS.
SO ARE YOU GOING TO HANG HERE UNTIL PRACTICE IS OVER, OR SHOULD I TAKE PICTURES OF THE AFTERMATH?
I WOULDN'T MISS IT. BUT YOU SHOULD TAKE PICTURES ANYWAY.

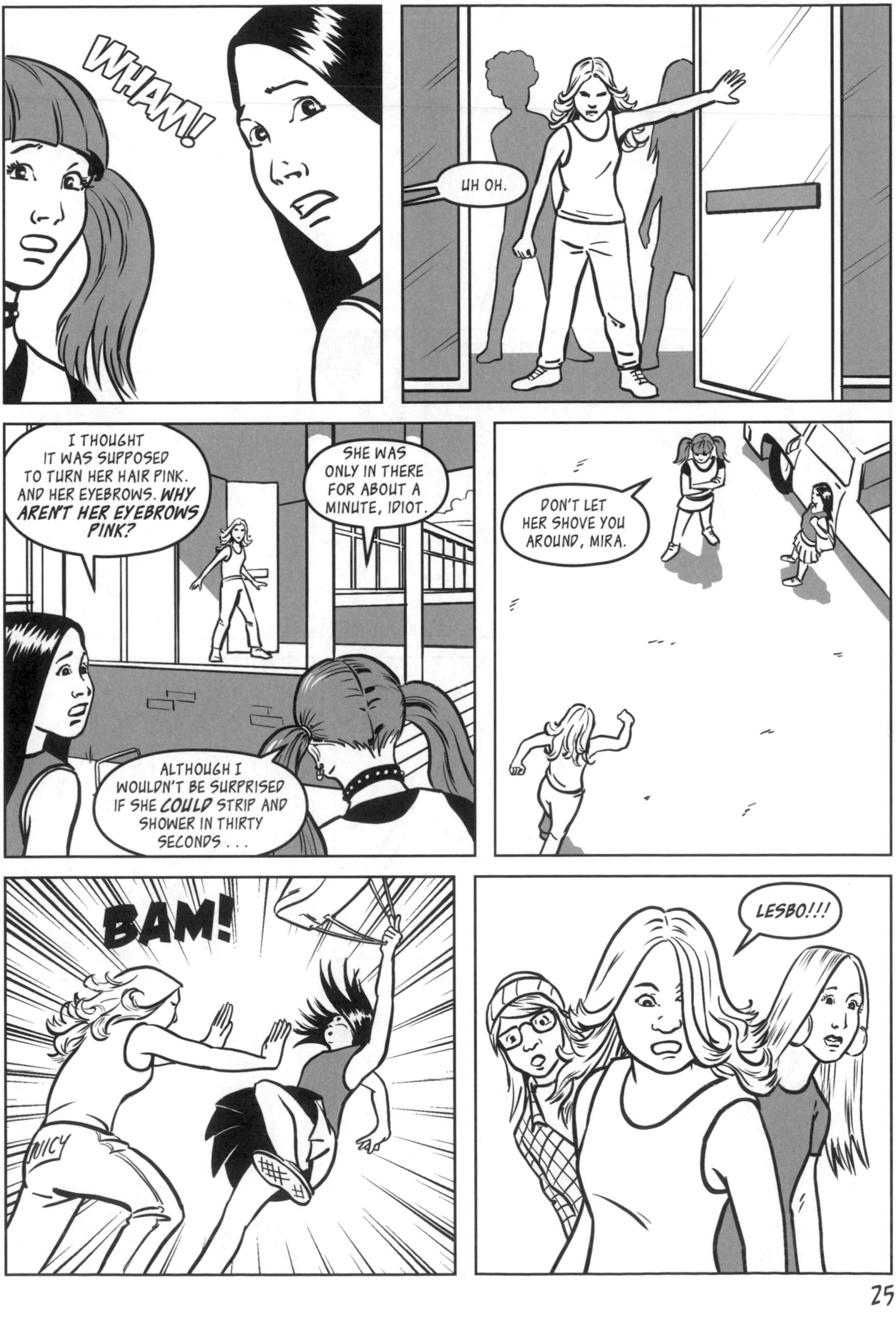
WHAM!
UH OH.
I THOUGHT IT WAS SUPPOSED TO TURN HER HAIR PINK. AND HER EYEBROWS. WHY AREN'T HER EYEBROWS PINK?
SHE WAS ONLY IN THERE FOR ABOUT A MINUTE, IDIOT.
ALTHOUGH I WOULDN'T BE SURPRISED IF SHE COULD STRIP AND SHOWER IN THIRTY SECONDS . . .
DON'T LET HER SHOVE YOU AROUND, MIRA.
BAM!
JUICY
LESBO!!!

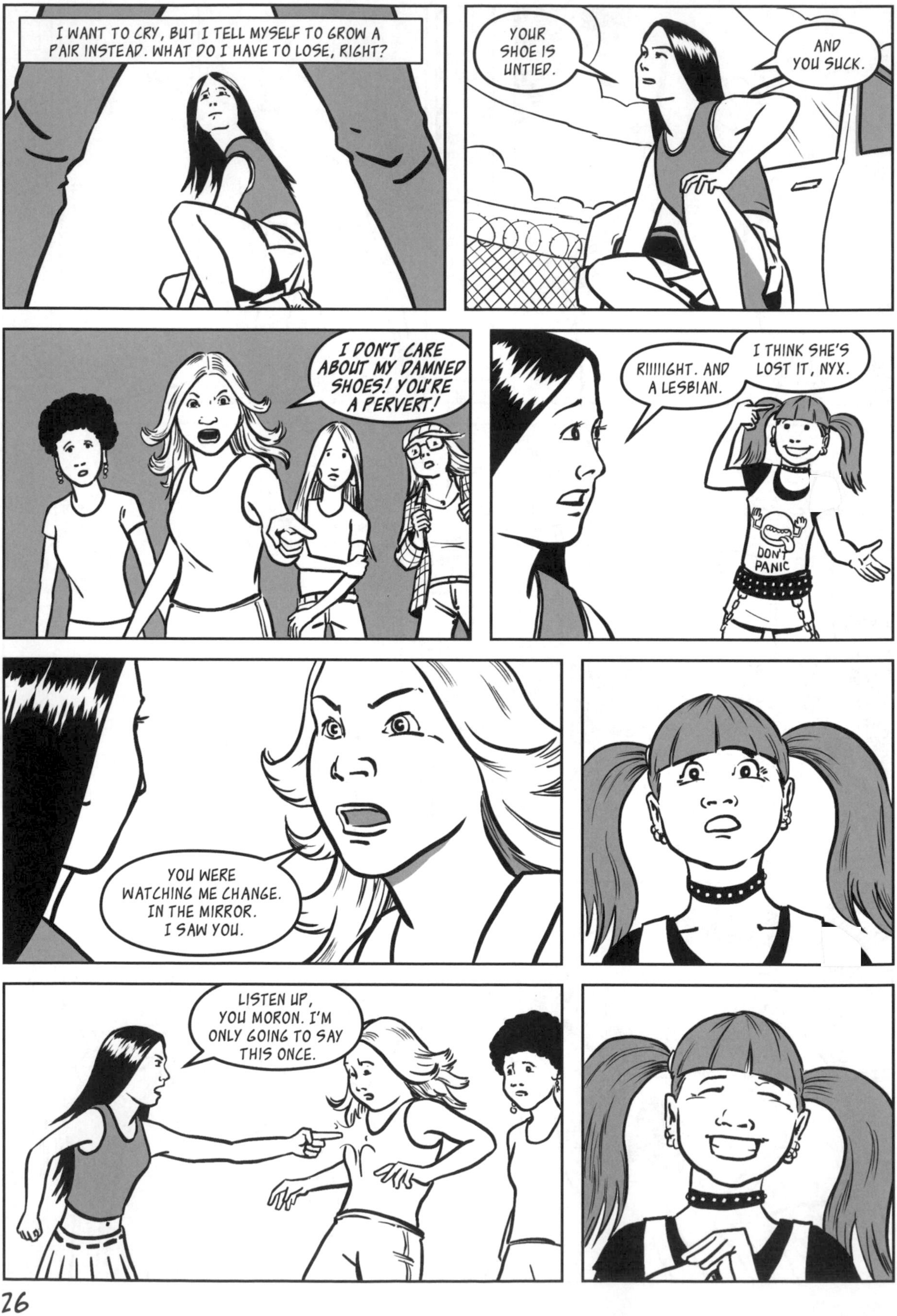
I WANT TO CRY, BUT I TELL MYSELF TO GROW A PAIR INSTEAD. WHAT DO I HAVE TO LOSE, RIGHT?
YOUR SHOE IS UNTIED.
AND YOU SUCK.
I DON'T CARE ABOUT MY DAMNED SHOES! YOU'RE A PERVERT!
RIIIIIGHT. AND A LESBIAN.
I THINK SHE'S LOST IT, NYX.
DON'T PANIC
YOU WERE WATCHING ME CHANGE. IN THE MIRROR. I SAW YOU.
LISTEN UP, YOU MORON. I'M ONLY GOING TO SAY THIS ONCE.

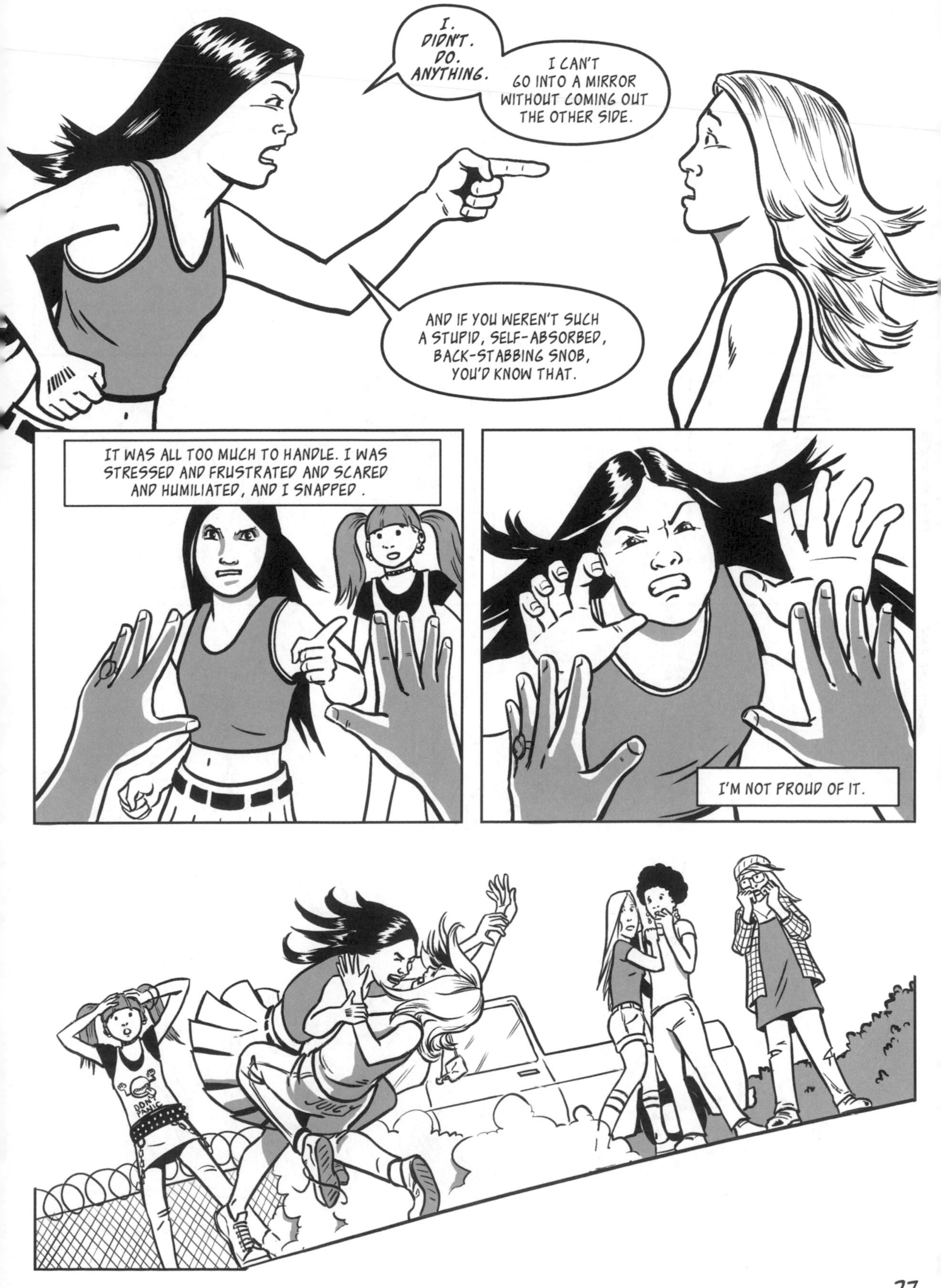
I. DIDN'T. DO. ANYTHING.
I CAN'T GO INTO A MIRROR WITHOUT COMING OUT THE OTHER SIDE.
AND IF YOU WEREN'T SUCH A STUPID, SELF-ABSORBED, BACK-STABBING SNOB, YOU'D KNOW THAT.
IT WAS ALL TOO MUCH TO HANDLE. I WAS STRESSED AND FRUSTRATED AND SCARED AND HUMILIATED, AND I SNAPPED .
I'M NOT PROUD OF IT.

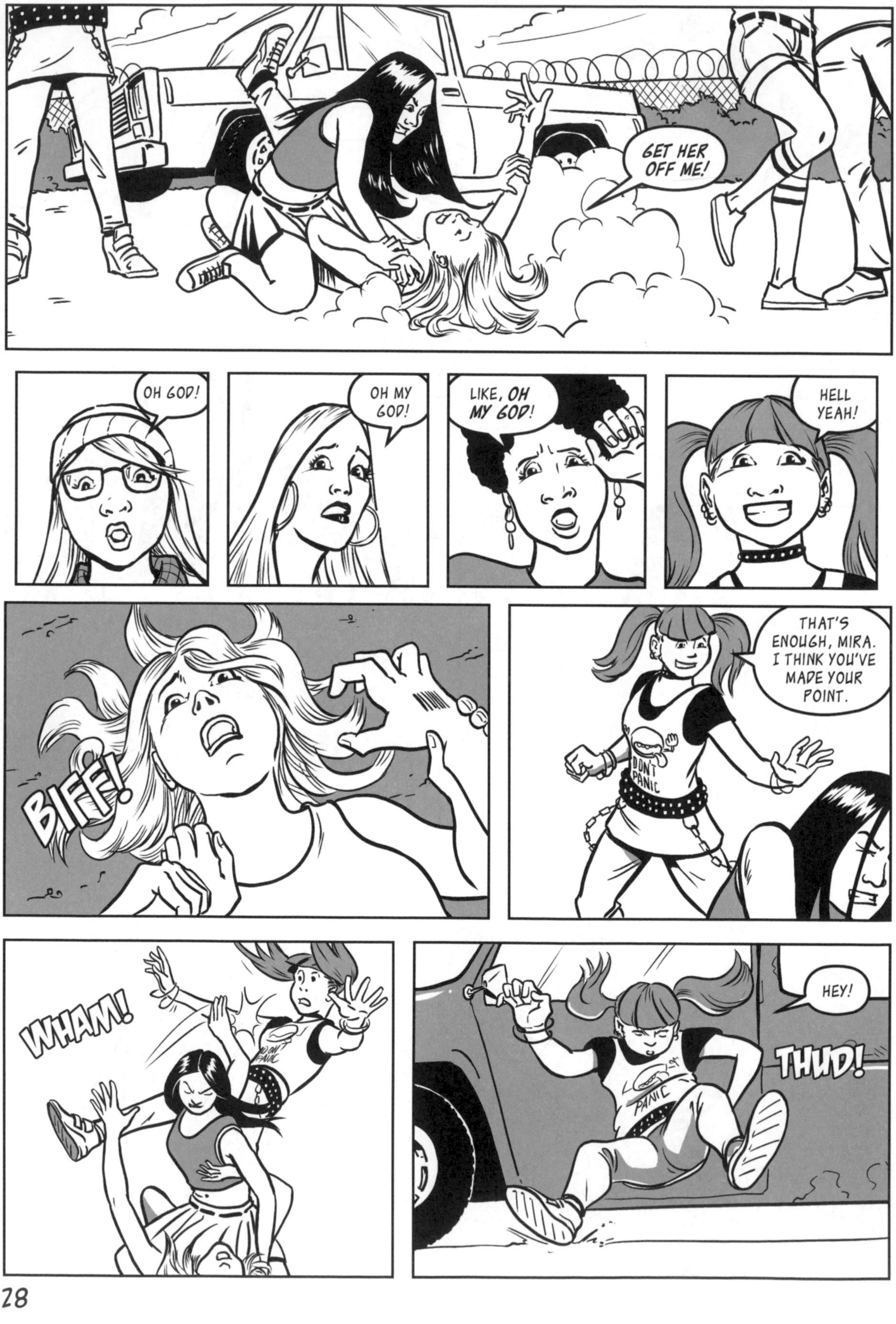
GET HER OFF ME!
OH GOD!
OH MY GOD!
LIKE, OH MY GOD!
HELL YEAH!
BIFF!
THAT'S ENOUGH, MIRA. I THINK YOU'VE MADE YOUR POINT.
DON'T PANIC
WHAM!
HEY!
THUD!

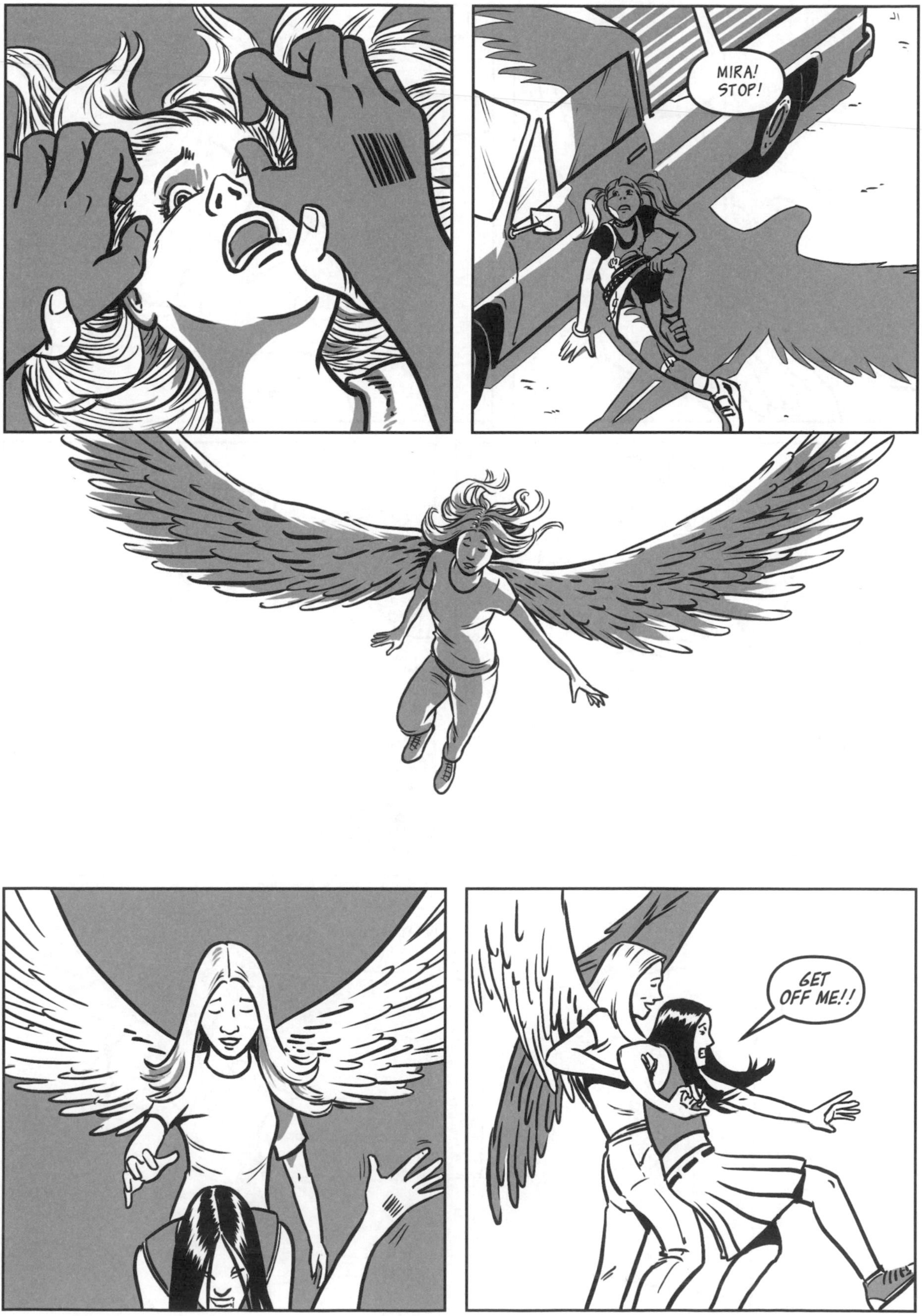
MIRA! STOP!
GET OFF ME!!

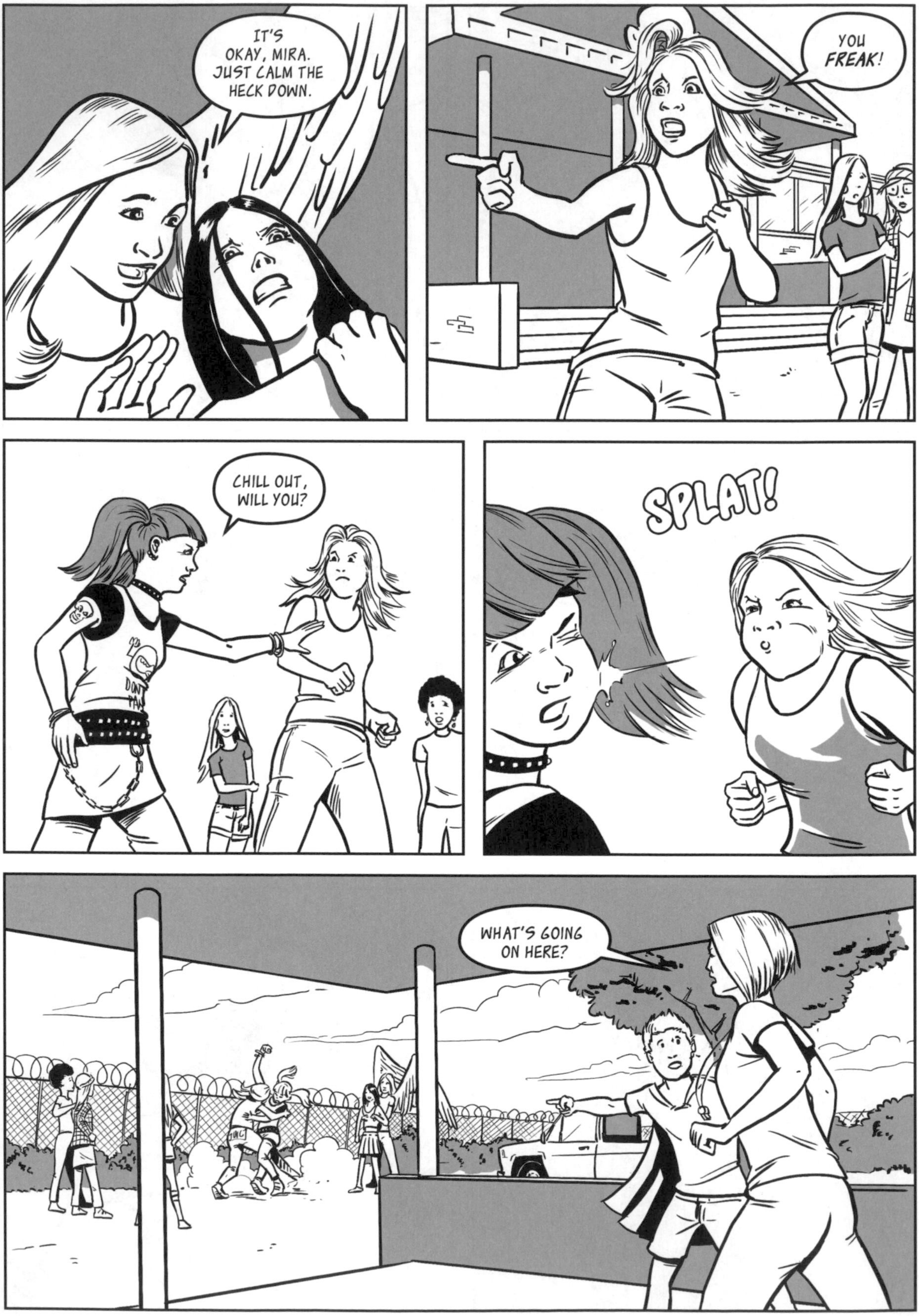
IT'S OKAY, MIRA. JUST CALM THE HECK DOWN.
YOU FREAK!
CHILL OUT, WILL YOU?
SPLAT!
WHAT'S GOING ON HERE?

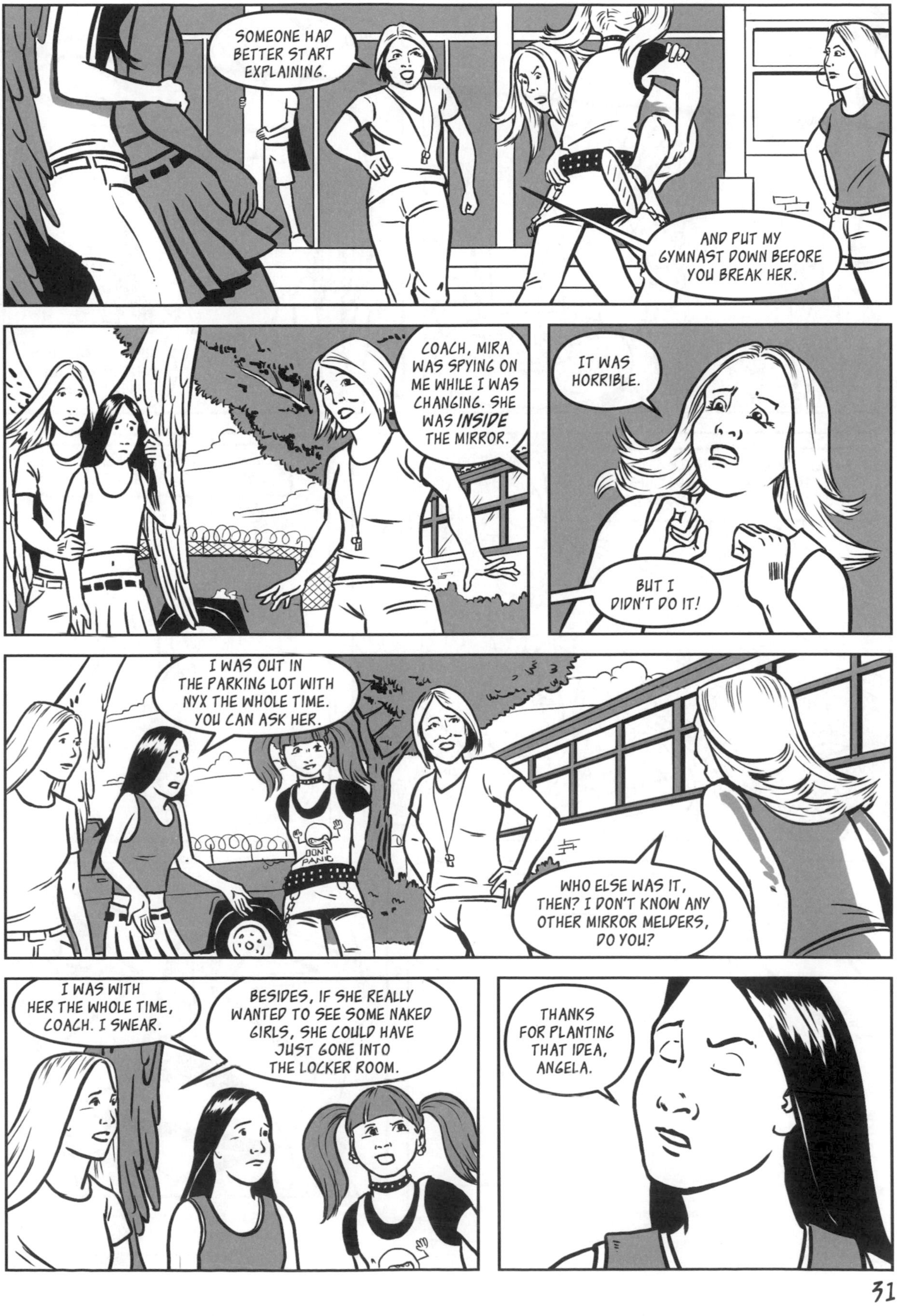
SOMEONE HAD BETTER START EXPLAINING.
AND PUT MY GYMNAST DOWN BEFORE YOU BREAK HER.
COACH, MIRA WAS SPYING ON ME WHILE I WAS CHANGING. SHE WAS *INSIDE* THE MIRROR.
IT WAS HORRIBLE.
BUT I DIDN'T DO IT!
I WAS OUT IN THE PARKING LOT WITH NYX THE WHOLE TIME. YOU CAN ASK HER.
DON'T PANIC
WHO ELSE WAS IT, THEN? I DON'T KNOW ANY OTHER MIRROR MELDERS, DO YOU?
I WAS WITH HER THE WHOLE TIME, COACH. I SWEAR.
BESIDES, IF SHE REALLY WANTED TO SEE SOME NAKED GIRLS, SHE COULD HAVE JUST GONE INTO THE LOCKER ROOM.
THANKS FOR PLANTING THAT IDEA, ANGELA.

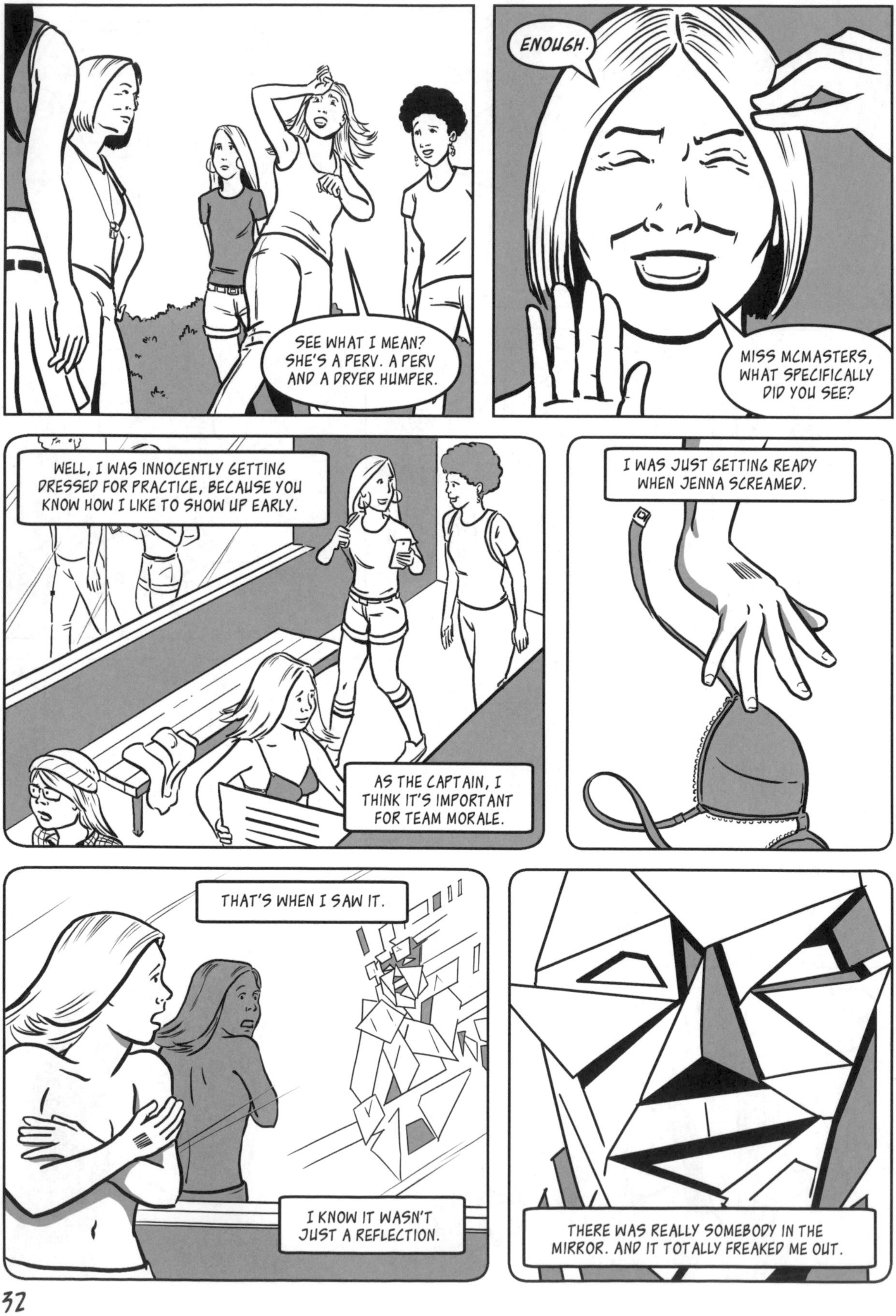
SEE WHAT I MEAN? SHE'S A PERV. A PERV AND A DRYER HUMPER.
ENOUGH.
MISS MCMASTERS, WHAT SPECIFICALLY DID YOU SEE?
WELL, I WAS INNOCENTLY GETTING DRESSED FOR PRACTICE, BECAUSE YOU KNOW HOW I LIKE TO SHOW UP EARLY.
AS THE CAPTAIN, I THINK IT'S IMPORTANT FOR TEAM MORALE.
I WAS JUST GETTING READY WHEN JENNA SCREAMED.
THAT'S WHEN I SAW IT.
I KNOW IT WASN'T JUST A REFLECTION.
THERE WAS REALLY SOMEBODY IN THE MIRROR. AND IT TOTALLY FREAKED ME OUT.

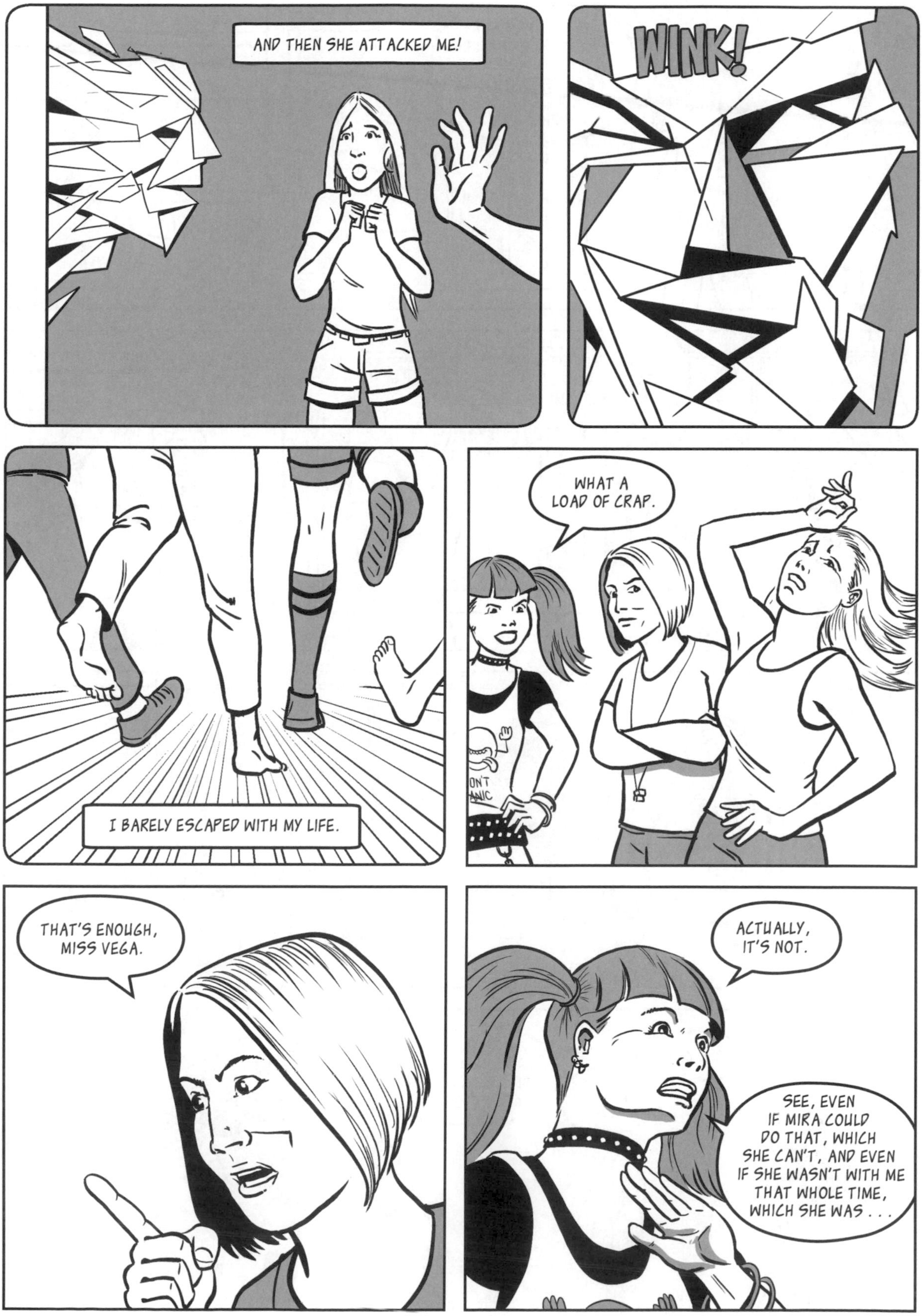
AND THEN SHE ATTACKED ME!
WINK!
I BARELY ESCAPED WITH MY LIFE.
WHAT A LOAD OF CRAP.
THAT'S ENOUGH, MISS VEGA.
ACTUALLY, IT'S NOT.
SEE, EVEN IF MIRA COULD DO THAT, WHICH SHE CAN'T, AND EVEN IF SHE WASN'T WITH ME THAT WHOLE TIME, WHICH SHE WAS . . .

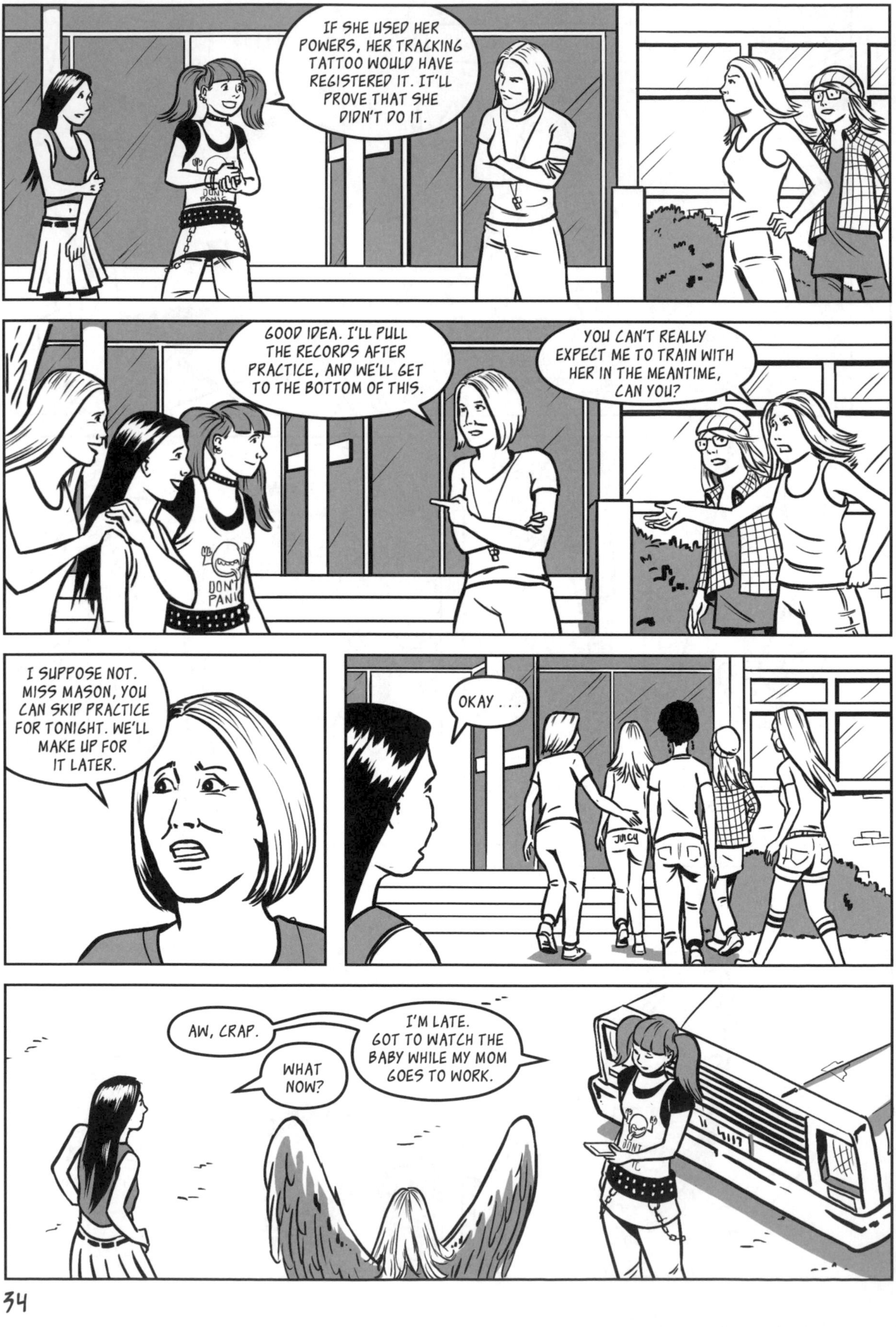
IF SHE USED HER POWERS, HER TRACKING TATTOO WOULD HAVE REGISTERED IT. IT'LL PROVE THAT SHE DIDN'T DO IT.
GOOD IDEA. I'LL PULL THE RECORDS AFTER PRACTICE, AND WE'LL GET TO THE BOTTOM OF THIS.
YOU CAN'T REALLY EXPECT ME TO TRAIN WITH HER IN THE MEANTIME, CAN YOU?
I SUPPOSE NOT. MISS MASON, YOU CAN SKIP PRACTICE FOR TONIGHT. WE'LL MAKE UP FOR IT LATER.
OKAY . . .
AW, CRAP.
I'M LATE. GOT TO WATCH THE BABY WHILE MY MOM GOES TO WORK.
WHAT NOW?

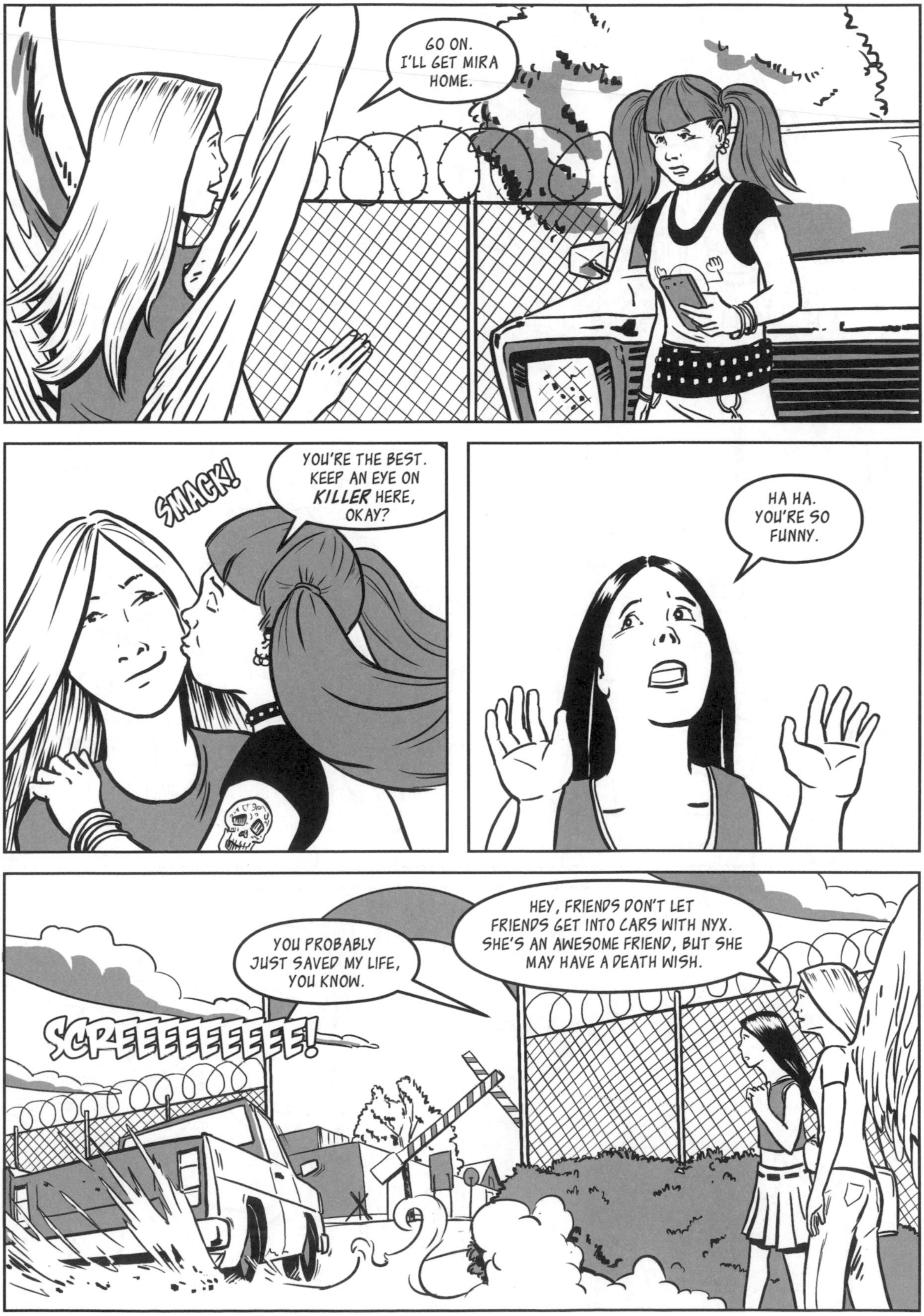
GO ON. I'LL GET MIRA HOME.
SMACK!
YOU'RE THE BEST. KEEP AN EYE ON KILLER HERE, OKAY?
HA HA. YOU'RE SO FUNNY.
YOU PROBABLY JUST SAVED MY LIFE, YOU KNOW.
HEY, FRIENDS DON'T LET FRIENDS GET INTO CARS WITH NYX. SHE'S AN AWESOME FRIEND, BUT SHE MAY HAVE A DEATH WISH.
SCREEEEEEEEEE!

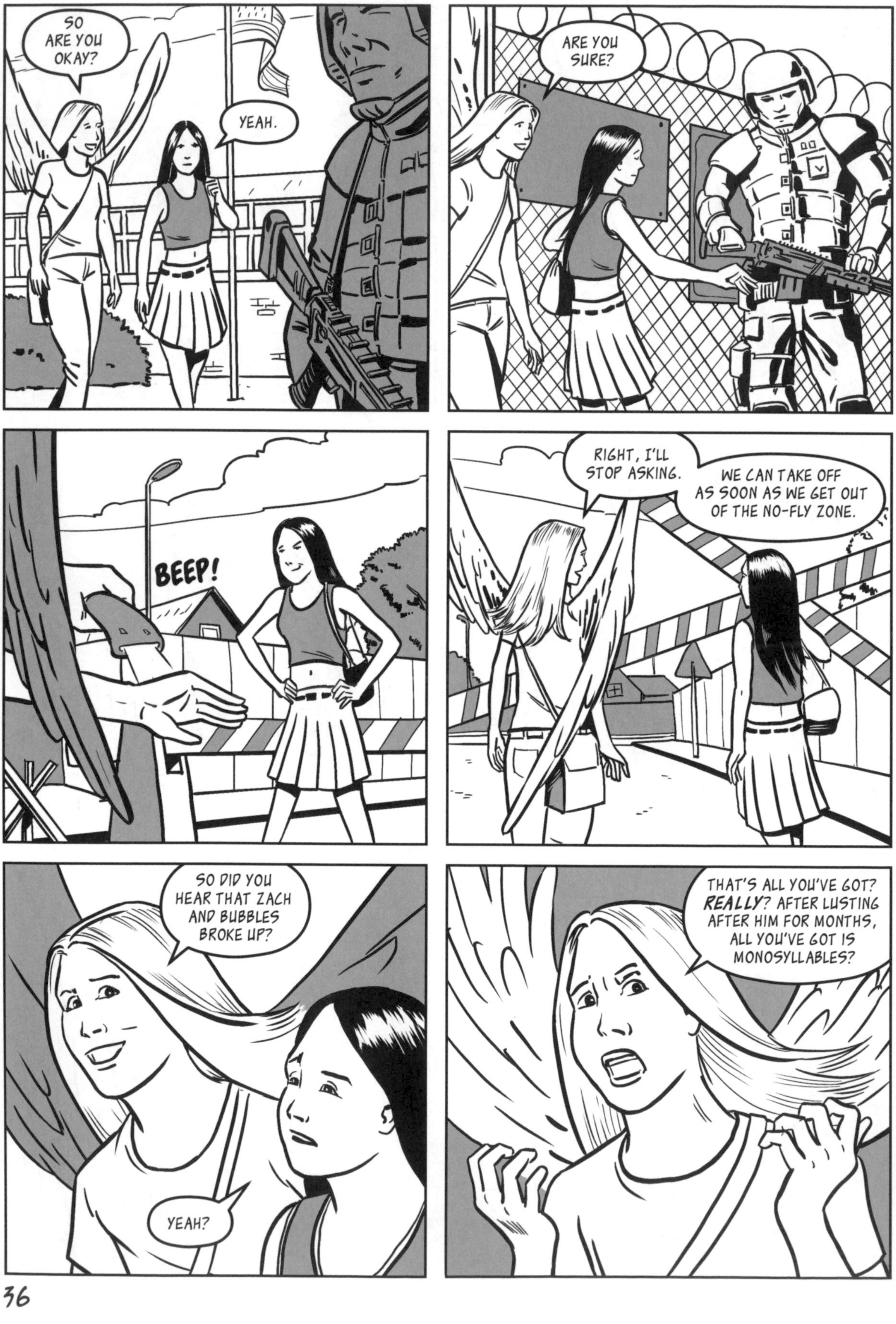
SO ARE YOU OKAY?
YEAH.
ARE YOU SURE?
BEEP!
RIGHT, I'LL STOP ASKING.
WE CAN TAKE OFF AS SOON AS WE GET OUT OF THE NO-FLY ZONE.
SO DID YOU HEAR THAT ZACH AND BUBBLES BROKE UP?
YEAH?
THAT'S ALL YOU'VE GOT? *REALLY*? AFTER LUSTING AFTER HIM FOR MONTHS, ALL YOU'VE GOT IS MONOSYLLABLES?

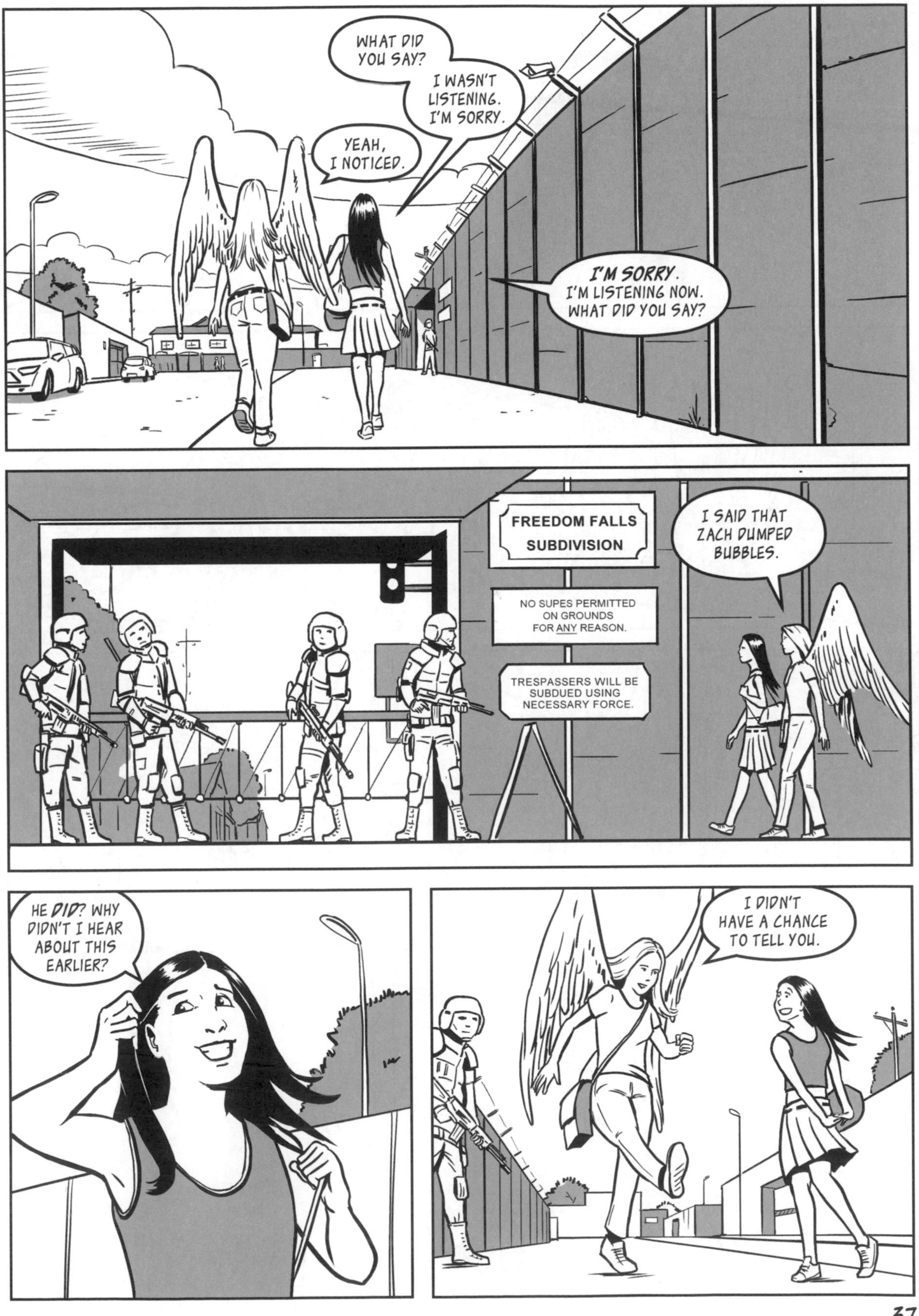

WHAT DID YOU SAY?
I WASN'T LISTENING. I'M SORRY.
YEAH, I NOTICED.
I'M SORRY. I'M LISTENING NOW. WHAT DID YOU SAY?
FREEDOM FALLS SUBDIVISION
NO SUPES PERMITTED ON GROUNDS FOR ANY REASON.
TRESPASSERS WILL BE SUBDUED USING NECESSARY FORCE.
I SAID THAT ZACH DUMPED BUBBLES.
HE DID? WHY DIDN'T I HEAR ABOUT THIS EARLIER?
I DIDN'T HAVE A CHANCE TO TELL YOU.

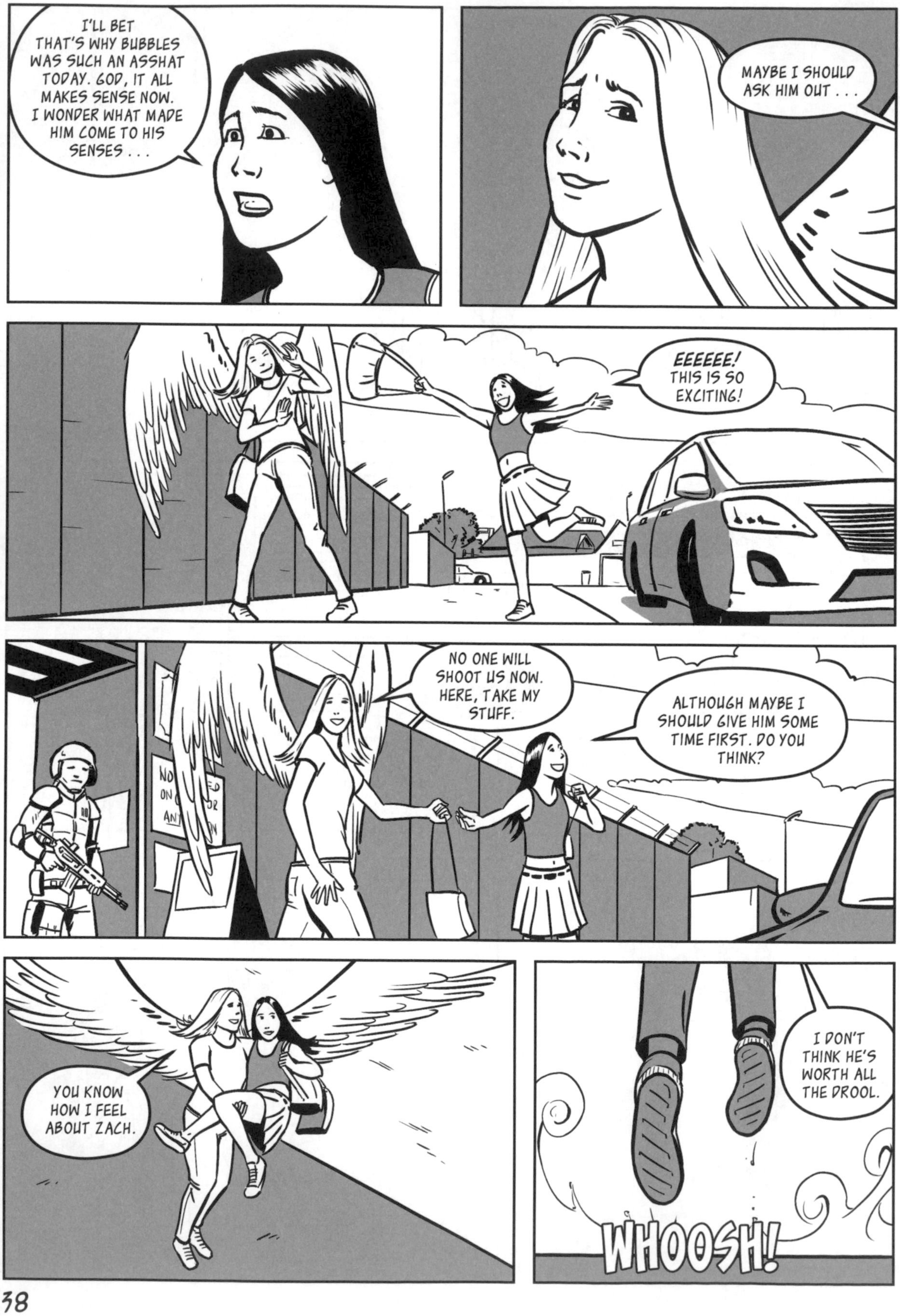

I'LL BET THAT'S WHY BUBBLES WAS SUCH AN ASSHAT TODAY. GOD, IT ALL MAKES SENSE NOW. I WONDER WHAT MADE HIM COME TO HIS SENSES . . .
MAYBE I SHOULD ASK HIM OUT . . .
EEEEEE! THIS IS SO EXCITING!
NO ONE WILL SHOOT US NOW. HERE, TAKE MY STUFF.
ALTHOUGH MAYBE I SHOULD GIVE HIM SOME TIME FIRST. DO YOU THINK?
YOU KNOW HOW I FEEL ABOUT ZACH.
I DON'T THINK HE'S WORTH ALL THE DROOL.
WHOOSH!

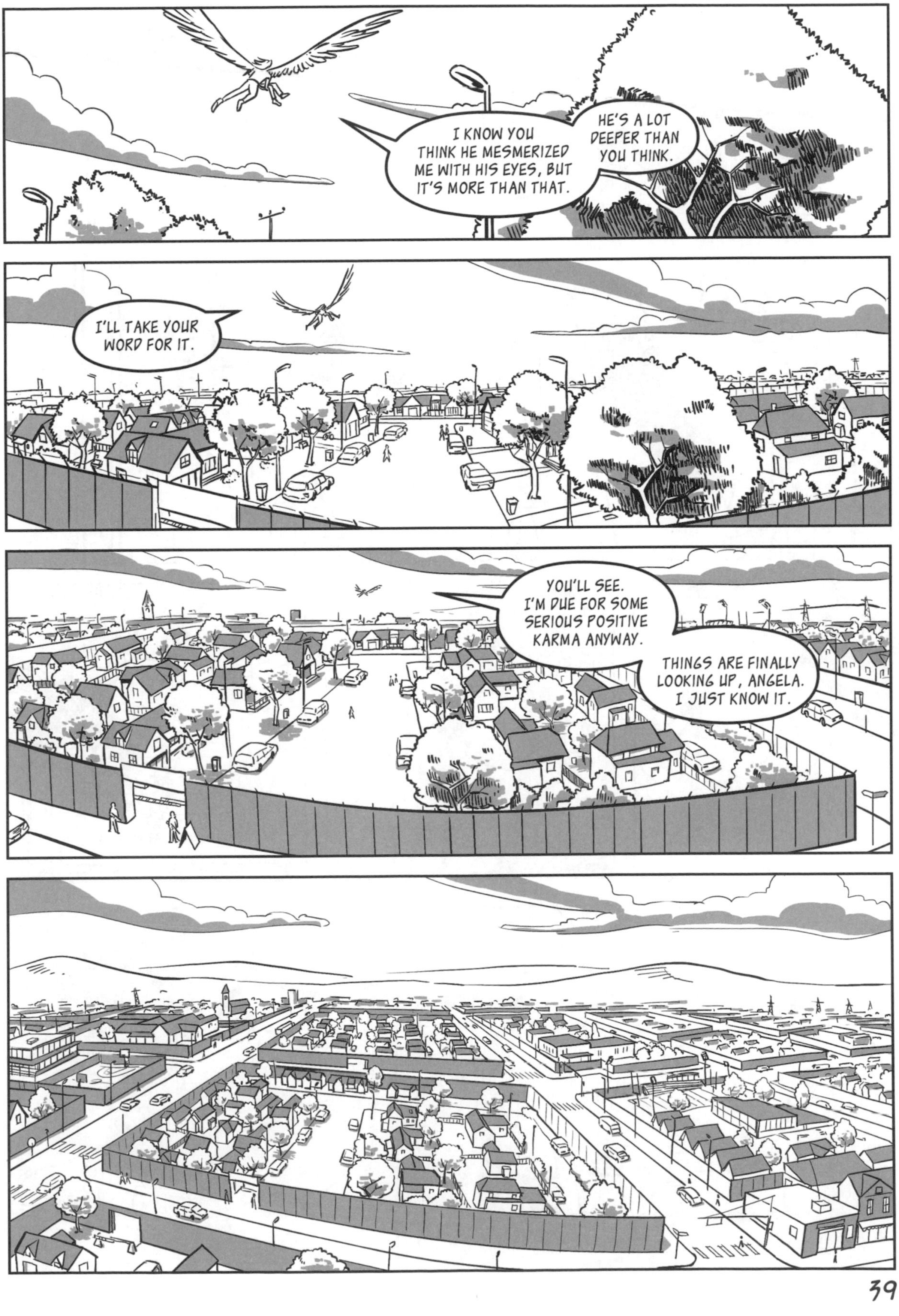
I KNOW YOU THINK HE MESMERIZED ME WITH HIS EYES, BUT IT'S MORE THAN THAT.
HE'S A LOT DEEPER THAN YOU THINK.
I'LL TAKE YOUR WORD FOR IT.
YOU'LL SEE. I'M DUE FOR SOME SERIOUS POSITIVE KARMA ANYWAY.
THINGS ARE FINALLY LOOKING UP, ANGELA. I JUST KNOW IT.

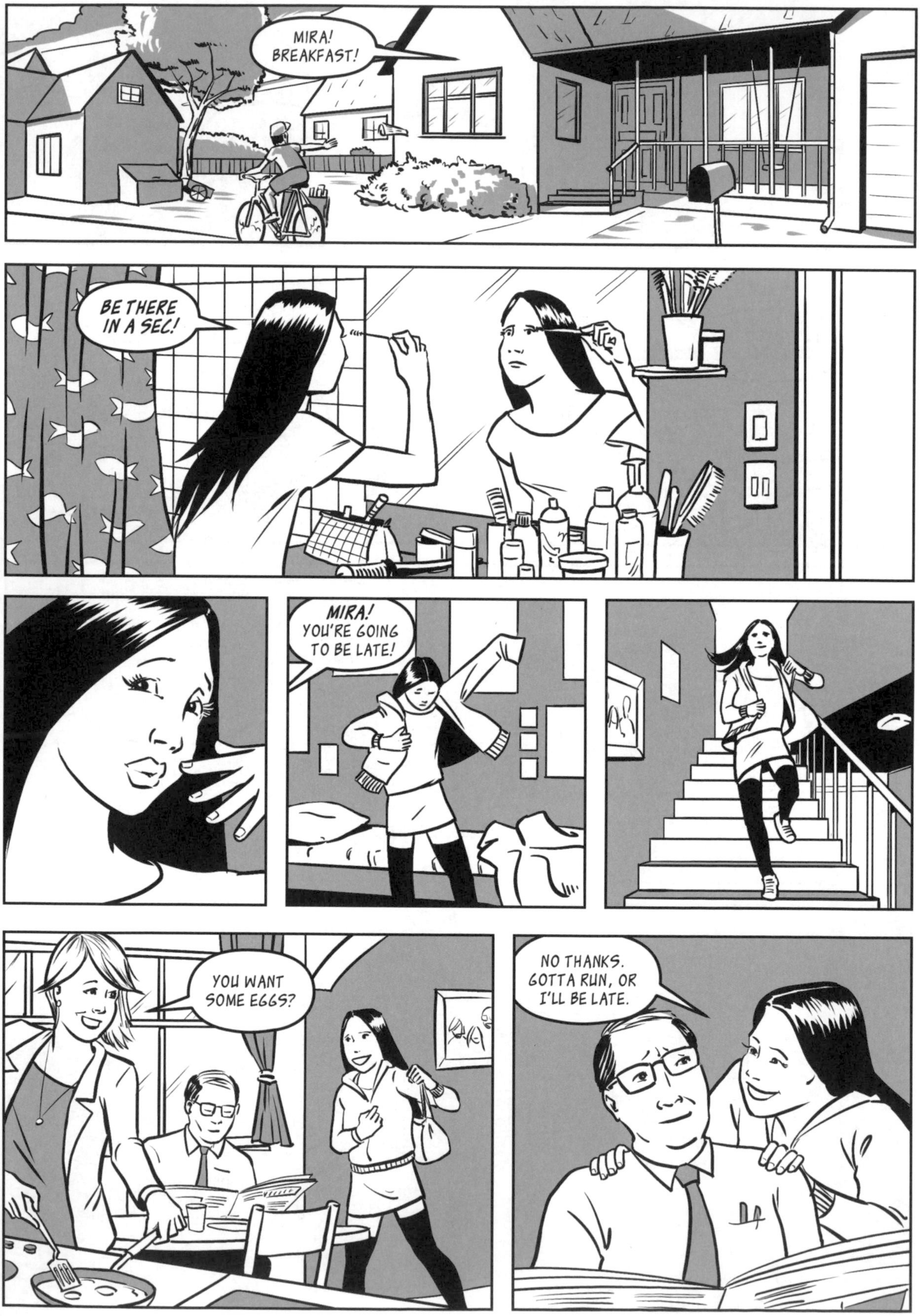
MIRA! BREAKFAST!
BE THERE IN A SEC!
MIRA! YOU'RE GOING TO BE LATE!
YOU WANT SOME EGGS?
NO THANKS. GOTTA RUN, OR I'LL BE LATE.

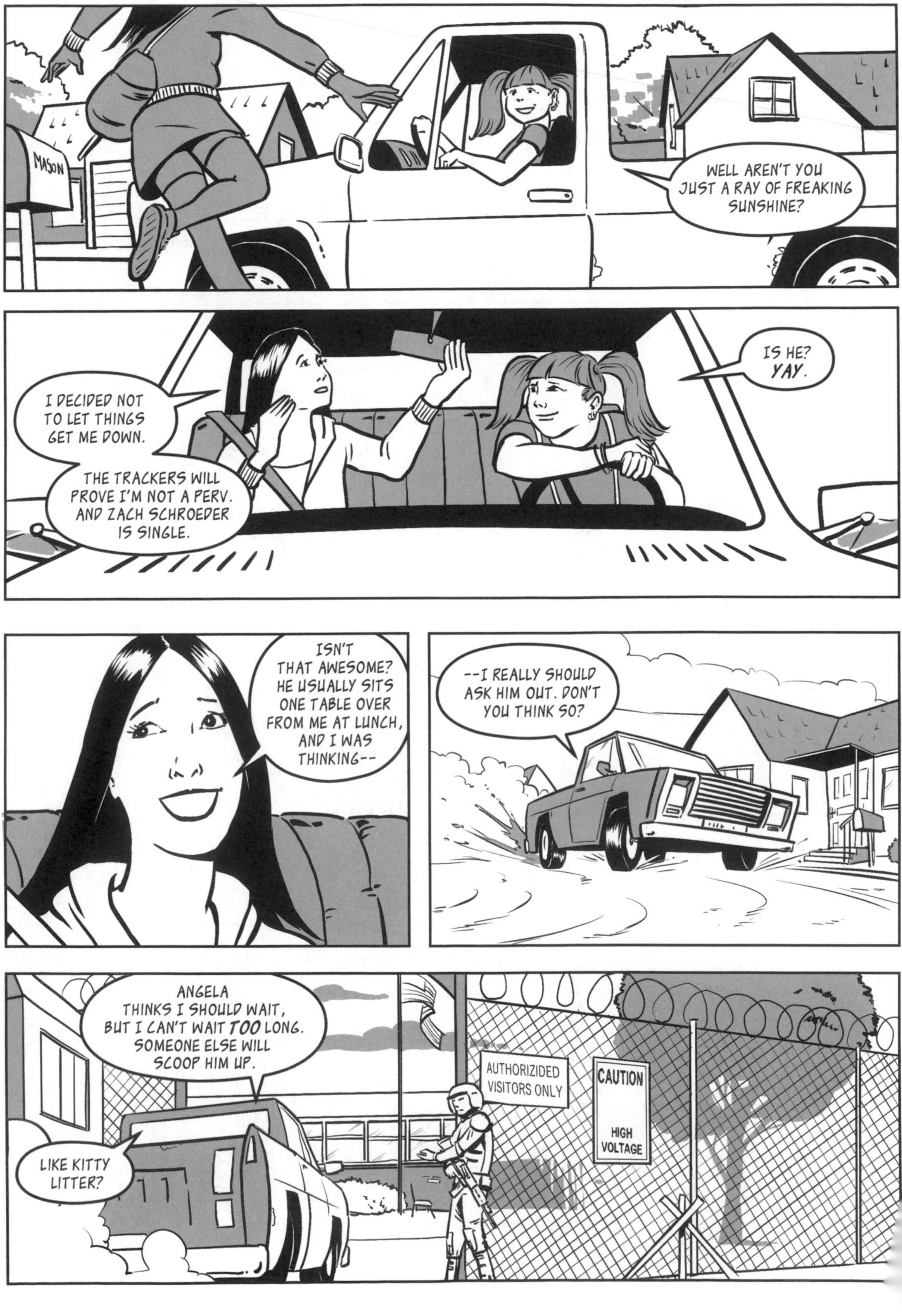
MASON
WELL AREN'T YOU JUST A RAY OF FREAKING SUNSHINE?
I DECIDED NOT TO LET THINGS GET ME DOWN.
THE TRACKERS WILL PROVE I'M NOT A PERV. AND ZACH SCHROEDER IS SINGLE.
IS HE? *YAY*.
ISN'T THAT AWESOME? HE USUALLY SITS ONE TABLE OVER FROM ME AT LUNCH, AND I WAS THINKING--
--I REALLY SHOULD ASK HIM OUT. DON'T YOU THINK SO?
ANGELA THINKS I SHOULD WAIT, BUT I CAN'T WAIT *TOO* LONG. SOMEONE ELSE WILL SCOOP HIM UP.
LIKE KITTY LITTER?
AUTHORIZIDED VISITORS ONLY
CAUTION
HIGH VOLTAGE

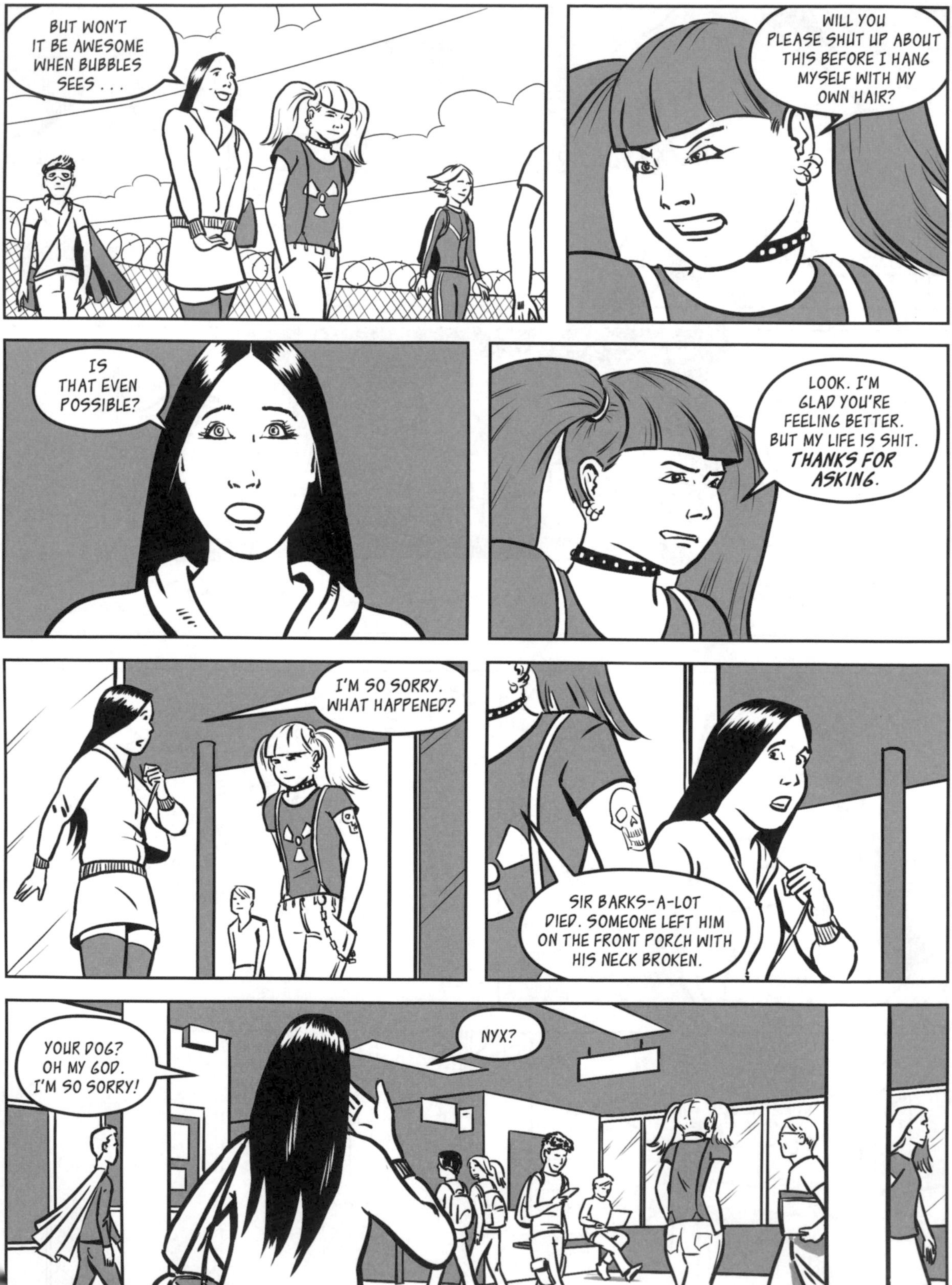
BUT WON'T IT BE AWESOME WHEN BUBBLES SEES . . .
WILL YOU PLEASE SHUT UP ABOUT THIS BEFORE I HANG MYSELF WITH MY OWN HAIR?
IS THAT EVEN POSSIBLE?
LOOK. I'M GLAD YOU'RE FEELING BETTER. BUT MY LIFE IS SHIT. *THANKS FOR ASKING*.
I'M SO SORRY. WHAT HAPPENED?
SIR BARKS-A-LOT DIED. SOMEONE LEFT HIM ON THE FRONT PORCH WITH HIS NECK BROKEN.
YOUR DOG? OH MY GOD. I'M SO SORRY!
NYX?

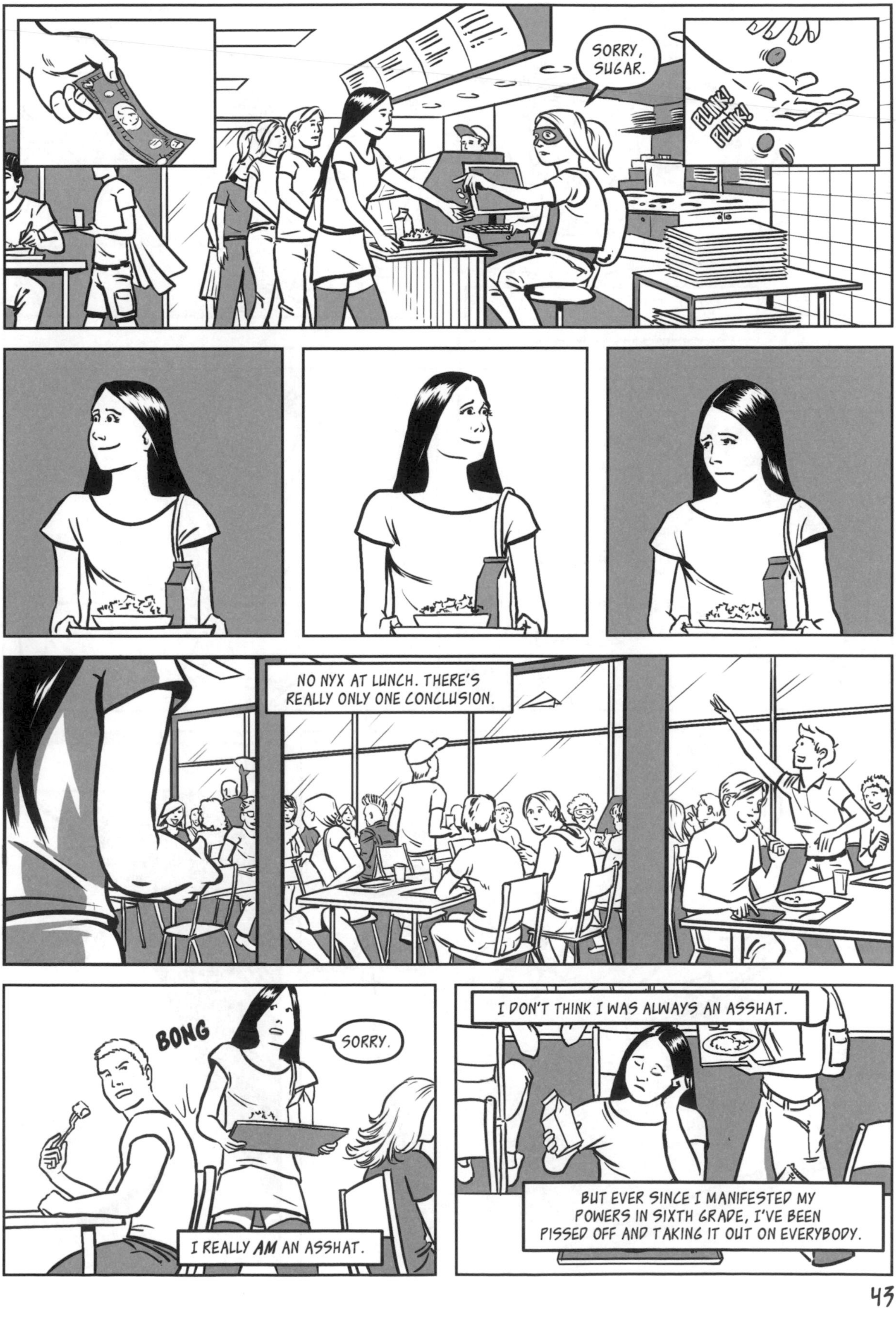
SORRY, SUGAR.
PLINK! PLINK!
NO NYX AT LUNCH. THERE'S REALLY ONLY ONE CONCLUSION.
BONG
SORRY.
I REALLY **AM** AN ASSHAT.
I DON'T THINK I WAS ALWAYS AN ASSHAT.
BUT EVER SINCE I MANIFESTED MY POWERS IN SIXTH GRADE, I'VE BEEN PISSED OFF AND TAKING IT OUT ON EVERYBODY.

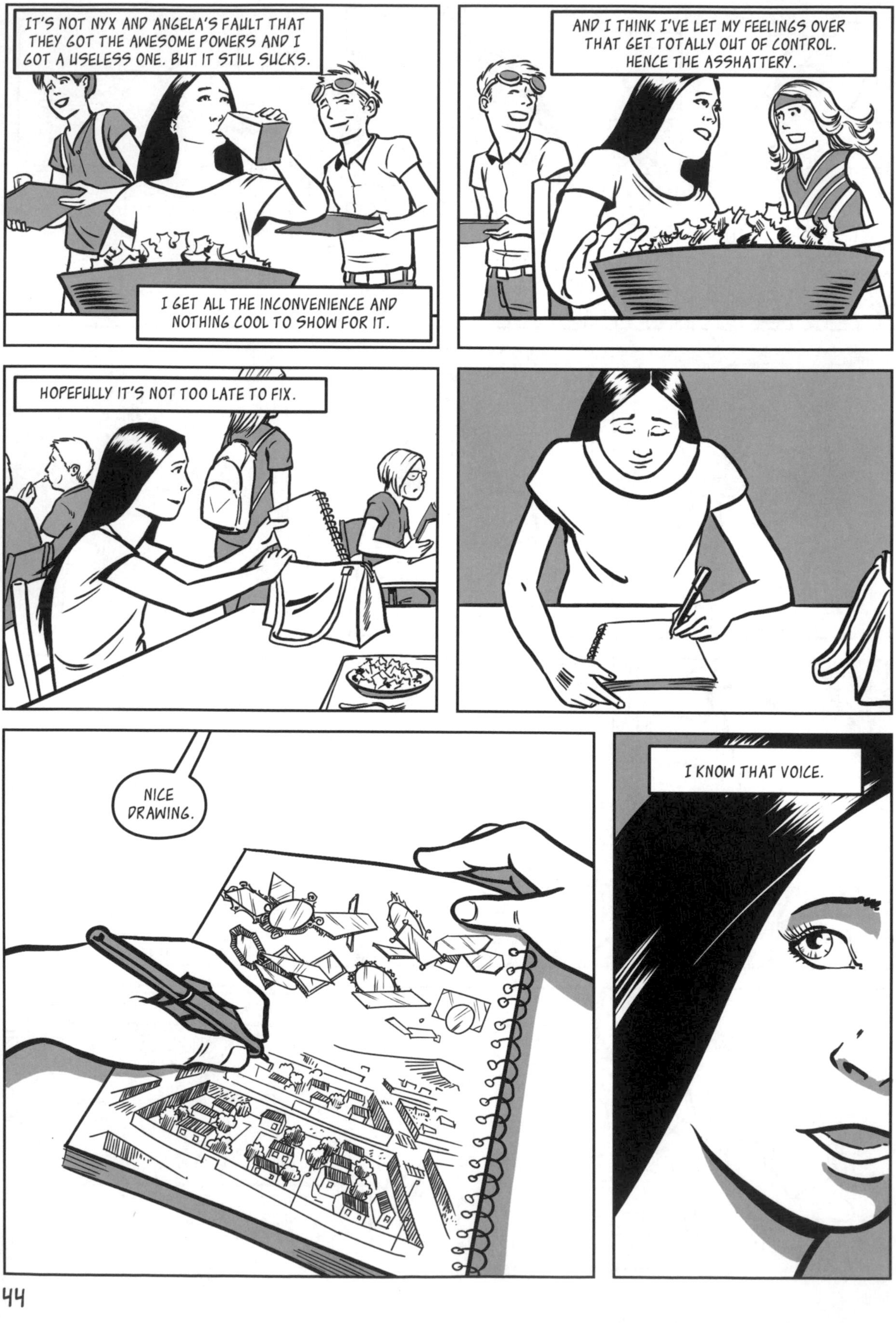
IT'S NOT NYX AND ANGELA'S FAULT THAT THEY GOT THE AWESOME POWERS AND I GOT A USELESS ONE. BUT IT STILL SUCKS.
I GET ALL THE INCONVENIENCE AND NOTHING COOL TO SHOW FOR IT.
AND I THINK I'VE LET MY FEELINGS OVER THAT GET TOTALLY OUT OF CONTROL. HENCE THE ASSHATTERY.
HOPEFULLY IT'S NOT TOO LATE TO FIX.
NICE DRAWING.
I KNOW THAT VOICE.

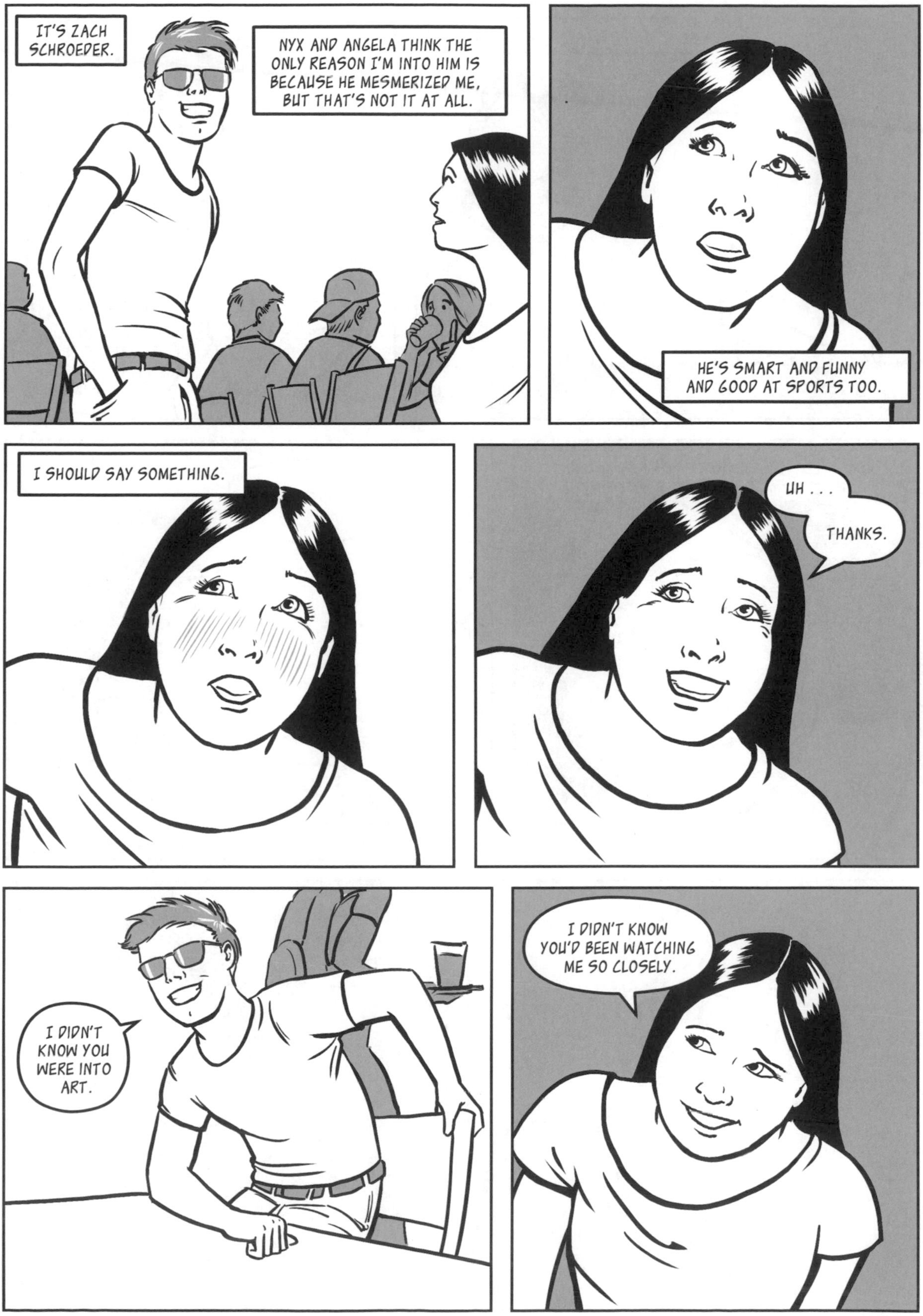
IT'S ZACH SCHROEDER.
NYX AND ANGELA THINK THE ONLY REASON I'M INTO HIM IS BECAUSE HE MESMERIZED ME, BUT THAT'S NOT IT AT ALL.
HE'S SMART AND FUNNY AND GOOD AT SPORTS TOO.
I SHOULD SAY SOMETHING.
UH . . .
THANKS.
I DIDN'T KNOW YOU WERE INTO ART.
I DIDN'T KNOW YOU'D BEEN WATCHING ME SO CLOSELY.

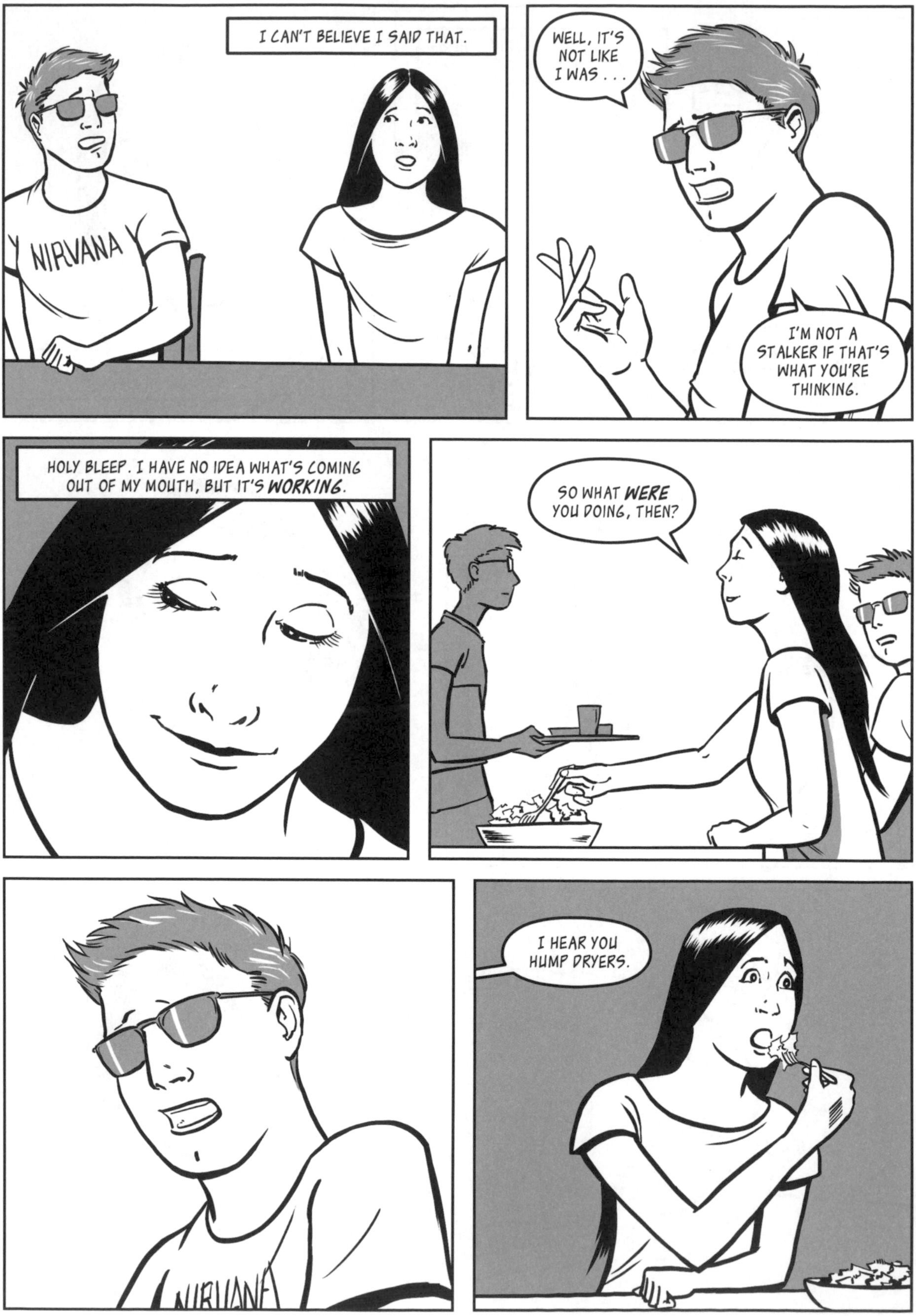
I CAN'T BELIEVE I SAID THAT.
NIRVANA
WELL, IT'S NOT LIKE I WAS . . .
I'M NOT A STALKER IF THAT'S WHAT YOU'RE THINKING.
HOLY BLEEP. I HAVE NO IDEA WHAT'S COMING OUT OF MY MOUTH, BUT IT'S **WORKING**.
SO WHAT **WERE** YOU DOING, THEN?
I HEAR YOU HUMP DRYERS.

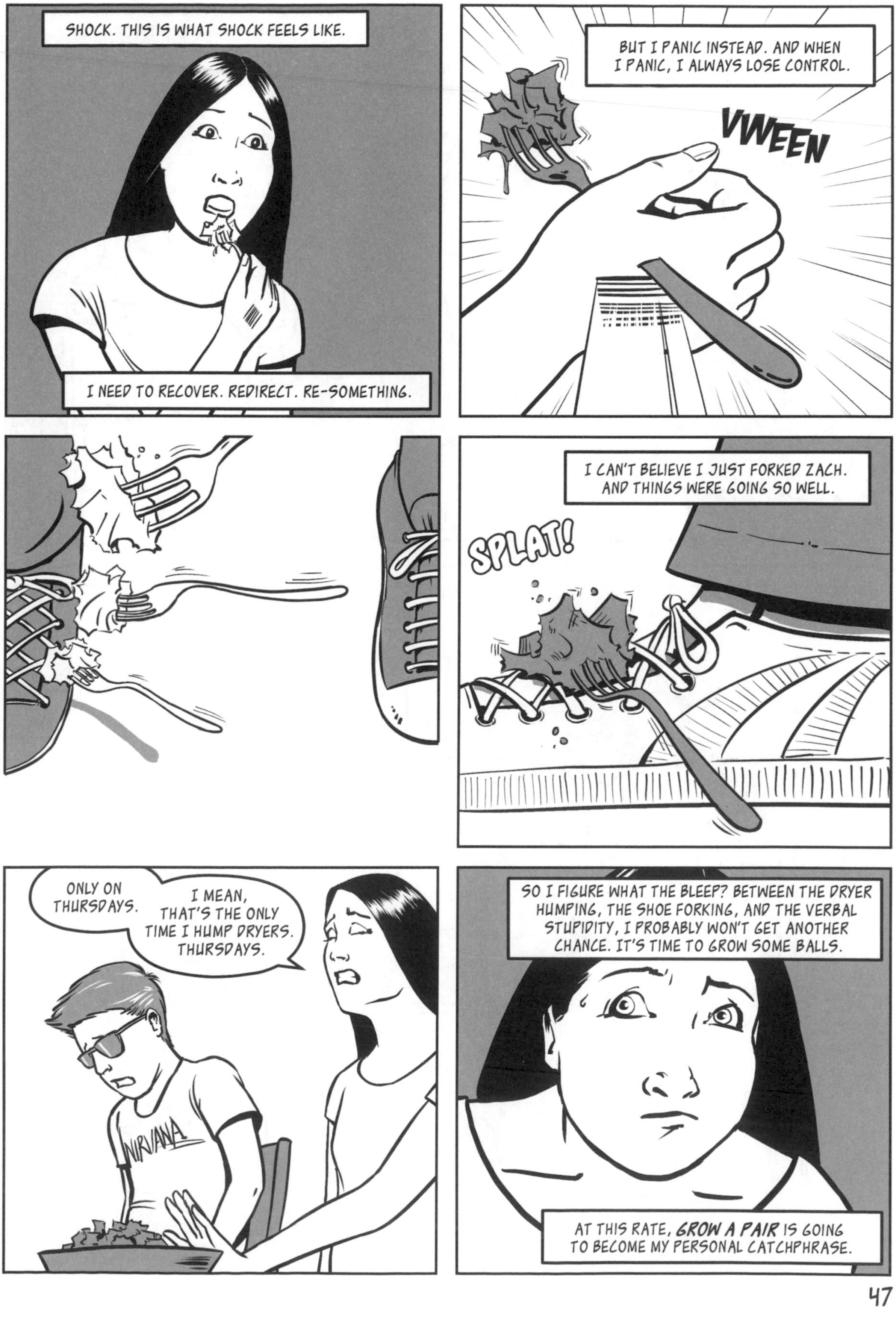
SHOCK. THIS IS WHAT SHOCK FEELS LIKE.
I NEED TO RECOVER. REDIRECT. RE-SOMETHING.
BUT I PANIC INSTEAD. AND WHEN I PANIC, I ALWAYS LOSE CONTROL.
VWEEN
I CAN'T BELIEVE I JUST FORKED ZACH. AND THINGS WERE GOING SO WELL.
SPLAT!
ONLY ON THURSDAYS.
I MEAN, THAT'S THE ONLY TIME I HUMP DRYERS. THURSDAYS.
NIRVANA
SO I FIGURE WHAT THE BLEEP? BETWEEN THE DRYER HUMPING, THE SHOE FORKING, AND THE VERBAL STUPIDITY, I PROBABLY WON'T GET ANOTHER CHANCE. IT'S TIME TO GROW SOME BALLS.
AT THIS RATE, ***GROW A PAIR*** IS GOING TO BECOME MY PERSONAL CATCHPHRASE.

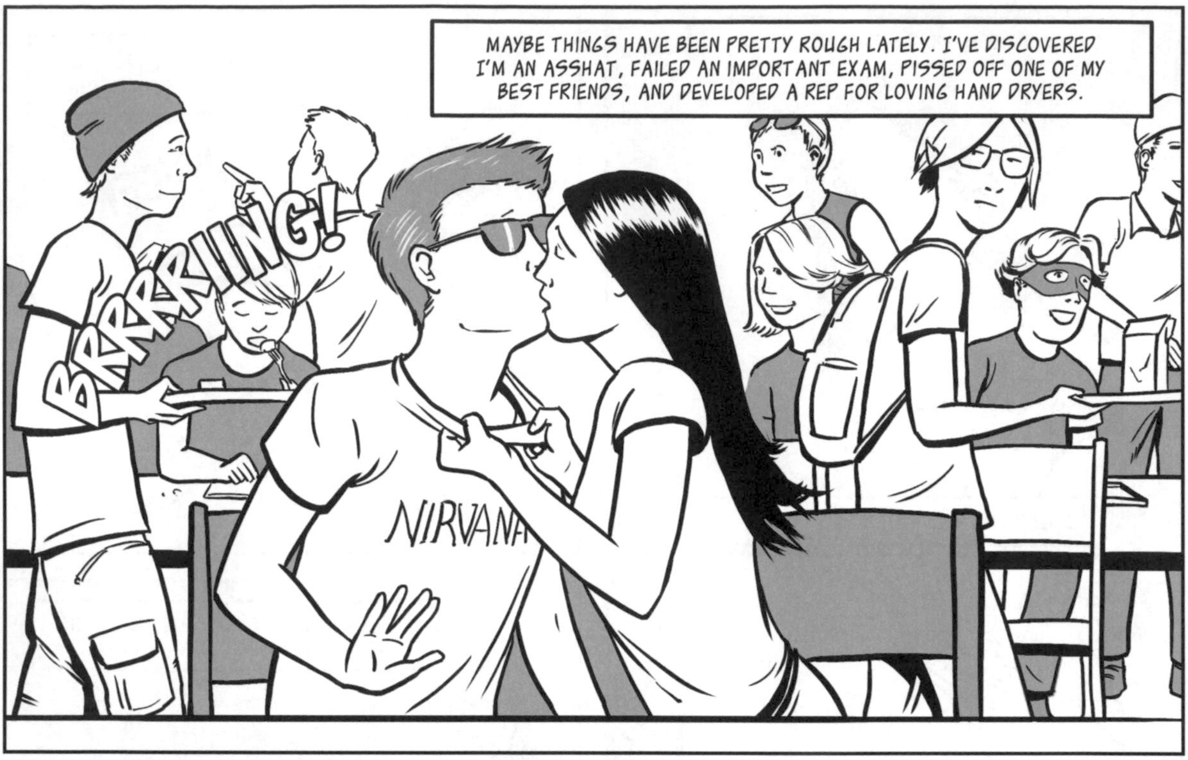
MAYBE THINGS HAVE BEEN PRETTY ROUGH LATELY. I'VE DISCOVERED I'M AN ASSHAT, FAILED AN IMPORTANT EXAM, PISSED OFF ONE OF MY BEST FRIENDS, AND DEVELOPED A REP FOR LOVING HAND DRYERS.
BRRRRIING!
NIRVANA

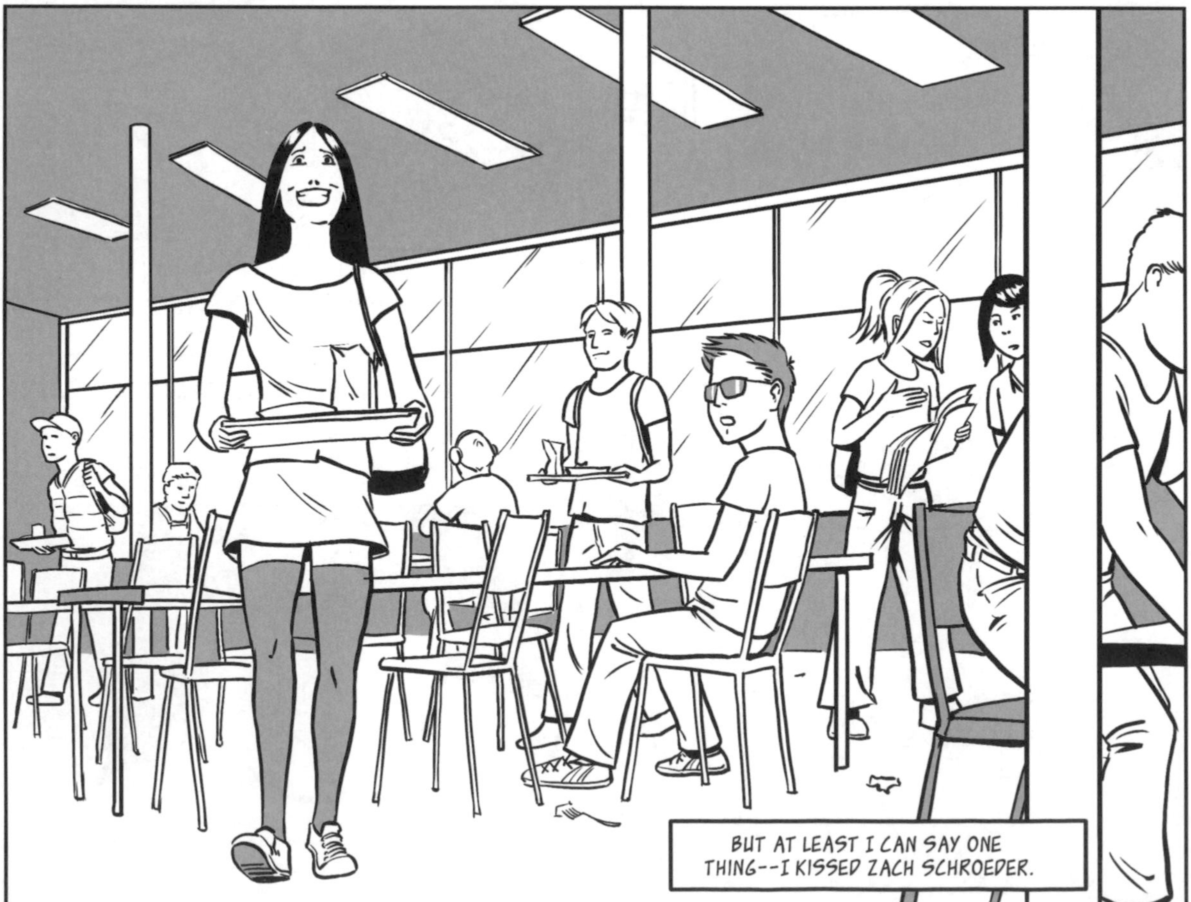
BUT AT LEAST I CAN SAY ONE THING--I KISSED ZACH SCHROEDER.

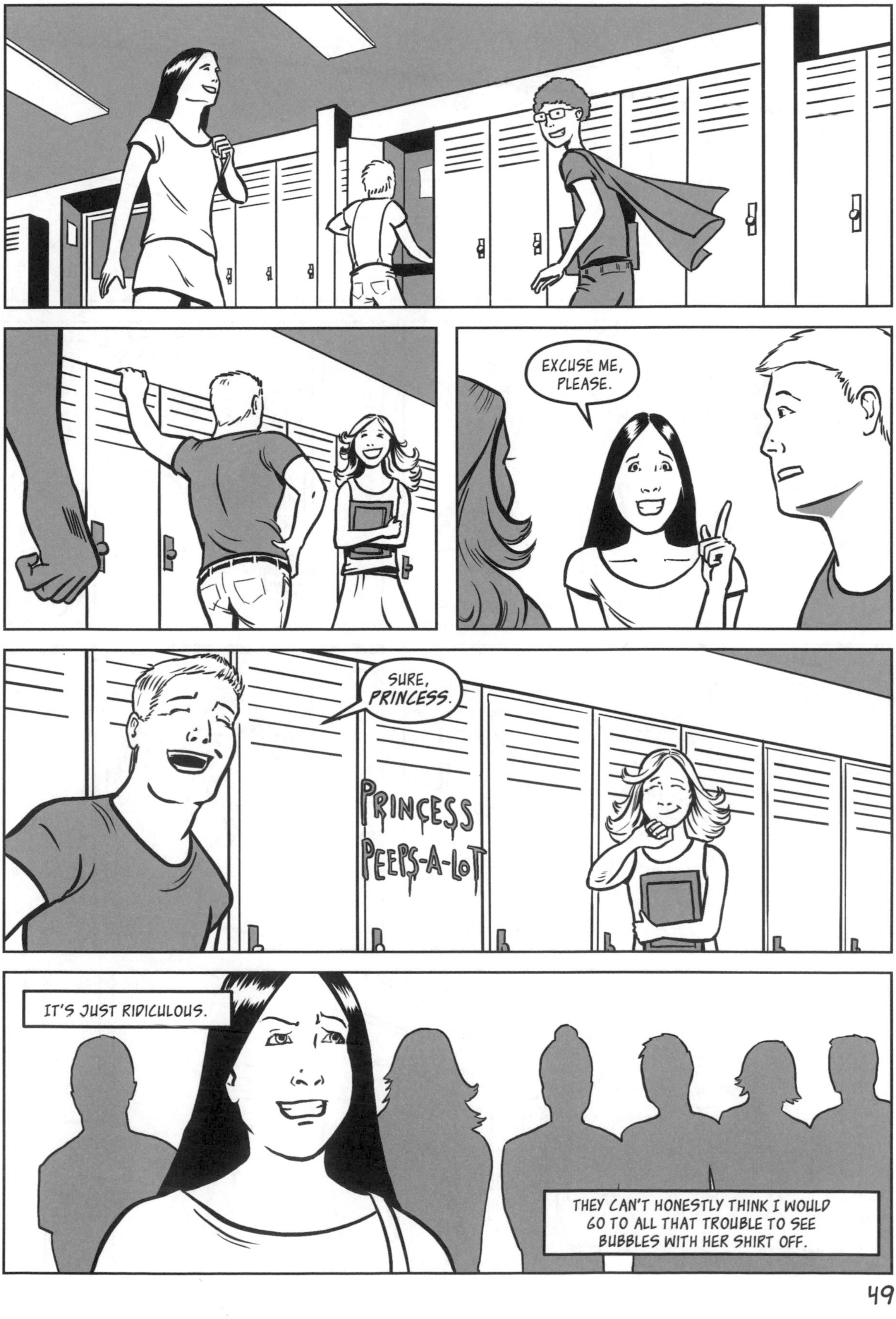
EXCUSE ME, PLEASE.
SURE, PRINCESS.
PRINCESS PEEPS-A-LOT
IT'S JUST RIDICULOUS.
THEY CAN'T HONESTLY THINK I WOULD GO TO ALL THAT TROUBLE TO SEE BUBBLES WITH HER SHIRT OFF.

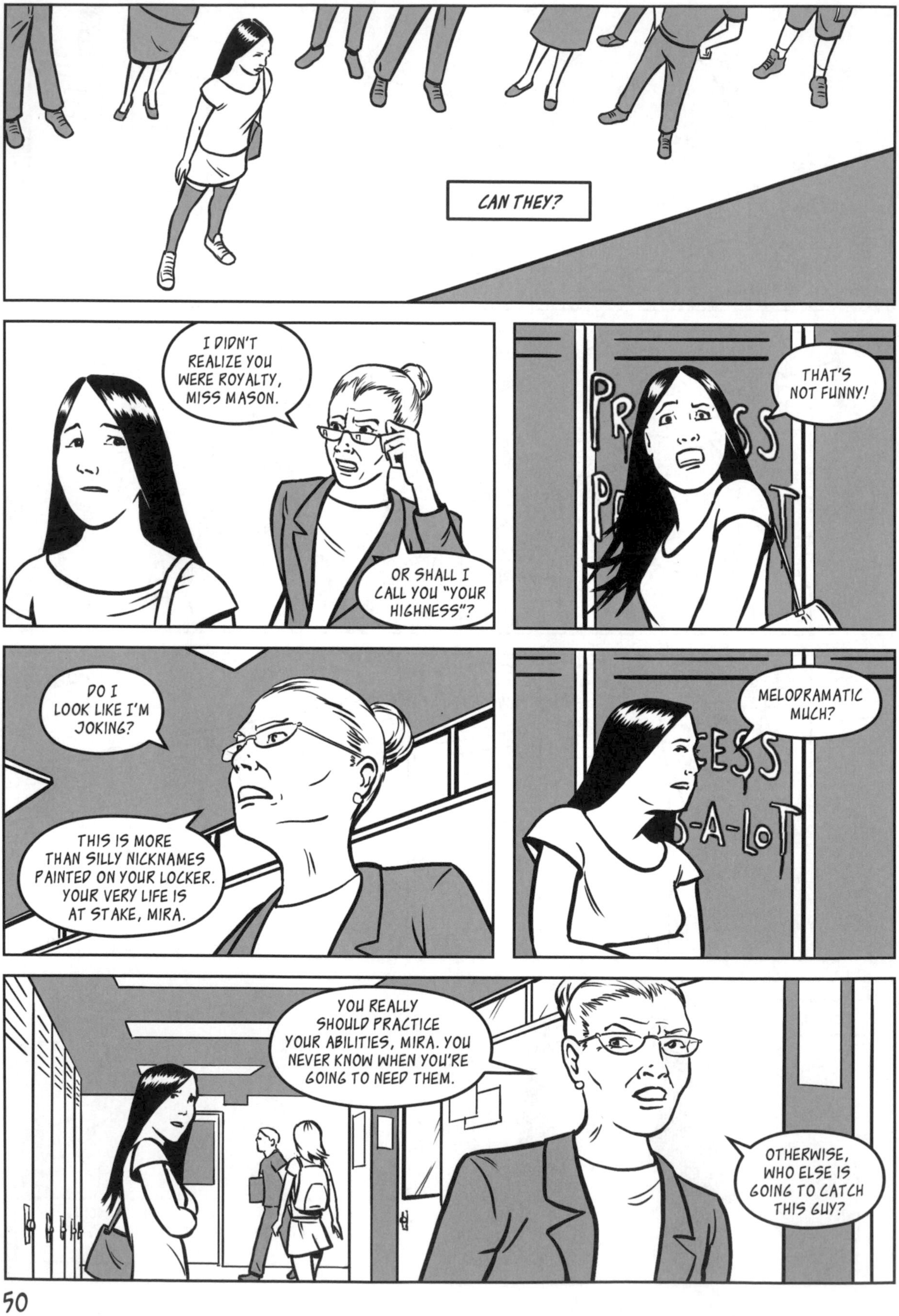
CAN THEY?
I DIDN'T REALIZE YOU WERE ROYALTY, MISS MASON.
OR SHALL I CALL YOU "YOUR HIGHNESS"?
THAT'S NOT FUNNY!
DO I LOOK LIKE I'M JOKING?
THIS IS MORE THAN SILLY NICKNAMES PAINTED ON YOUR LOCKER. YOUR VERY LIFE IS AT STAKE, MIRA.
MELODRAMATIC MUCH?
YOU REALLY SHOULD PRACTICE YOUR ABILITIES, MIRA. YOU NEVER KNOW WHEN YOU'RE GOING TO NEED THEM.
OTHERWISE, WHO ELSE IS GOING TO CATCH THIS GUY?

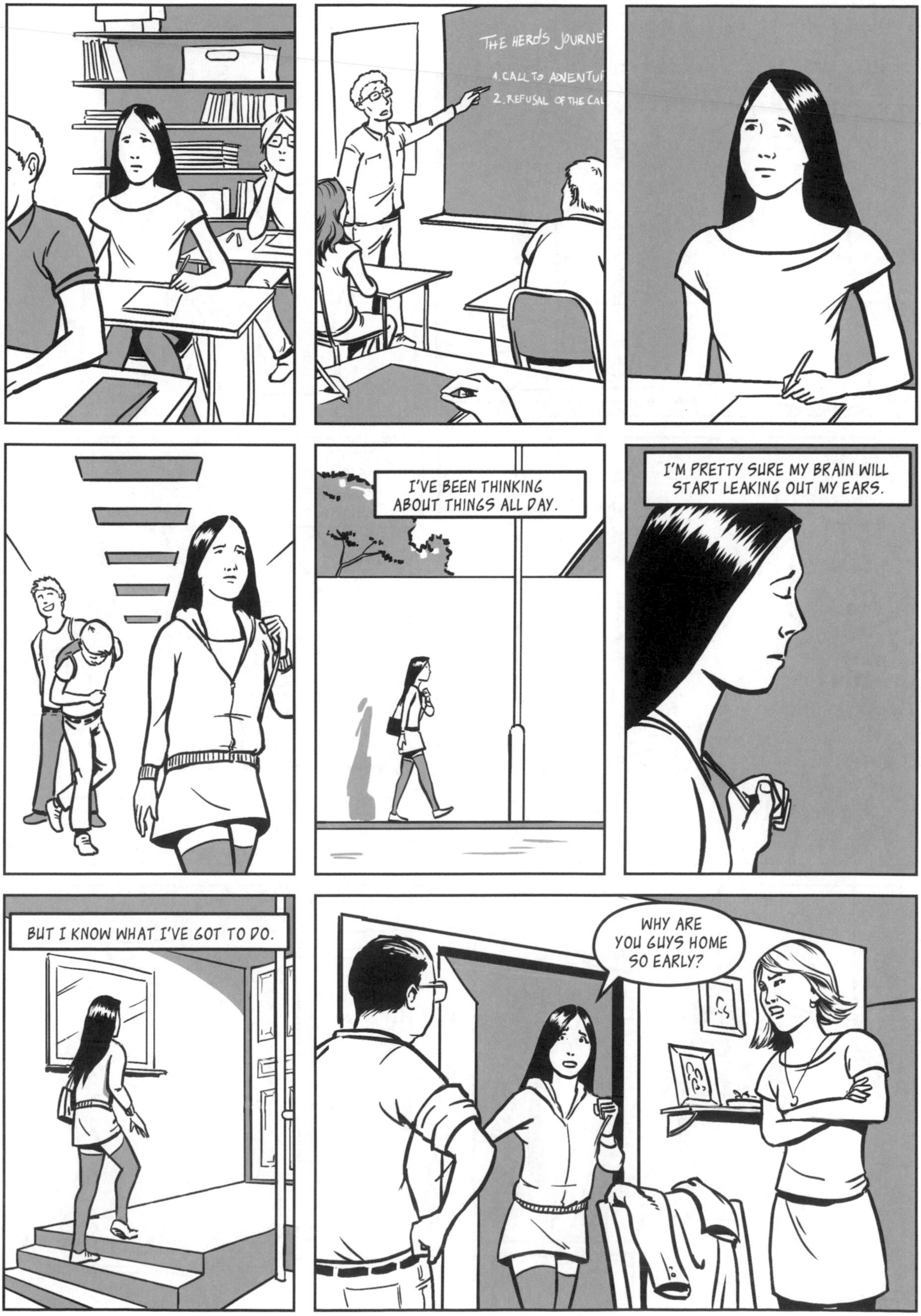
THE HERO'S JOURNE
1. CALL TO ADVENTU
2. REFUSAL OF THE CAL
I'VE BEEN THINKING ABOUT THINGS ALL DAY.
I'M PRETTY SURE MY BRAIN WILL START LEAKING OUT MY EARS.
BUT I KNOW WHAT I'VE GOT TO DO.
WHY ARE YOU GUYS HOME SO EARLY?

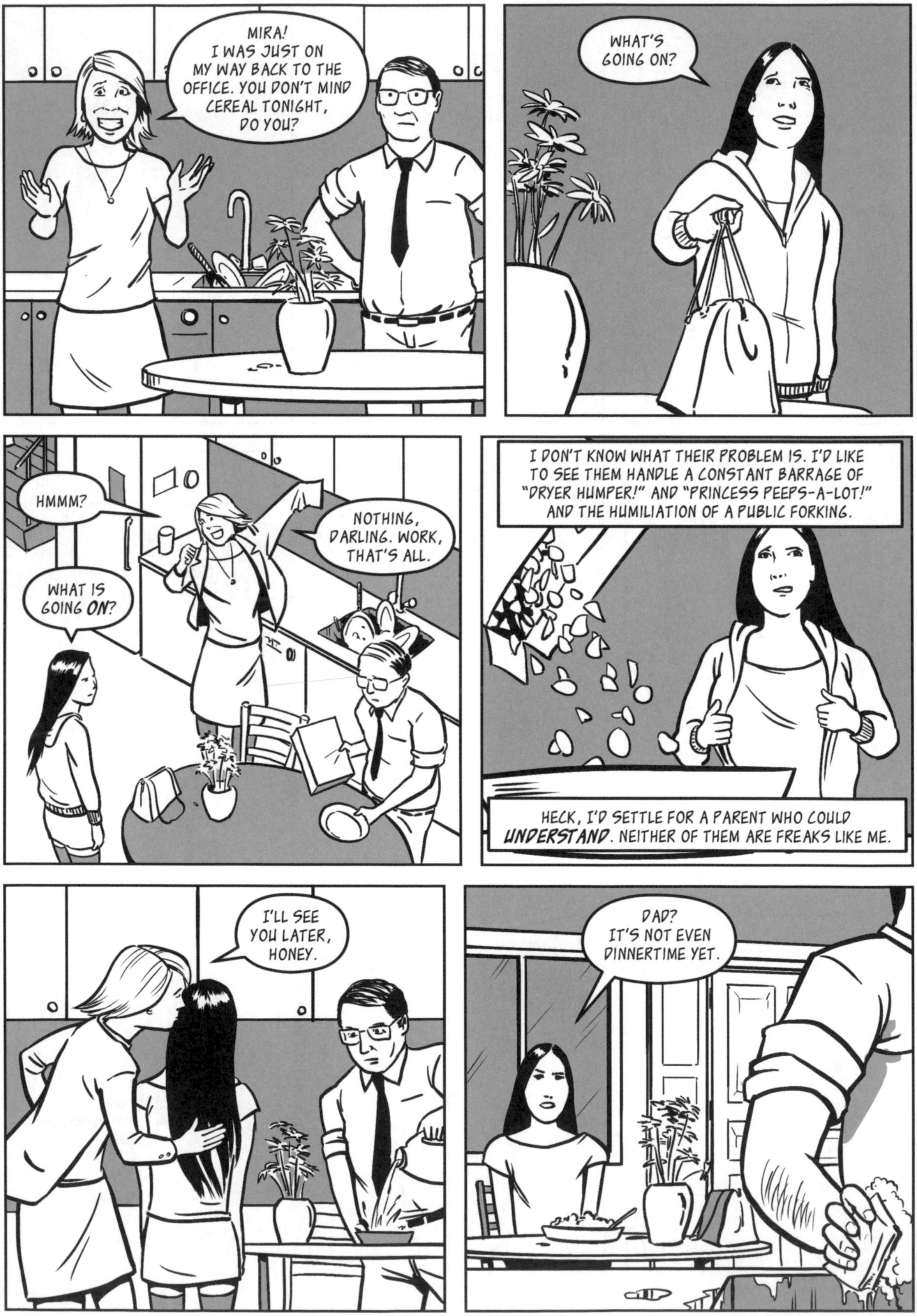
MIRA! I WAS JUST ON MY WAY BACK TO THE OFFICE. YOU DON'T MIND CEREAL TONIGHT, DO YOU?
WHAT'S GOING ON?
HMMM?
NOTHING, DARLING. WORK, THAT'S ALL.
WHAT IS GOING ON?
I DON'T KNOW WHAT THEIR PROBLEM IS. I'D LIKE TO SEE THEM HANDLE A CONSTANT BARRAGE OF "DRYER HUMPER!" AND "PRINCESS PEEPS-A-LOT!" AND THE HUMILIATION OF A PUBLIC FORKING.
HECK, I'D SETTLE FOR A PARENT WHO COULD UNDERSTAND. NEITHER OF THEM ARE FREAKS LIKE ME.
I'LL SEE YOU LATER, HONEY.
DAD? IT'S NOT EVEN DINNERTIME YET.

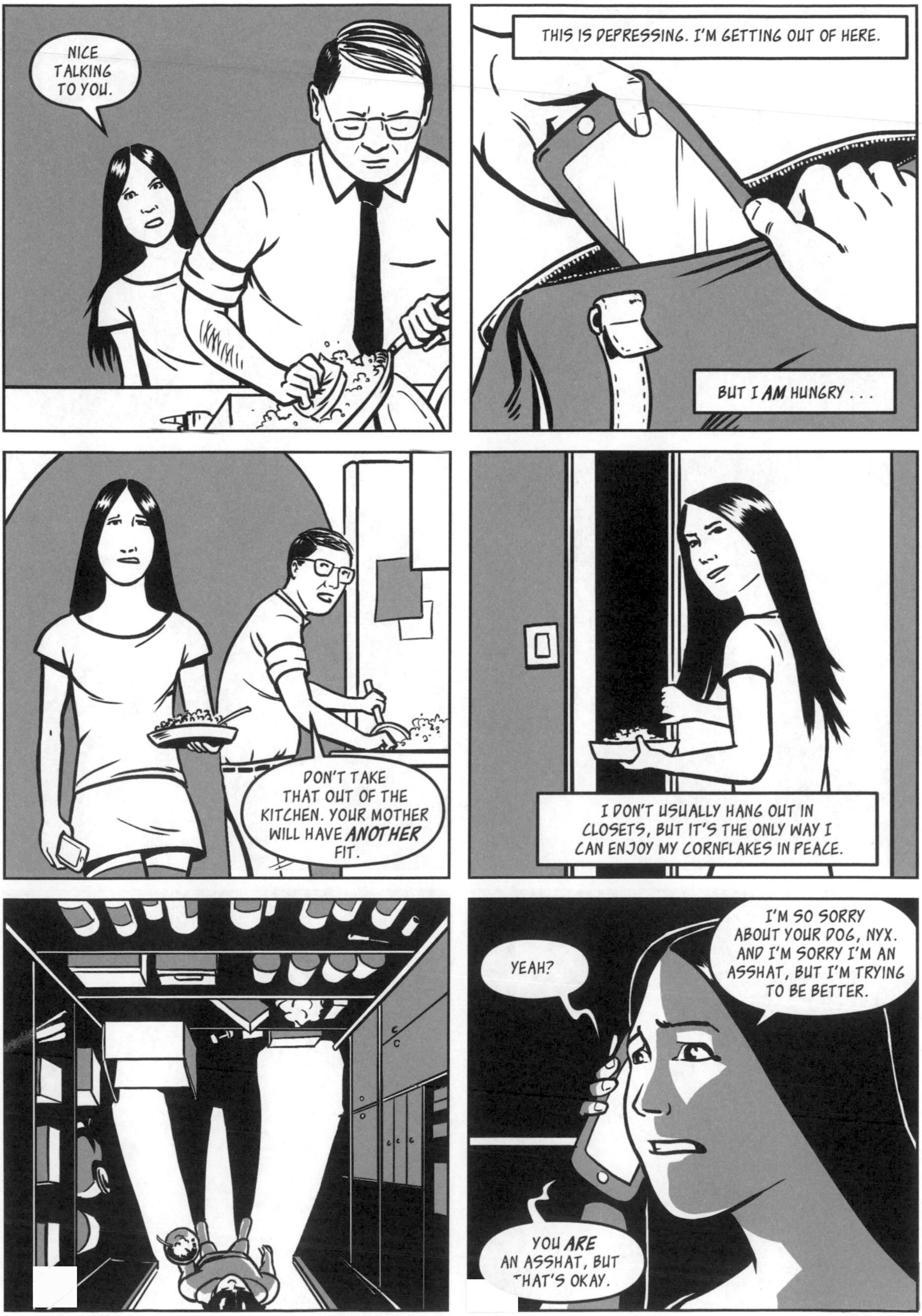
NICE TALKING TO YOU.
THIS IS DEPRESSING. I'M GETTING OUT OF HERE.
BUT I **AM** HUNGRY . . .
DON'T TAKE THAT OUT OF THE KITCHEN. YOUR MOTHER WILL HAVE **ANOTHER** FIT.
I DON'T USUALLY HANG OUT IN CLOSETS, BUT IT'S THE ONLY WAY I CAN ENJOY MY CORNFLAKES IN PEACE.
YEAH?
I'M SO SORRY ABOUT YOUR DOG, NYX. AND I'M SORRY I'M AN ASSHAT, BUT I'M TRYING TO BE BETTER.
YOU **ARE** AN ASSHAT, BUT THAT'S OKAY.

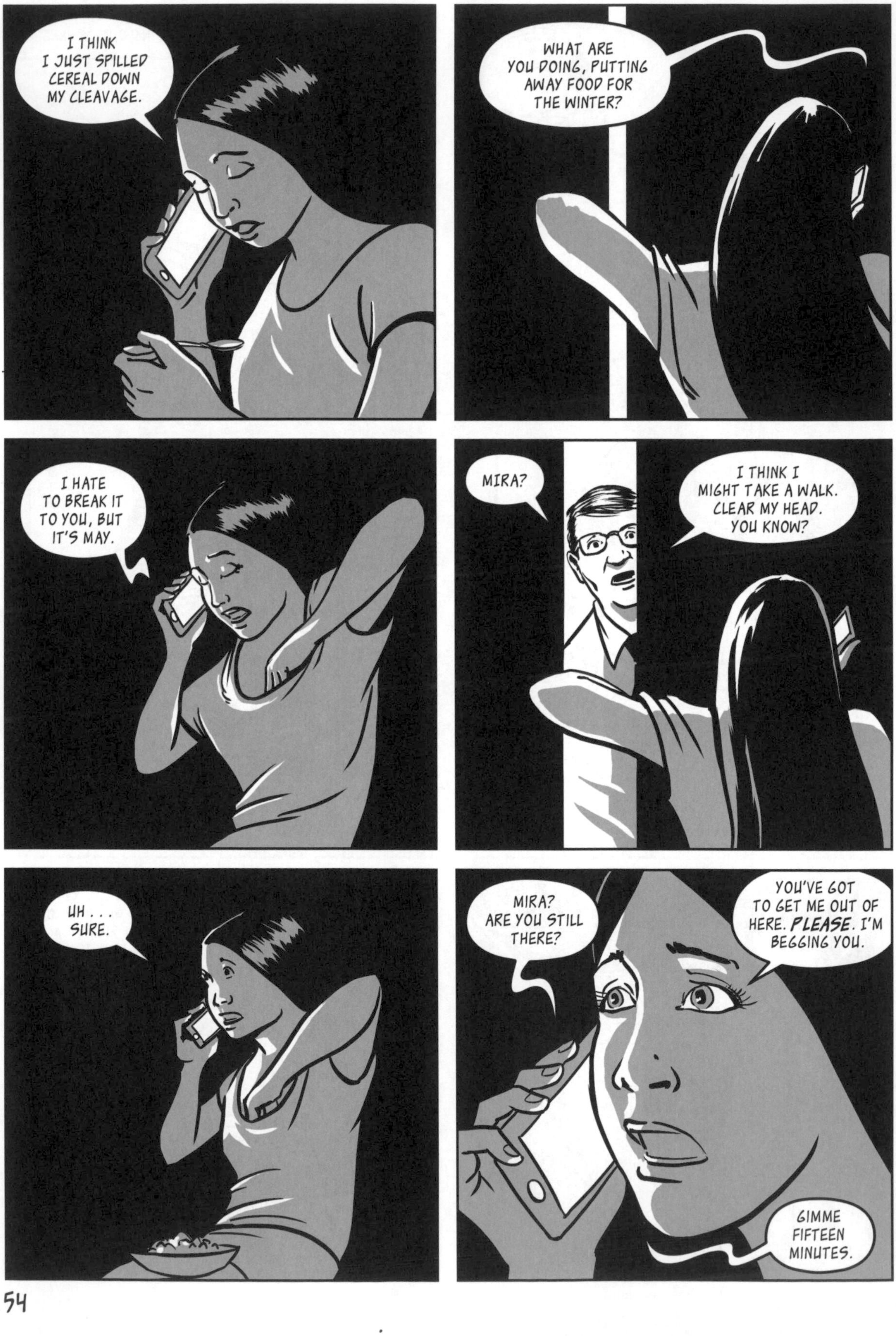
I THINK I JUST SPILLED CEREAL DOWN MY CLEAVAGE.
WHAT ARE YOU DOING, PUTTING AWAY FOOD FOR THE WINTER?
I HATE TO BREAK IT TO YOU, BUT IT'S MAY.
MIRA?
I THINK I MIGHT TAKE A WALK. CLEAR MY HEAD. YOU KNOW?
UH . . . SURE.
MIRA? ARE YOU STILL THERE?
YOU'VE GOT TO GET ME OUT OF HERE. PLEASE. I'M BEGGING YOU.
GIMME FIFTEEN MINUTES.

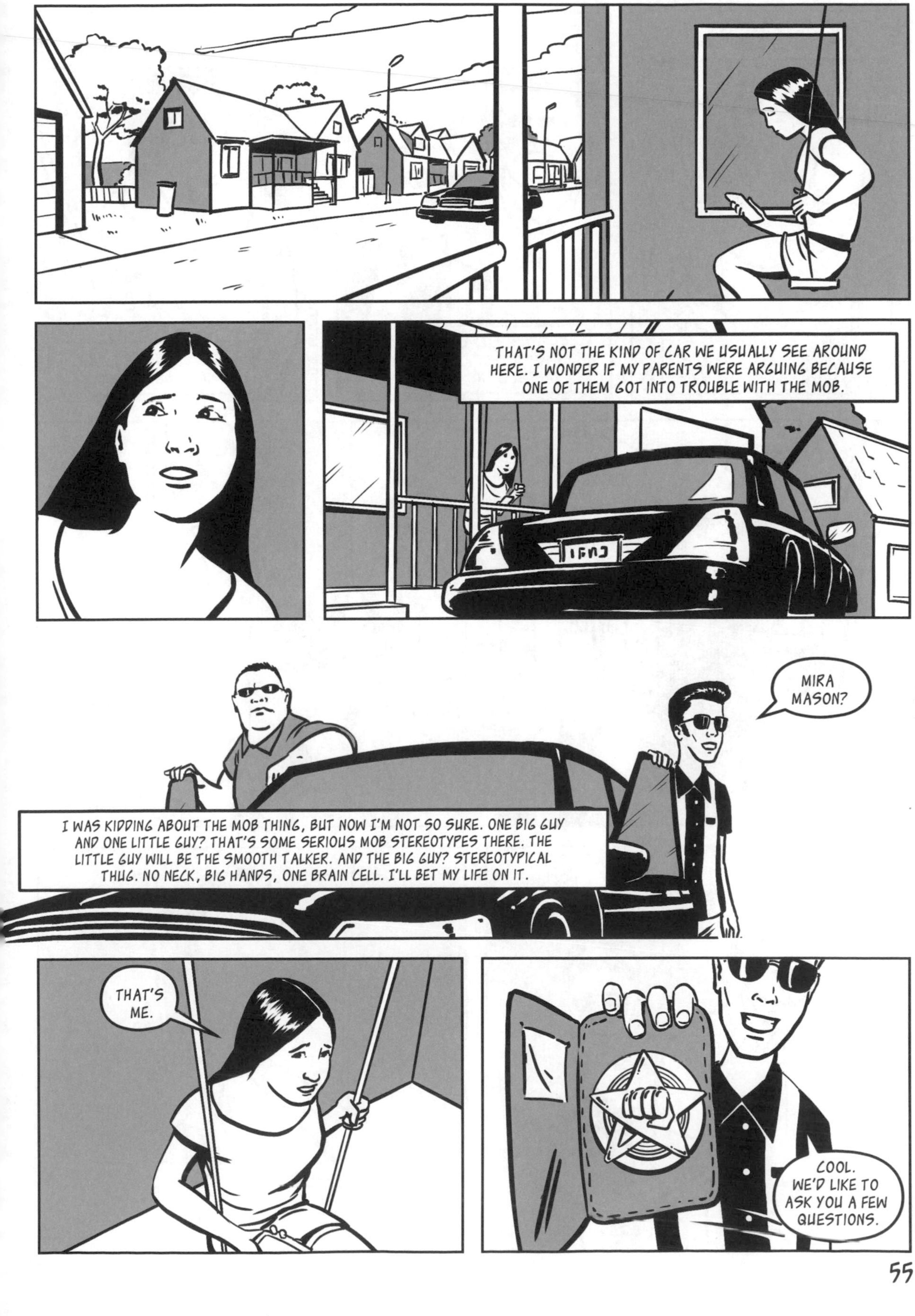
THAT'S NOT THE KIND OF CAR WE USUALLY SEE AROUND HERE. I WONDER IF MY PARENTS WERE ARGUING BECAUSE ONE OF THEM GOT INTO TROUBLE WITH THE MOB.
MIRA MASON?
I WAS KIDDING ABOUT THE MOB THING, BUT NOW I'M NOT SO SURE. ONE BIG GUY AND ONE LITTLE GUY? THAT'S SOME SERIOUS MOB STEREOTYPES THERE. THE LITTLE GUY WILL BE THE SMOOTH TALKER. AND THE BIG GUY? STEREOTYPICAL THUG. NO NECK, BIG HANDS, ONE BRAIN CELL. I'LL BET MY LIFE ON IT.
THAT'S ME.
COOL. WE'D LIKE TO ASK YOU A FEW QUESTIONS.

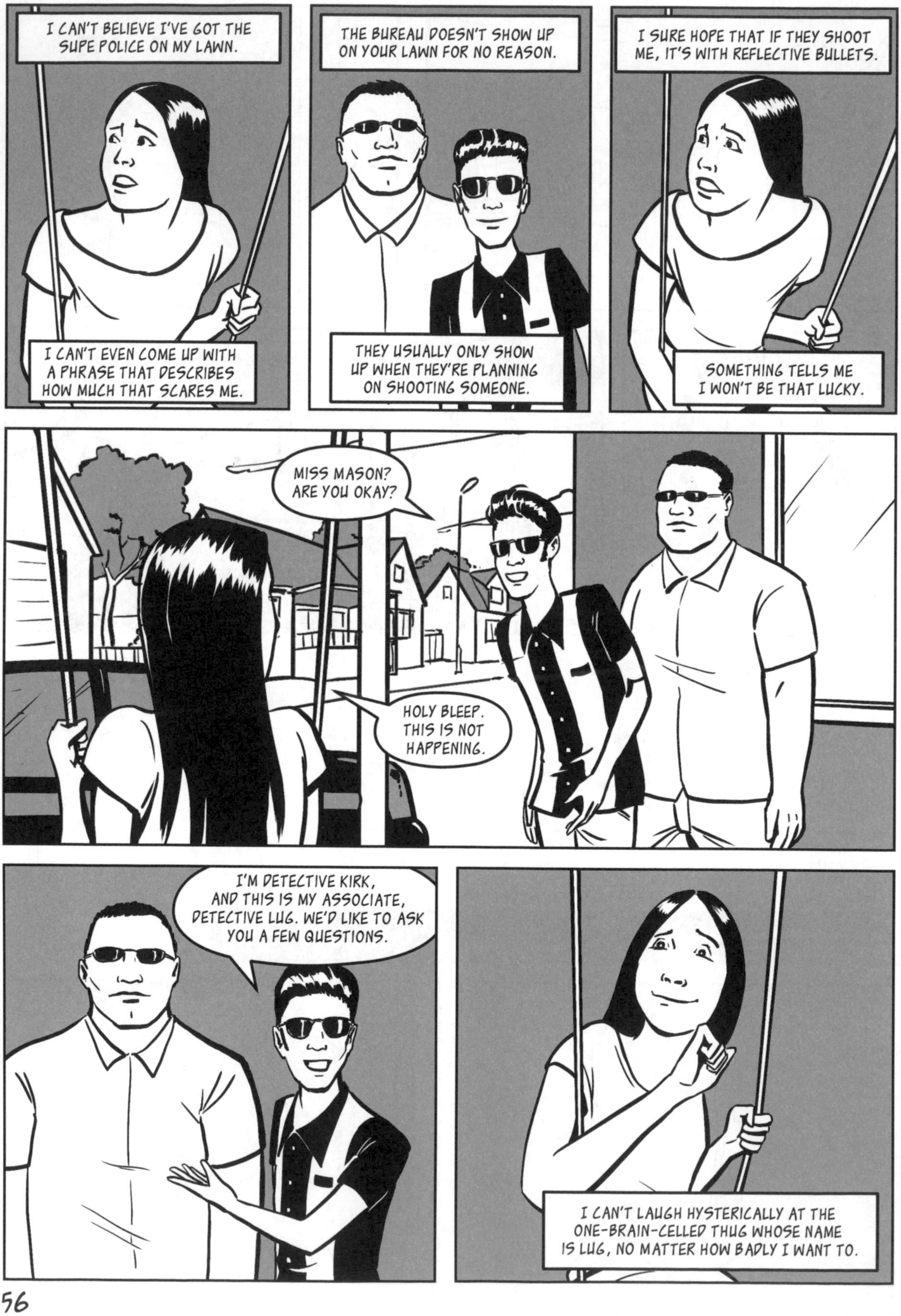
I CAN'T BELIEVE I'VE GOT THE SUPE POLICE ON MY LAWN.
I CAN'T EVEN COME UP WITH A PHRASE THAT DESCRIBES HOW MUCH THAT SCARES ME.
THE BUREAU DOESN'T SHOW UP ON YOUR LAWN FOR NO REASON.
THEY USUALLY ONLY SHOW UP WHEN THEY'RE PLANNING ON SHOOTING SOMEONE.
I SURE HOPE THAT IF THEY SHOOT ME, IT'S WITH REFLECTIVE BULLETS.
SOMETHING TELLS ME I WON'T BE THAT LUCKY.
MISS MASON? ARE YOU OKAY?
HOLY BLEEP. THIS IS NOT HAPPENING.
I'M DETECTIVE KIRK, AND THIS IS MY ASSOCIATE, DETECTIVE LUG. WE'D LIKE TO ASK YOU A FEW QUESTIONS.
I CAN'T LAUGH HYSTERICALLY AT THE ONE-BRAIN-CELLED THUG WHOSE NAME IS LUG, NO MATTER HOW BADLY I WANT TO.

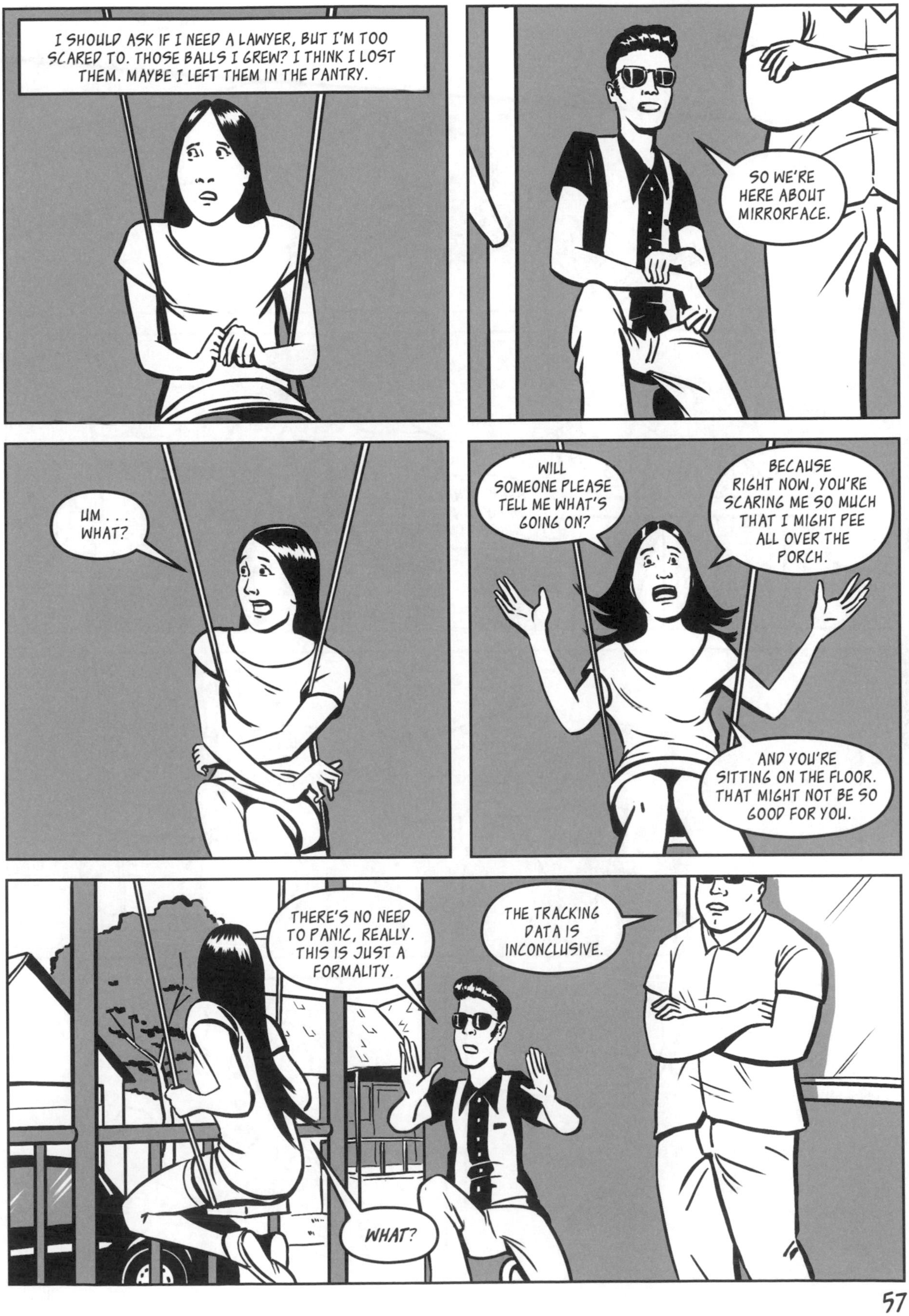
I SHOULD ASK IF I NEED A LAWYER, BUT I'M TOO SCARED TO. THOSE BALLS I GREW? I THINK I LOST THEM. MAYBE I LEFT THEM IN THE PANTRY.
SO WE'RE HERE ABOUT MIRRORFACE.
UM . . . WHAT?
WILL SOMEONE PLEASE TELL ME WHAT'S GOING ON?
BECAUSE RIGHT NOW, YOU'RE SCARING ME SO MUCH THAT I MIGHT PEE ALL OVER THE PORCH.
AND YOU'RE SITTING ON THE FLOOR. THAT MIGHT NOT BE SO GOOD FOR YOU.
THERE'S NO NEED TO PANIC, REALLY. THIS IS JUST A FORMALITY.
THE TRACKING DATA IS INCONCLUSIVE.
WHAT?

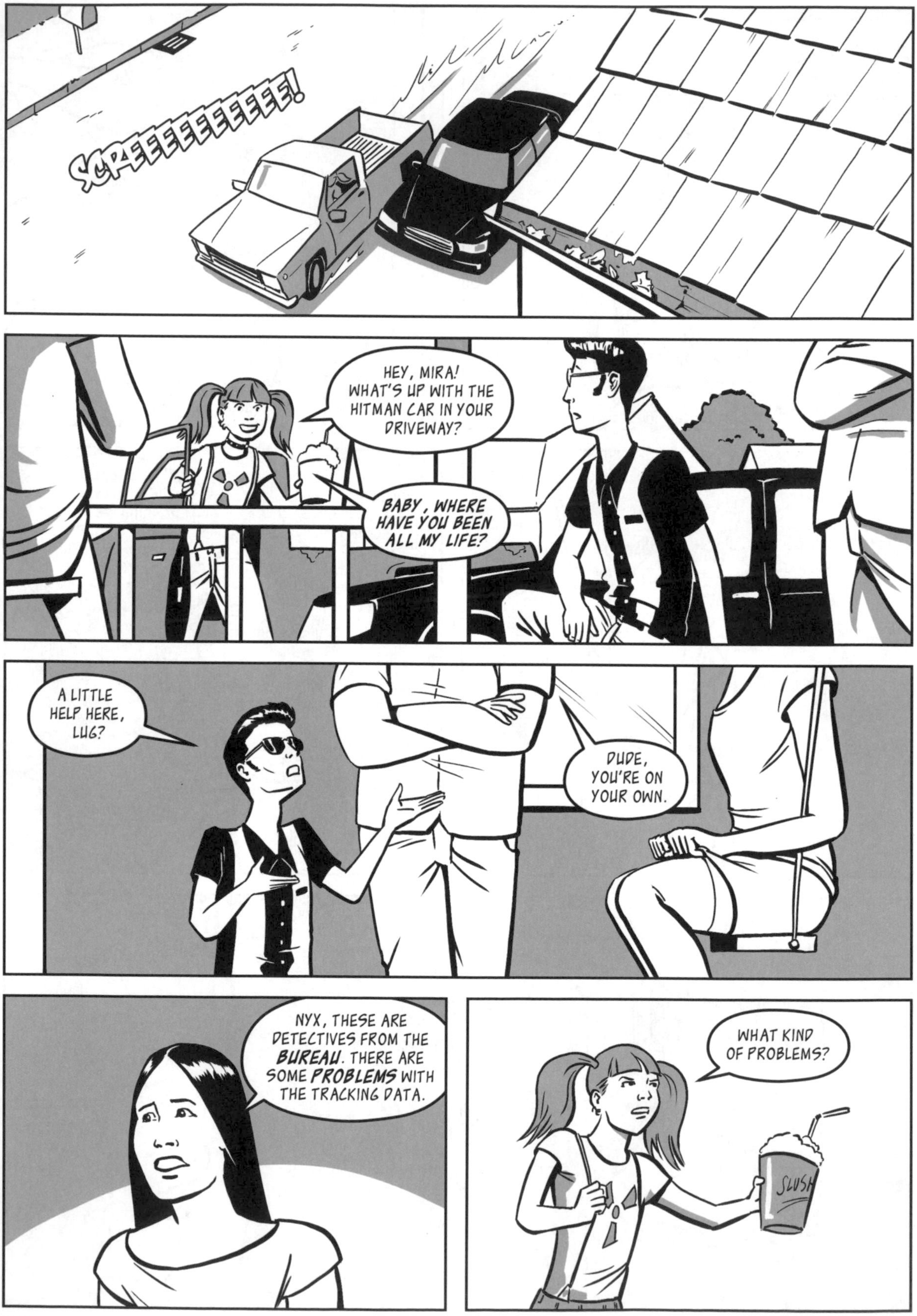
SCREEEEEEEEEEE!
HEY, MIRA! WHAT'S UP WITH THE HITMAN CAR IN YOUR DRIVEWAY?
BABY, WHERE HAVE YOU BEEN ALL MY LIFE?
A LITTLE HELP HERE, LUG?
DUDE, YOU'RE ON YOUR OWN.
NYX, THESE ARE DETECTIVES FROM THE BUREAU. THERE ARE SOME PROBLEMS WITH THE TRACKING DATA.
WHAT KIND OF PROBLEMS?
SLUSH

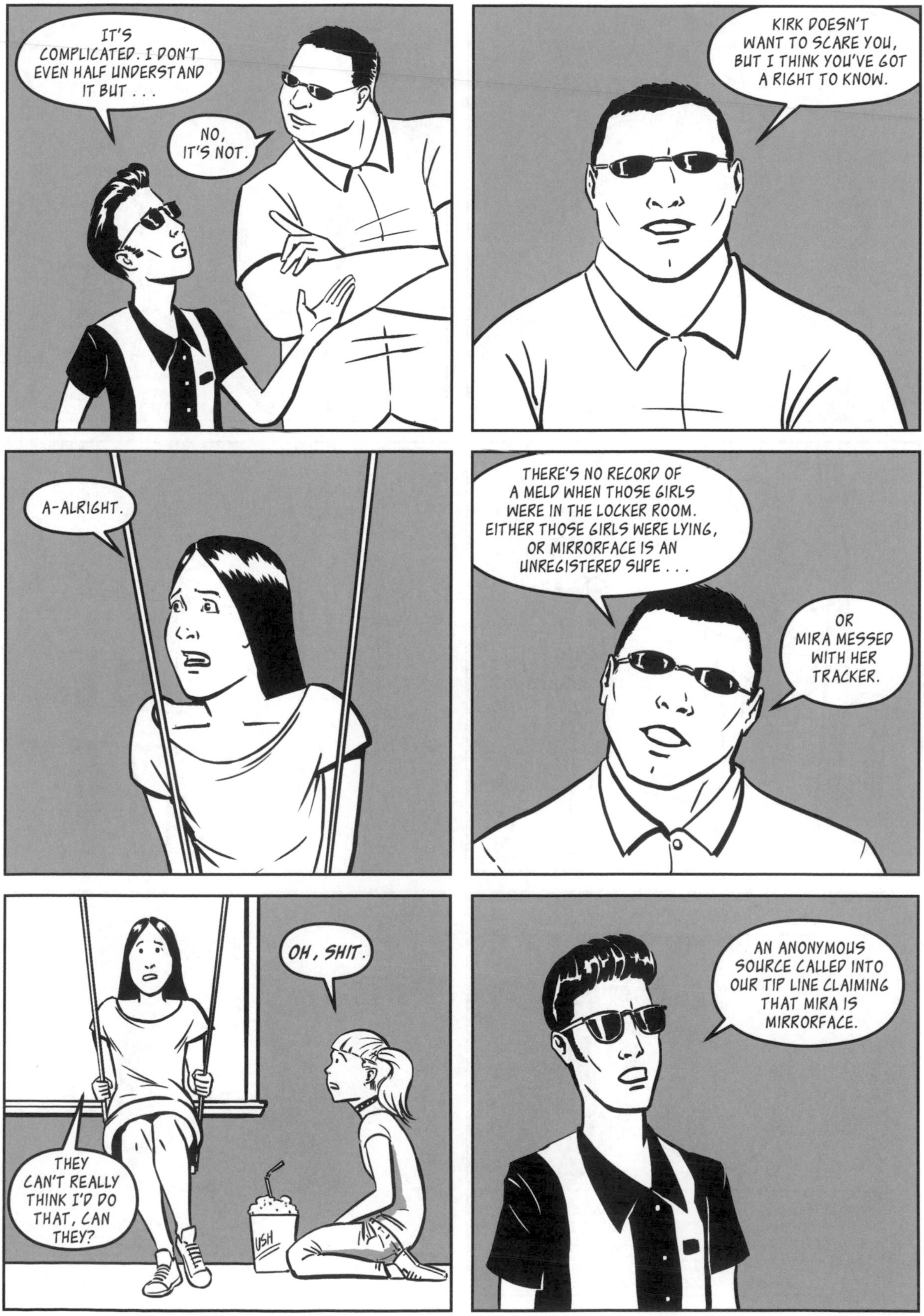
IT'S COMPLICATED. I DON'T EVEN HALF UNDERSTAND IT BUT . . .
NO, IT'S NOT.
KIRK DOESN'T WANT TO SCARE YOU, BUT I THINK YOU'VE GOT A RIGHT TO KNOW.
A-ALRIGHT.
THERE'S NO RECORD OF A MELD WHEN THOSE GIRLS WERE IN THE LOCKER ROOM. EITHER THOSE GIRLS WERE LYING, OR MIRRORFACE IS AN UNREGISTERED SUPE . . .
OR MIRA MESSED WITH HER TRACKER.
OH, SHIT.
THEY CAN'T REALLY THINK I'D DO THAT, CAN THEY?
AN ANONYMOUS SOURCE CALLED INTO OUR TIP LINE CLAIMING THAT MIRA IS MIRRORFACE.

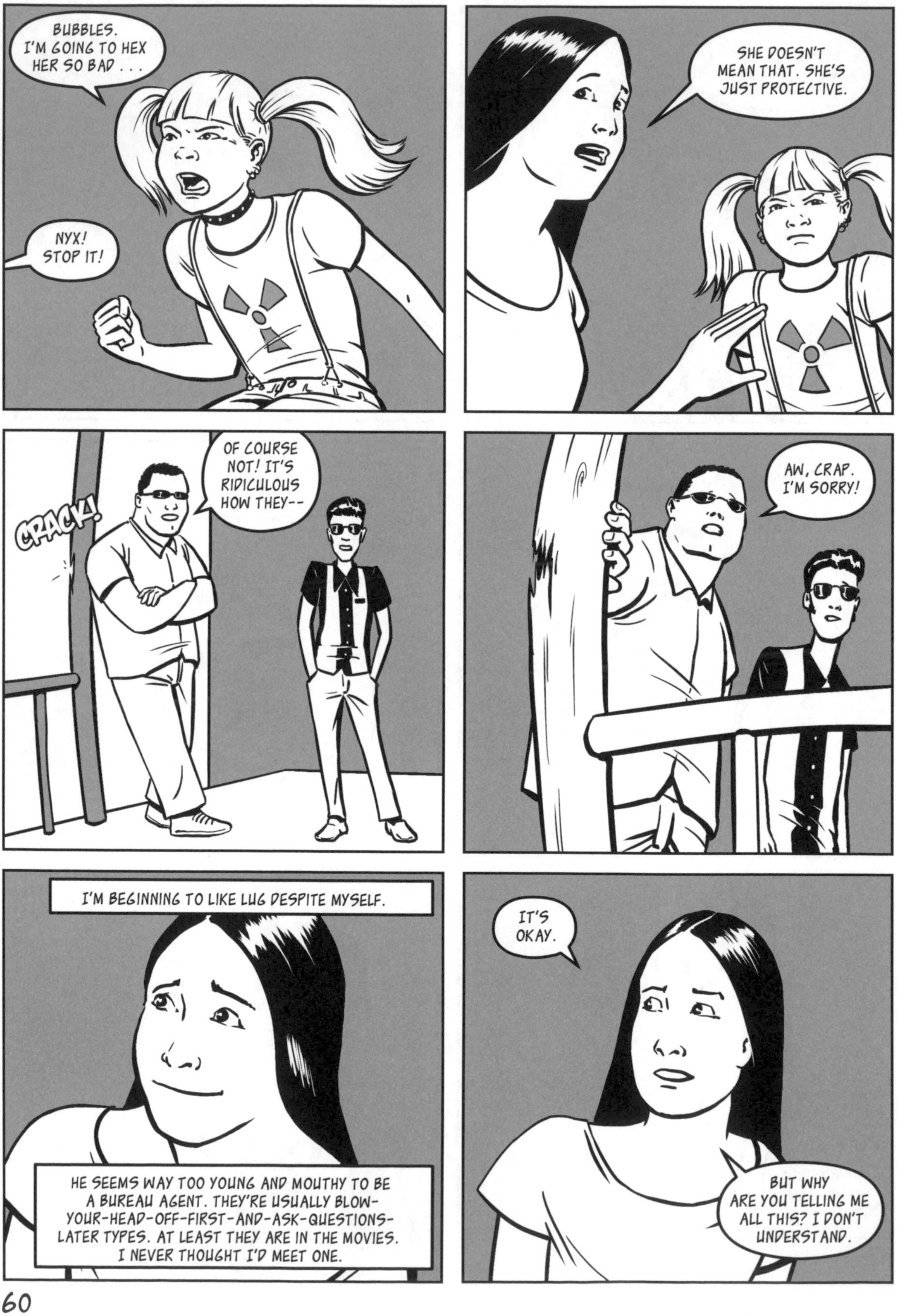

BUBBLES. I'M GOING TO HEX HER SO BAD . . .
NYX! STOP IT!
SHE DOESN'T MEAN THAT. SHE'S JUST PROTECTIVE.
OF COURSE NOT! IT'S RIDICULOUS HOW THEY--
CRACK!
AW, CRAP. I'M SORRY!
I'M BEGINNING TO LIKE LUG DESPITE MYSELF.
HE SEEMS WAY TOO YOUNG AND MOUTHY TO BE A BUREAU AGENT. THEY'RE USUALLY BLOW-YOUR-HEAD-OFF-FIRST-AND-ASK-QUESTIONS-LATER TYPES. AT LEAST THEY ARE IN THE MOVIES. I NEVER THOUGHT I'D MEET ONE.
IT'S OKAY.
BUT WHY ARE YOU TELLING ME ALL THIS? I DON'T UNDERSTAND.

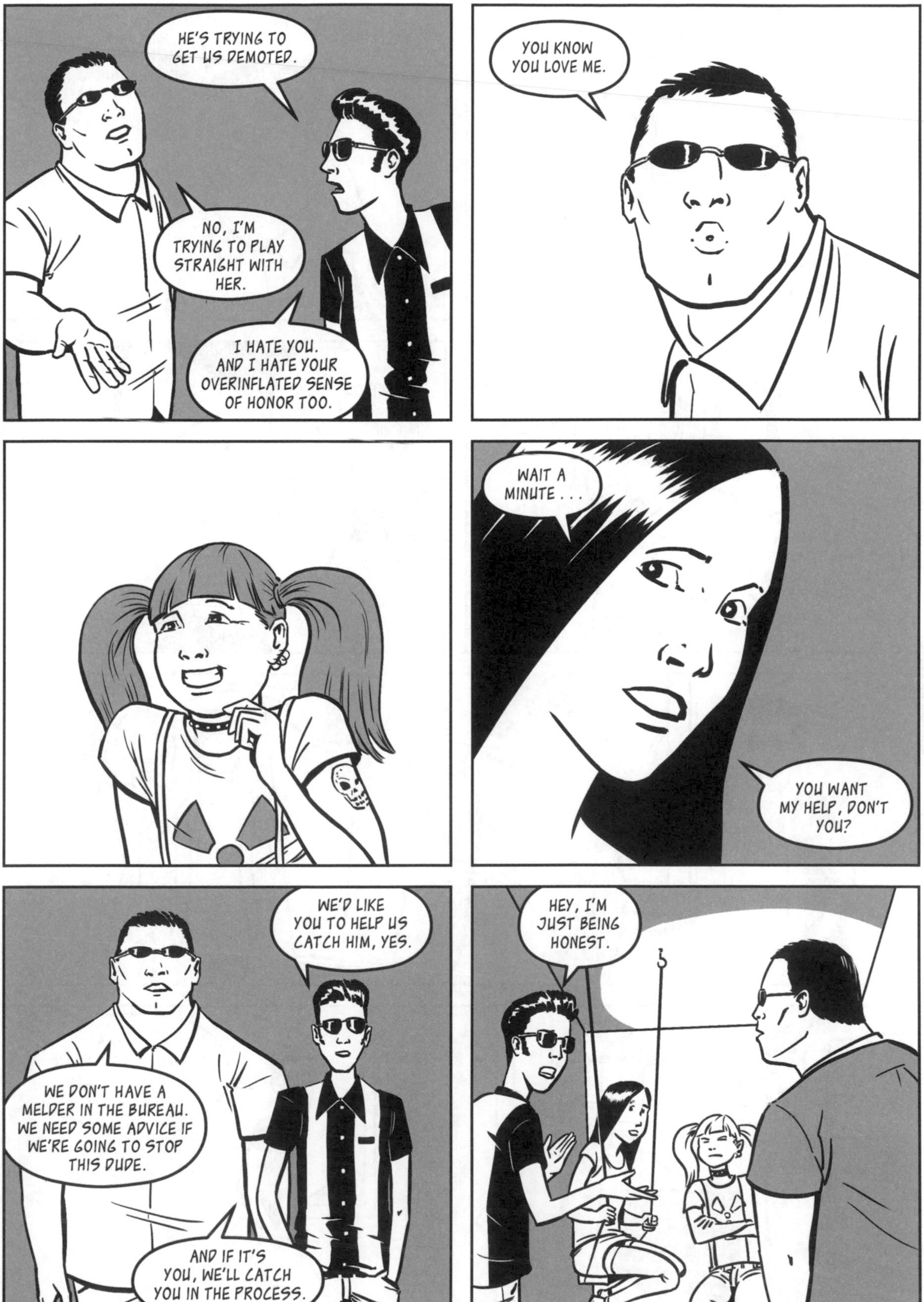
HE'S TRYING TO GET US DEMOTED.
NO, I'M TRYING TO PLAY STRAIGHT WITH HER.
I HATE YOU. AND I HATE YOUR OVERINFLATED SENSE OF HONOR TOO.
YOU KNOW YOU LOVE ME.
WAIT A MINUTE . . .
YOU WANT MY HELP, DON'T YOU?
WE'D LIKE YOU TO HELP US CATCH HIM, YES.
WE DON'T HAVE A MELDER IN THE BUREAU. WE NEED SOME ADVICE IF WE'RE GOING TO STOP THIS DUDE.
AND IF IT'S YOU, WE'LL CATCH YOU IN THE PROCESS.
HEY, I'M JUST BEING HONEST.

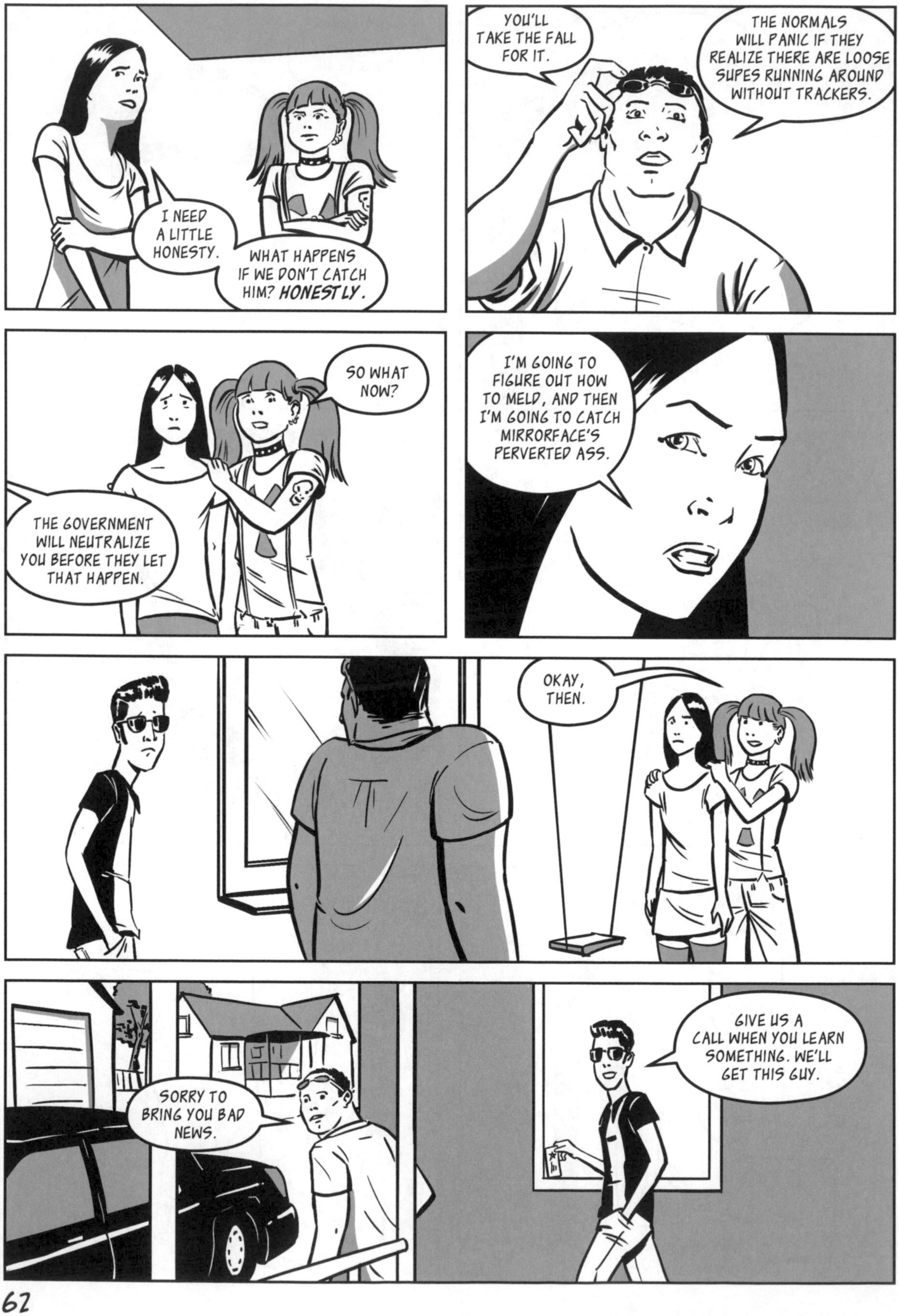
I NEED A LITTLE HONESTY.
WHAT HAPPENS IF WE DON'T CATCH HIM? HONESTLY.
YOU'LL TAKE THE FALL FOR IT.
THE NORMALS WILL PANIC IF THEY REALIZE THERE ARE LOOSE SUPES RUNNING AROUND WITHOUT TRACKERS.
SO WHAT NOW?
THE GOVERNMENT WILL NEUTRALIZE YOU BEFORE THEY LET THAT HAPPEN.
I'M GOING TO FIGURE OUT HOW TO MELD, AND THEN I'M GOING TO CATCH MIRRORFACE'S PERVERTED ASS.
OKAY, THEN.
SORRY TO BRING YOU BAD NEWS.
GIVE US A CALL WHEN YOU LEARN SOMETHING. WE'LL GET THIS GUY.

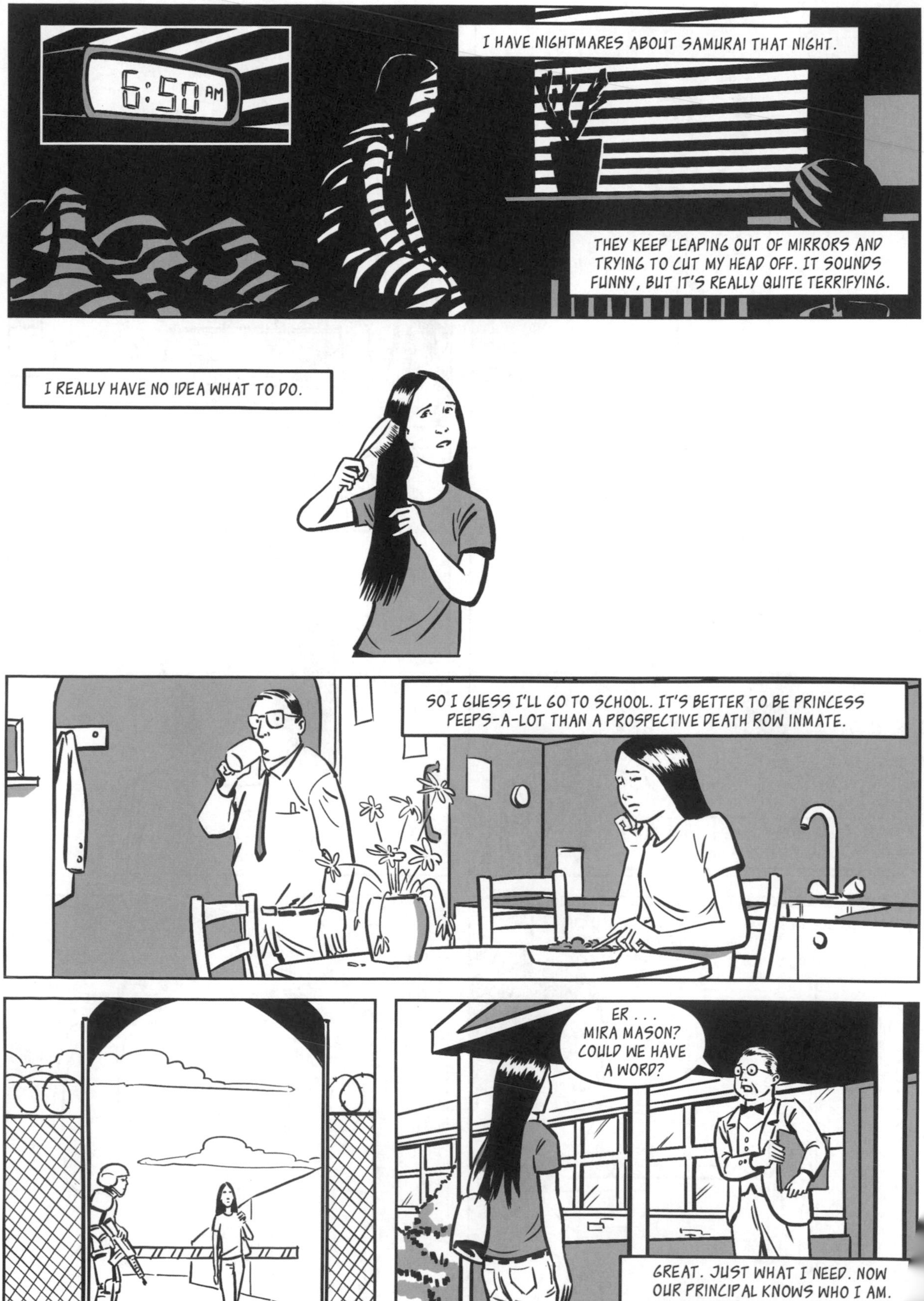
6:50 AM
I HAVE NIGHTMARES ABOUT SAMURAI THAT NIGHT.
THEY KEEP LEAPING OUT OF MIRRORS AND TRYING TO CUT MY HEAD OFF. IT SOUNDS FUNNY, BUT IT'S REALLY QUITE TERRIFYING.
I REALLY HAVE NO IDEA WHAT TO DO.
SO I GUESS I'LL GO TO SCHOOL. IT'S BETTER TO BE PRINCESS PEEPS-A-LOT THAN A PROSPECTIVE DEATH ROW INMATE.
ER . . . MIRA MASON? COULD WE HAVE A WORD?
GREAT. JUST WHAT I NEED. NOW OUR PRINCIPAL KNOWS WHO I AM.

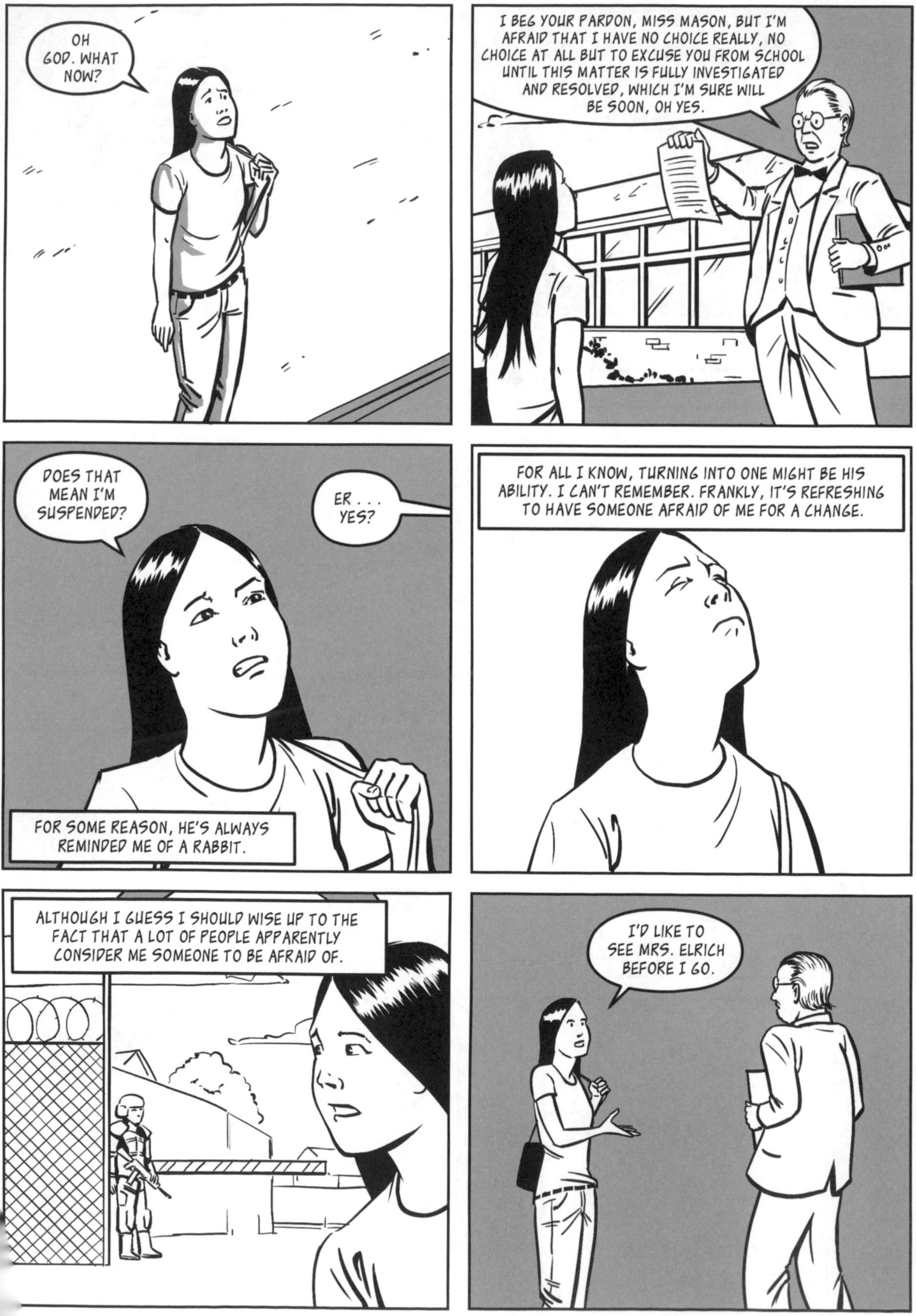
OH GOD. WHAT NOW?
I BEG YOUR PARDON, MISS MASON, BUT I'M AFRAID THAT I HAVE NO CHOICE REALLY, NO CHOICE AT ALL BUT TO EXCUSE YOU FROM SCHOOL UNTIL THIS MATTER IS FULLY INVESTIGATED AND RESOLVED, WHICH I'M SURE WILL BE SOON, OH YES.
DOES THAT MEAN I'M SUSPENDED?
ER . . . YES?
FOR SOME REASON, HE'S ALWAYS REMINDED ME OF A RABBIT.
FOR ALL I KNOW, TURNING INTO ONE MIGHT BE HIS ABILITY. I CAN'T REMEMBER. FRANKLY, IT'S REFRESHING TO HAVE SOMEONE AFRAID OF ME FOR A CHANGE.
ALTHOUGH I GUESS I SHOULD WISE UP TO THE FACT THAT A LOT OF PEOPLE APPARENTLY CONSIDER ME SOMEONE TO BE AFRAID OF.
I'D LIKE TO SEE MRS. ELRICH BEFORE I GO.

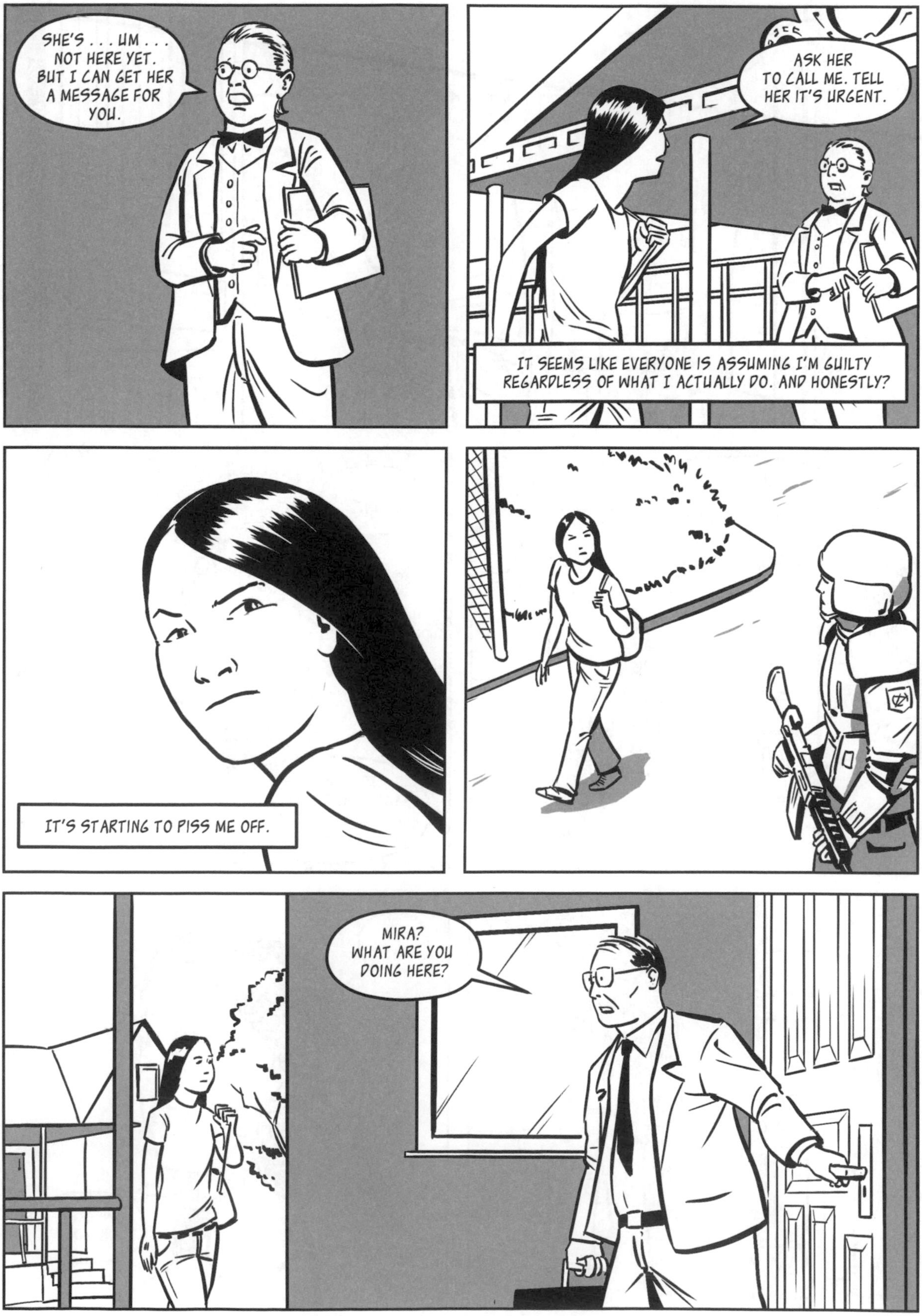

SHE'S . . . UM . . . NOT HERE YET. BUT I CAN GET HER A MESSAGE FOR YOU.
ASK HER TO CALL ME. TELL HER IT'S URGENT.
IT SEEMS LIKE EVERYONE IS ASSUMING I'M GUILTY REGARDLESS OF WHAT I ACTUALLY DO. AND HONESTLY?
IT'S STARTING TO PISS ME OFF.
MIRA? WHAT ARE YOU DOING HERE?

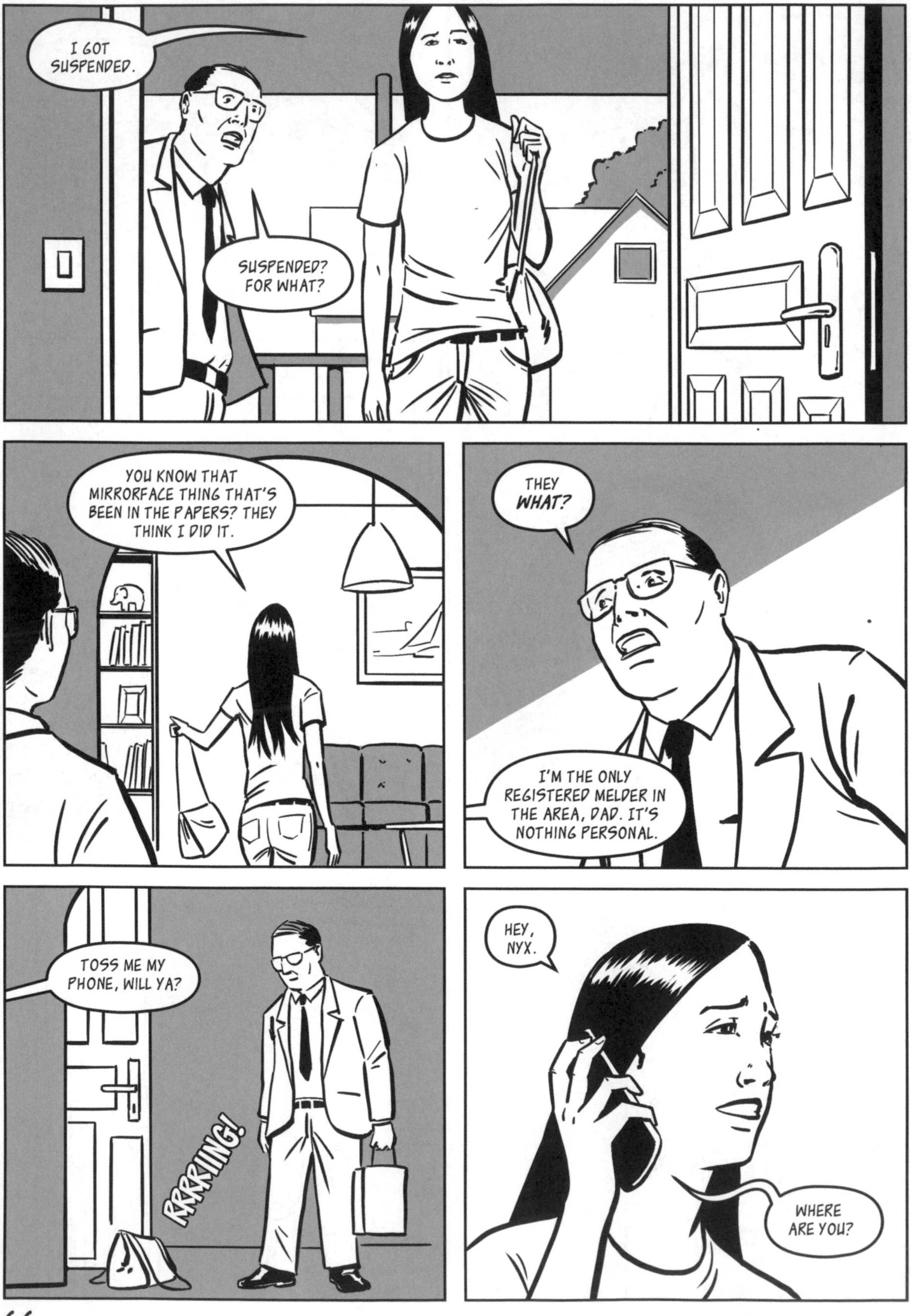
I GOT SUSPENDED.
SUSPENDED? FOR WHAT?
YOU KNOW THAT MIRRORFACE THING THAT'S BEEN IN THE PAPERS? THEY THINK I DID IT.
THEY *WHAT?*
I'M THE ONLY REGISTERED MELDER IN THE AREA, DAD. IT'S NOTHING PERSONAL.
TOSS ME MY PHONE, WILL YA?
RRRRING!
HEY, NYX.
WHERE ARE YOU?

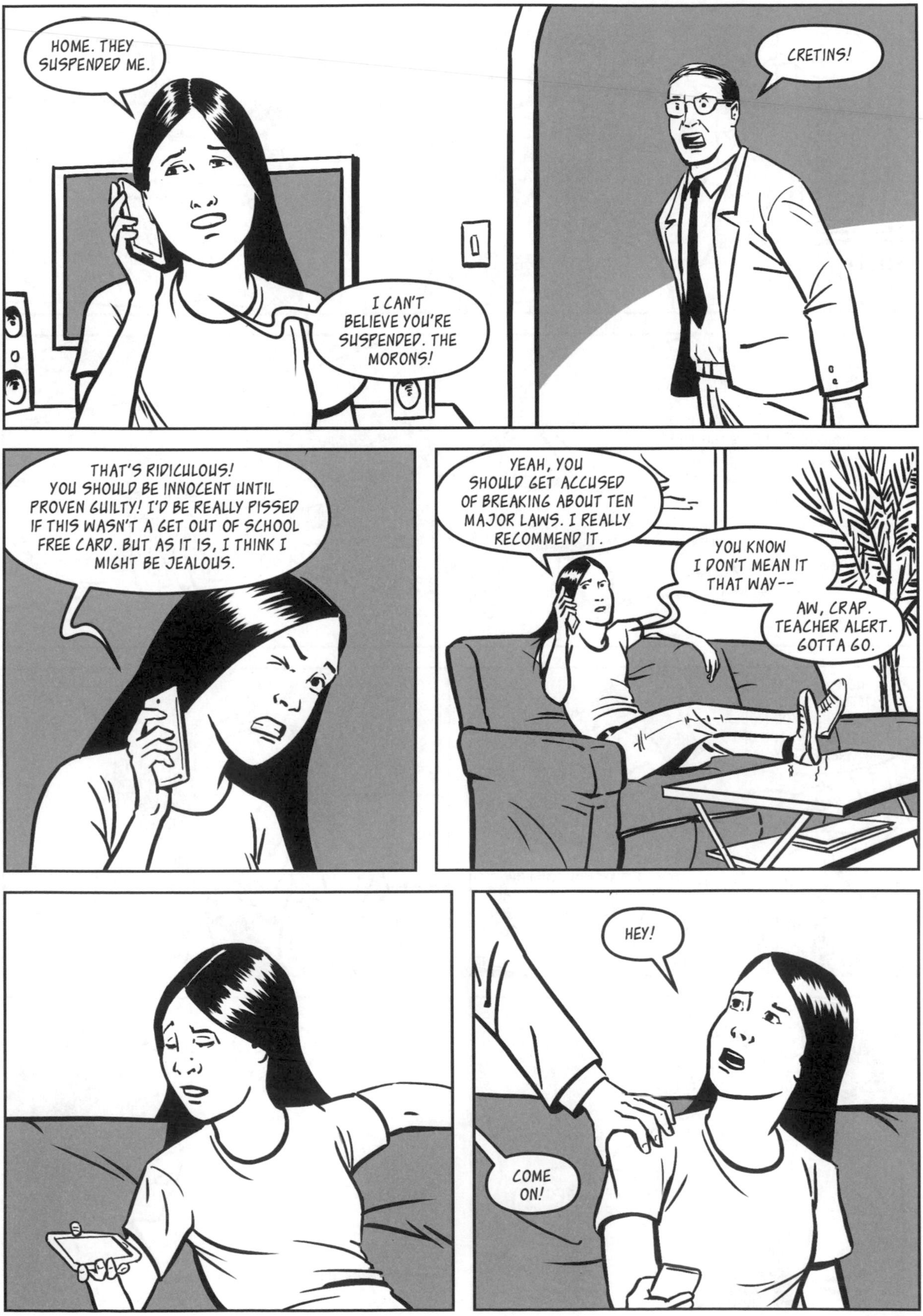
HOME. THEY SUSPENDED ME.
I CAN'T BELIEVE YOU'RE SUSPENDED. THE MORONS!
CRETINS!
THAT'S RIDICULOUS! YOU SHOULD BE INNOCENT UNTIL PROVEN GUILTY! I'D BE REALLY PISSED IF THIS WASN'T A GET OUT OF SCHOOL FREE CARD. BUT AS IT IS, I THINK I MIGHT BE JEALOUS.
YEAH, YOU SHOULD GET ACCUSED OF BREAKING ABOUT TEN MAJOR LAWS. I REALLY RECOMMEND IT.
YOU KNOW I DON'T MEAN IT THAT WAY--
AW, CRAP. TEACHER ALERT. GOTTA GO.
HEY!
COME ON!

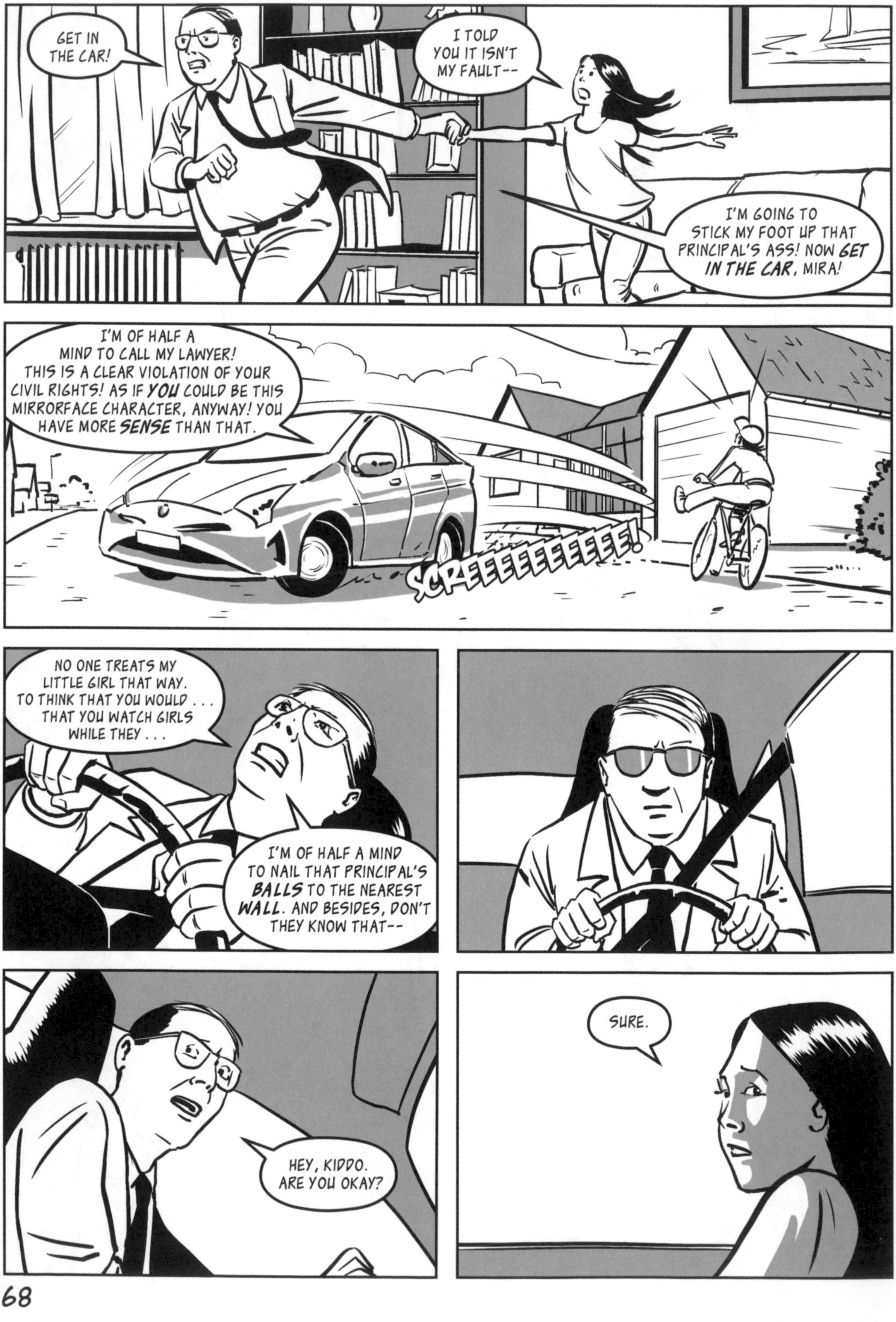
GET IN THE CAR!
I TOLD YOU IT ISN'T MY FAULT--
I'M GOING TO STICK MY FOOT UP THAT PRINCIPAL'S ASS! NOW GET IN THE CAR, MIRA!
I'M OF HALF A MIND TO CALL MY LAWYER! THIS IS A CLEAR VIOLATION OF YOUR CIVIL RIGHTS! AS IF YOU COULD BE THIS MIRRORFACE CHARACTER, ANYWAY! YOU HAVE MORE SENSE THAN THAT.
SCREEEEEEEEEEE!
NO ONE TREATS MY LITTLE GIRL THAT WAY. TO THINK THAT YOU WOULD . . . THAT YOU WATCH GIRLS WHILE THEY . . .
I'M OF HALF A MIND TO NAIL THAT PRINCIPAL'S BALLS TO THE NEAREST WALL. AND BESIDES, DON'T THEY KNOW THAT--
HEY, KIDDO. ARE YOU OKAY?
SURE.

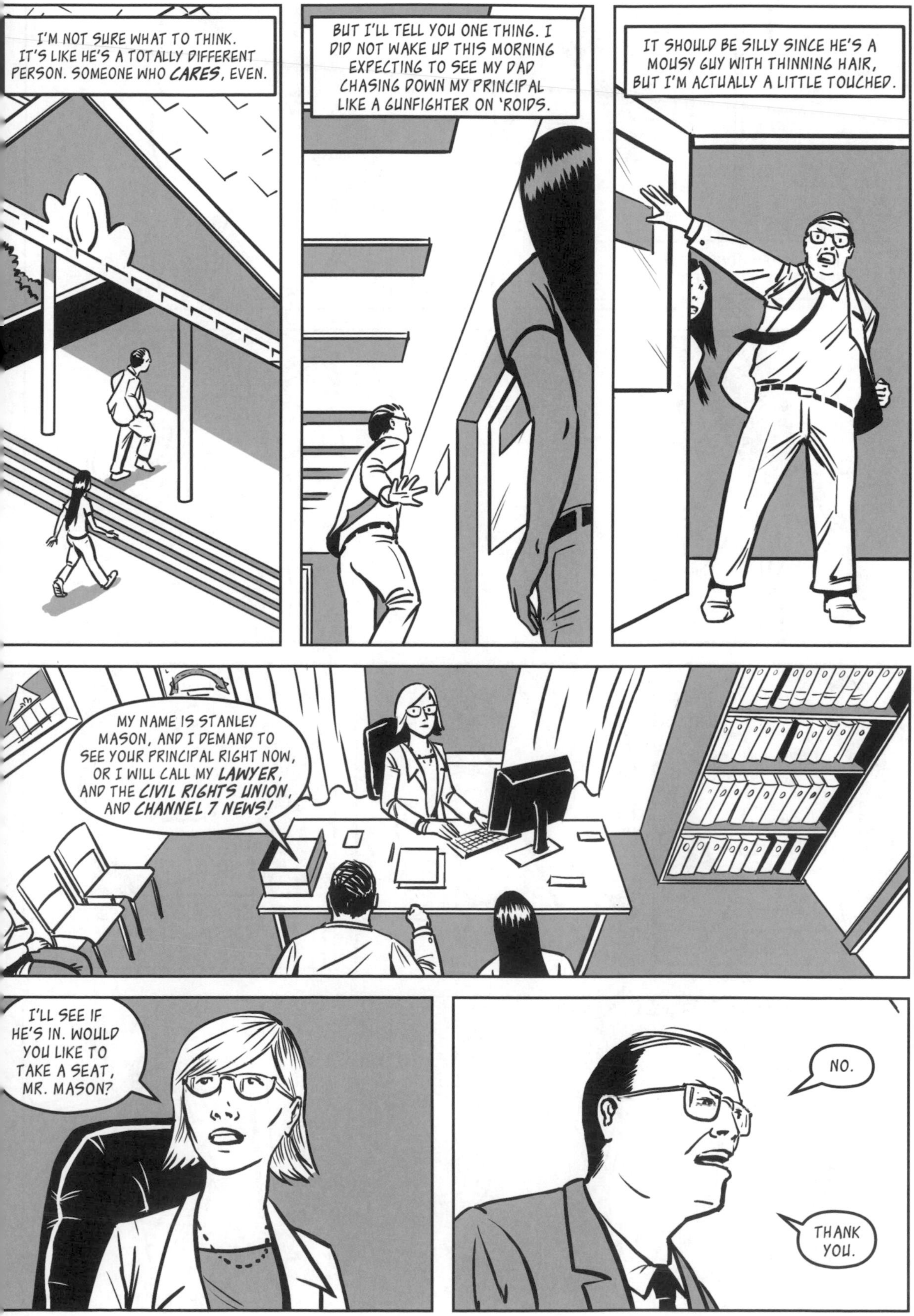
I'M NOT SURE WHAT TO THINK. IT'S LIKE HE'S A TOTALLY DIFFERENT PERSON. SOMEONE WHO CARES, EVEN.
BUT I'LL TELL YOU ONE THING. I DID NOT WAKE UP THIS MORNING EXPECTING TO SEE MY DAD CHASING DOWN MY PRINCIPAL LIKE A GUNFIGHTER ON 'ROIDS.
IT SHOULD BE SILLY SINCE HE'S A MOUSY GUY WITH THINNING HAIR, BUT I'M ACTUALLY A LITTLE TOUCHED.
MY NAME IS STANLEY MASON, AND I DEMAND TO SEE YOUR PRINCIPAL RIGHT NOW, OR I WILL CALL MY LAWYER, AND THE CIVIL RIGHTS UNION, AND CHANNEL 7 NEWS!
I'LL SEE IF HE'S IN. WOULD YOU LIKE TO TAKE A SEAT, MR. MASON?
NO.
THANK YOU.

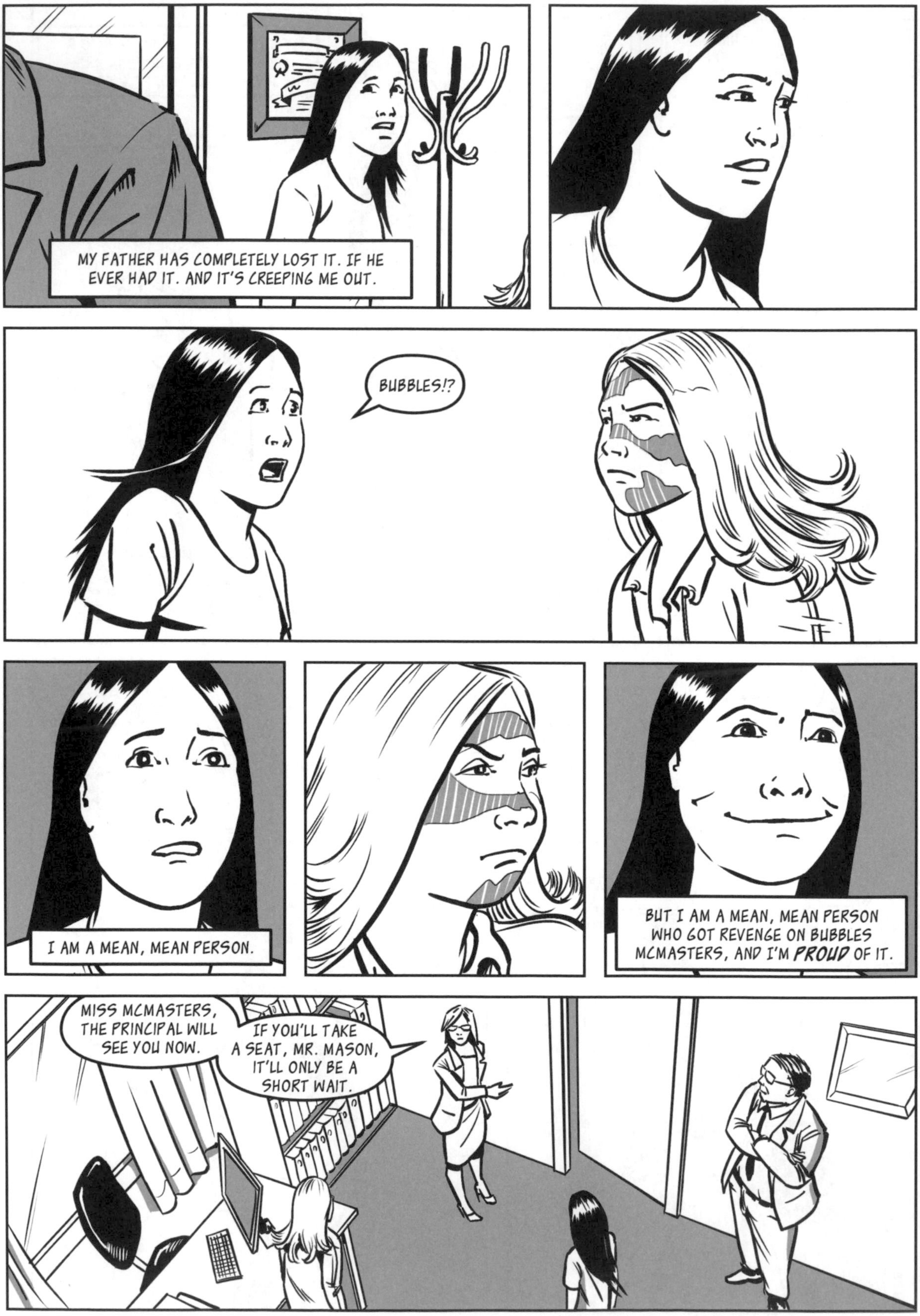
MY FATHER HAS COMPLETELY LOST IT. IF HE EVER HAD IT. AND IT'S CREEPING ME OUT.
BUBBLES!?
I AM A MEAN, MEAN PERSON.
BUT I AM A MEAN, MEAN PERSON WHO GOT REVENGE ON BUBBLES MCMASTERS, AND I'M PROUD OF IT.
MISS MCMASTERS, THE PRINCIPAL WILL SEE YOU NOW.
IF YOU'LL TAKE A SEAT, MR. MASON, IT'LL ONLY BE A SHORT WAIT.

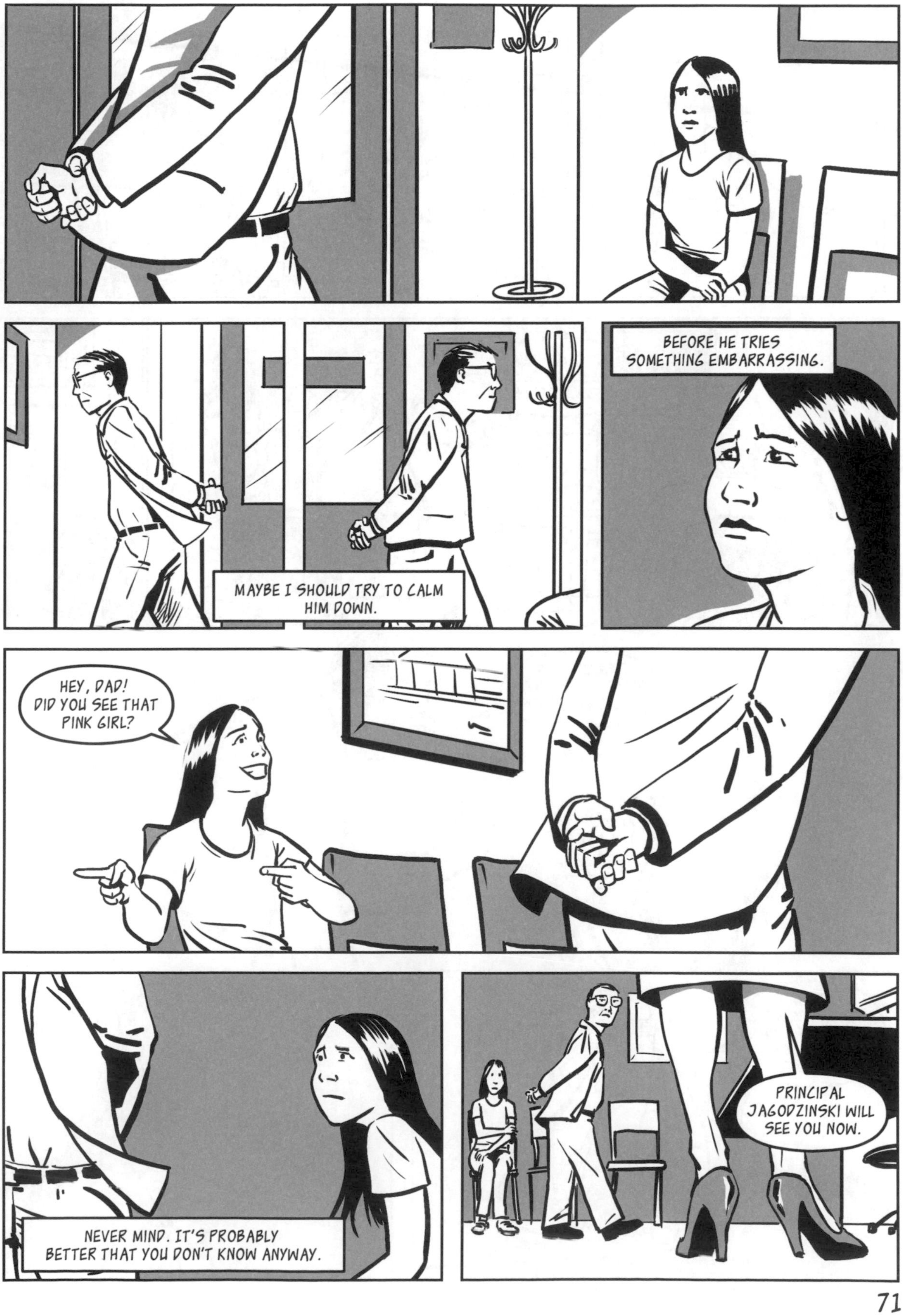
MAYBE I SHOULD TRY TO CALM HIM DOWN.
BEFORE HE TRIES SOMETHING EMBARRASSING.
HEY, DAD! DID YOU SEE THAT PINK GIRL?
NEVER MIND. IT'S PROBABLY BETTER THAT YOU DON'T KNOW ANYWAY.
PRINCIPAL JAGODZINSKI WILL SEE YOU NOW.

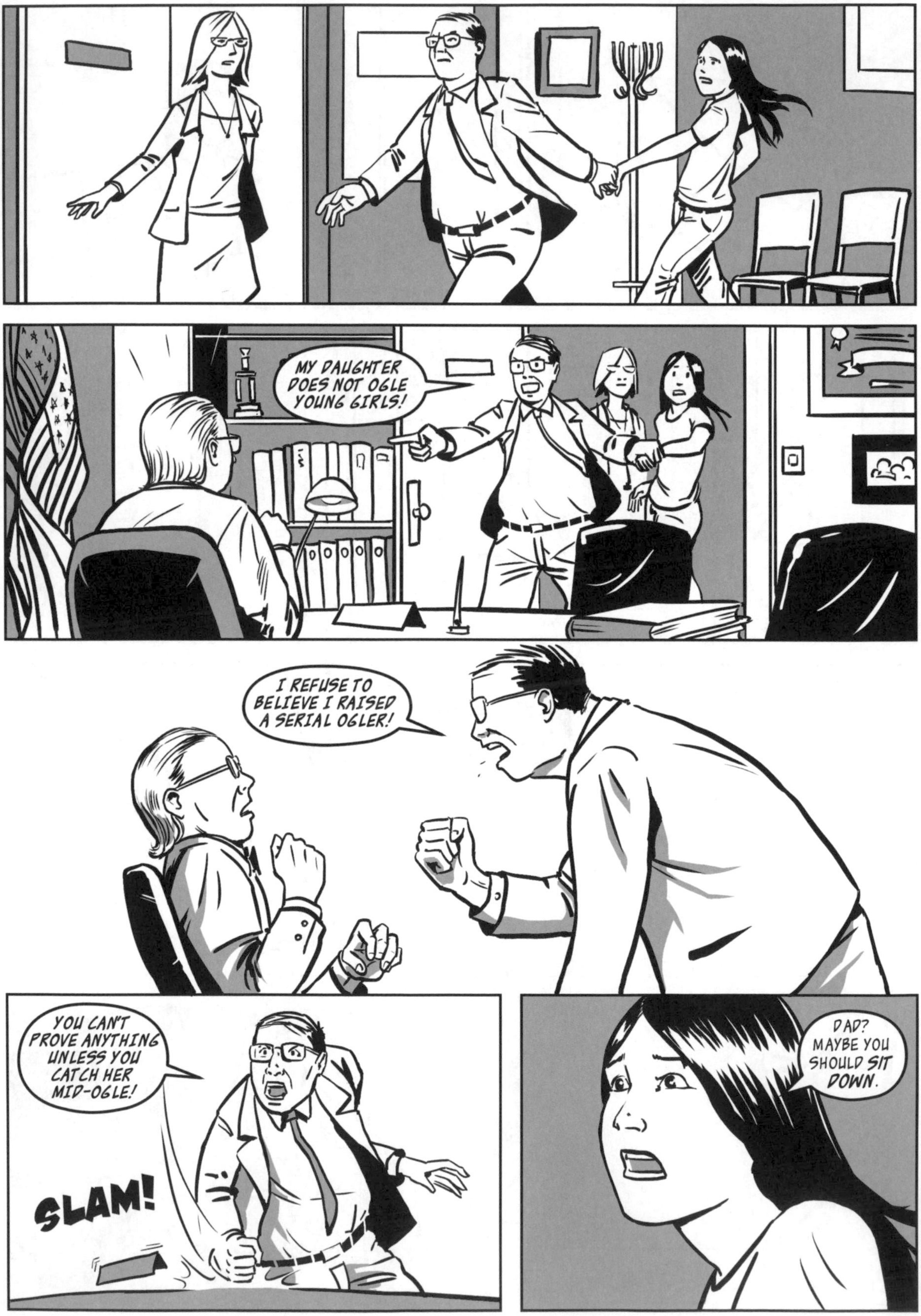
MY DAUGHTER DOES NOT OGLE YOUNG GIRLS!
I REFUSE TO BELIEVE I RAISED A SERIAL OGLER!
YOU CAN'T PROVE ANYTHING UNLESS YOU CATCH HER MID-OGLE!
SLAM!
DAD? MAYBE YOU SHOULD SIT DOWN.

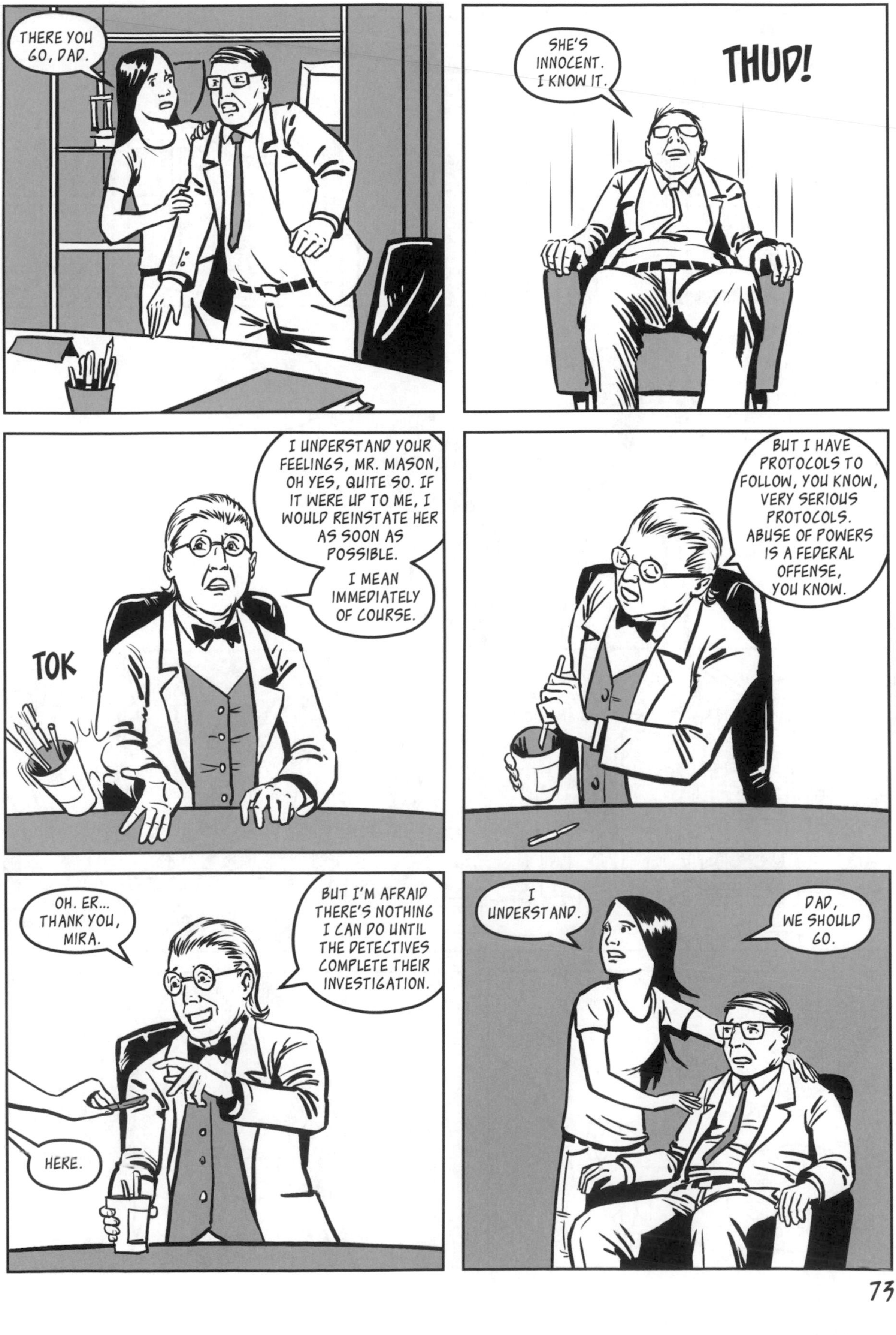
THERE YOU GO, DAD.
SHE'S INNOCENT. I KNOW IT.
THUD!
I UNDERSTAND YOUR FEELINGS, MR. MASON, OH YES, QUITE SO. IF IT WERE UP TO ME, I WOULD REINSTATE HER AS SOON AS POSSIBLE.
I MEAN IMMEDIATELY OF COURSE.
TOK
BUT I HAVE PROTOCOLS TO FOLLOW, YOU KNOW, VERY SERIOUS PROTOCOLS. ABUSE OF POWERS IS A FEDERAL OFFENSE, YOU KNOW.
HERE.
OH. ER... THANK YOU, MIRA.
BUT I'M AFRAID THERE'S NOTHING I CAN DO UNTIL THE DETECTIVES COMPLETE THEIR INVESTIGATION.
I UNDERSTAND.
DAD, WE SHOULD GO.

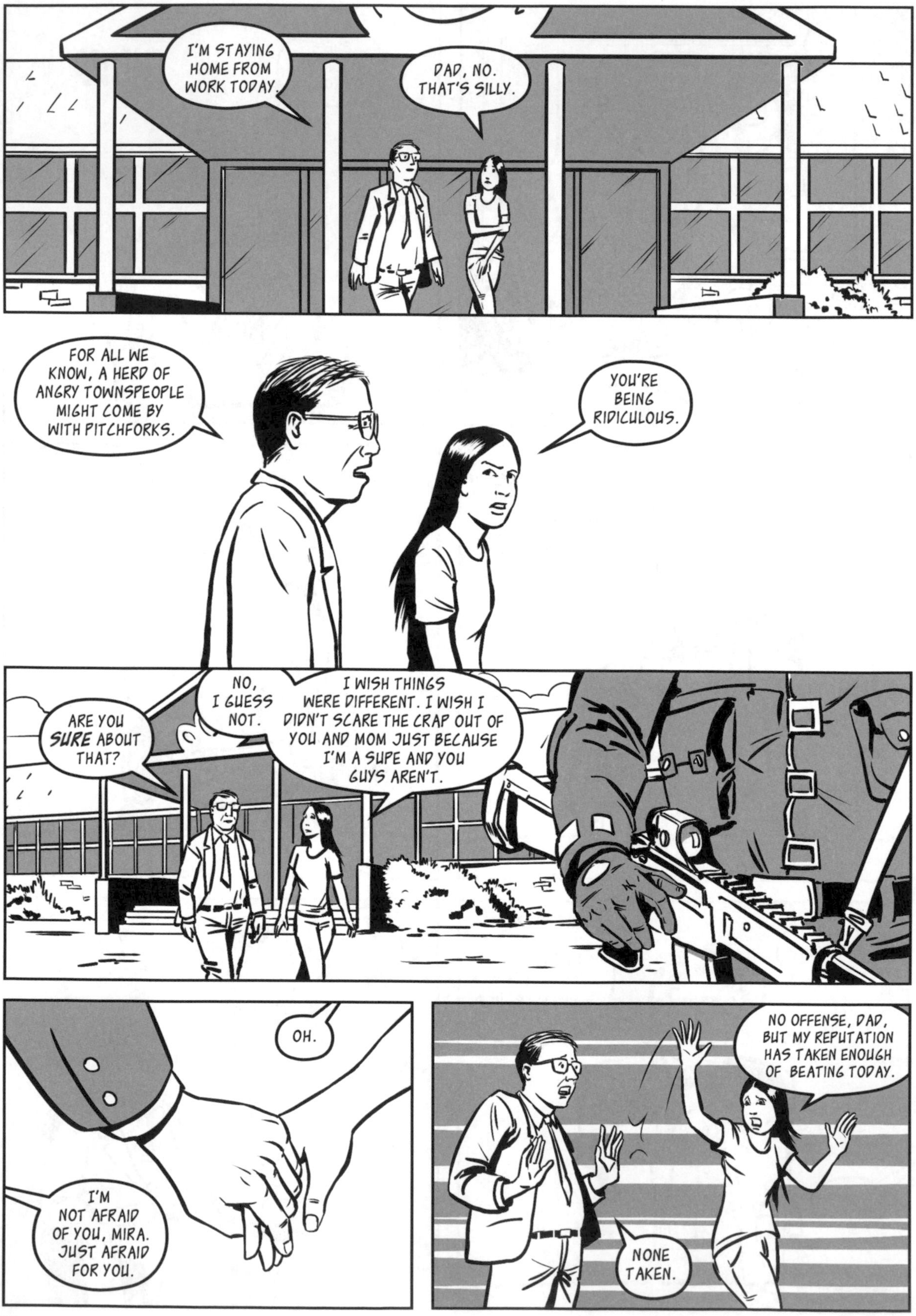
I'M STAYING HOME FROM WORK TODAY.
DAD, NO. THAT'S SILLY.
FOR ALL WE KNOW, A HERD OF ANGRY TOWNSPEOPLE MIGHT COME BY WITH PITCHFORKS.
YOU'RE BEING RIDICULOUS.
ARE YOU *SURE* ABOUT THAT?
NO, I GUESS NOT.
I WISH THINGS WERE DIFFERENT. I WISH I DIDN'T SCARE THE CRAP OUT OF YOU AND MOM JUST BECAUSE I'M A SUPE AND YOU GUYS AREN'T.
OH.
I'M NOT AFRAID OF YOU, MIRA. JUST AFRAID FOR YOU.
NO OFFENSE, DAD, BUT MY REPUTATION HAS TAKEN ENOUGH OF BEATING TODAY.
NONE TAKEN.

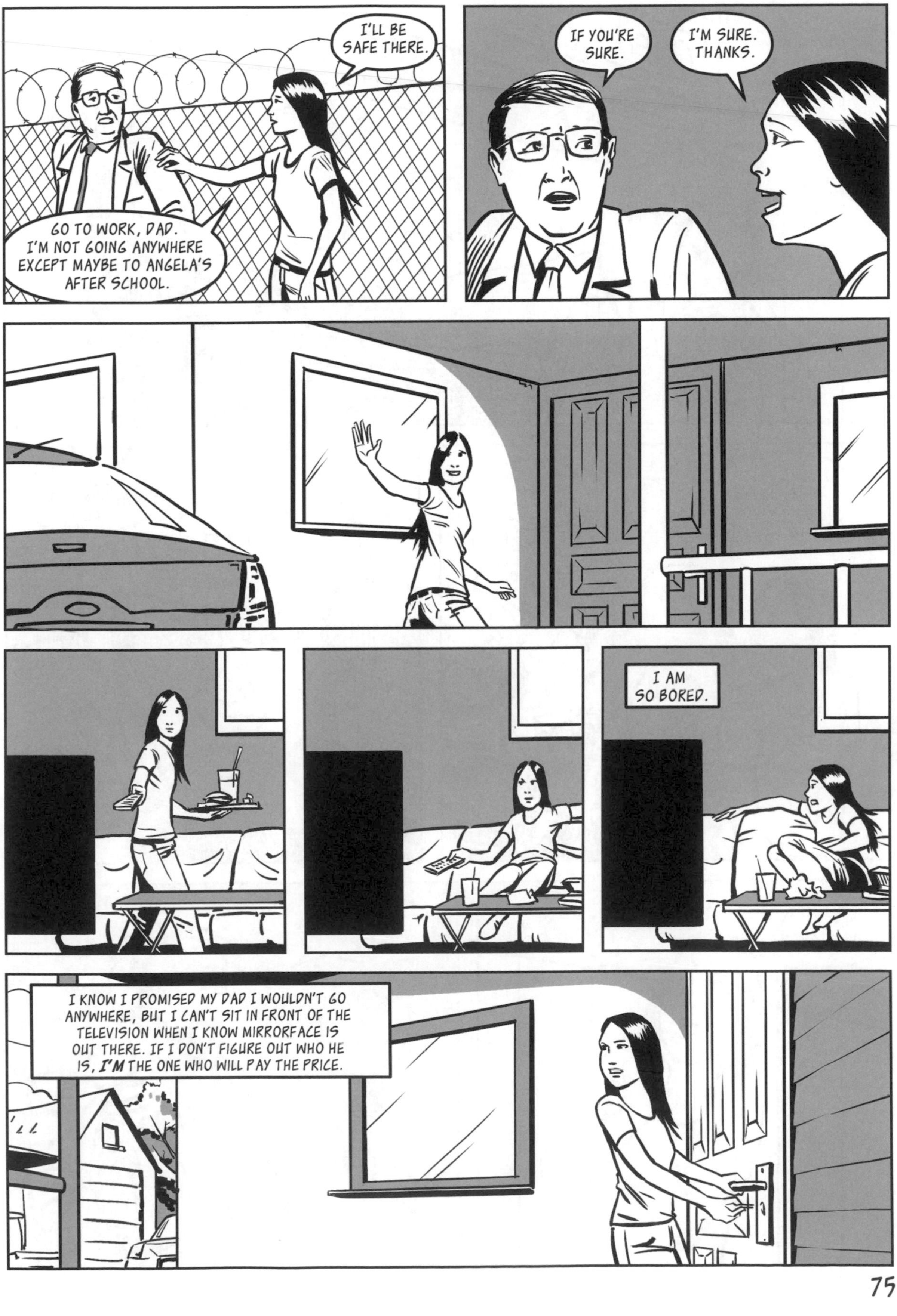
I'LL BE SAFE THERE.
GO TO WORK, DAD. I'M NOT GOING ANYWHERE EXCEPT MAYBE TO ANGELA'S AFTER SCHOOL.
IF YOU'RE SURE.
I'M SURE. THANKS.
I AM SO BORED.
I KNOW I PROMISED MY DAD I WOULDN'T GO ANYWHERE, BUT I CAN'T SIT IN FRONT OF THE TELEVISION WHEN I KNOW MIRRORFACE IS OUT THERE. IF I DON'T FIGURE OUT WHO HE IS, I'M THE ONE WHO WILL PAY THE PRICE.

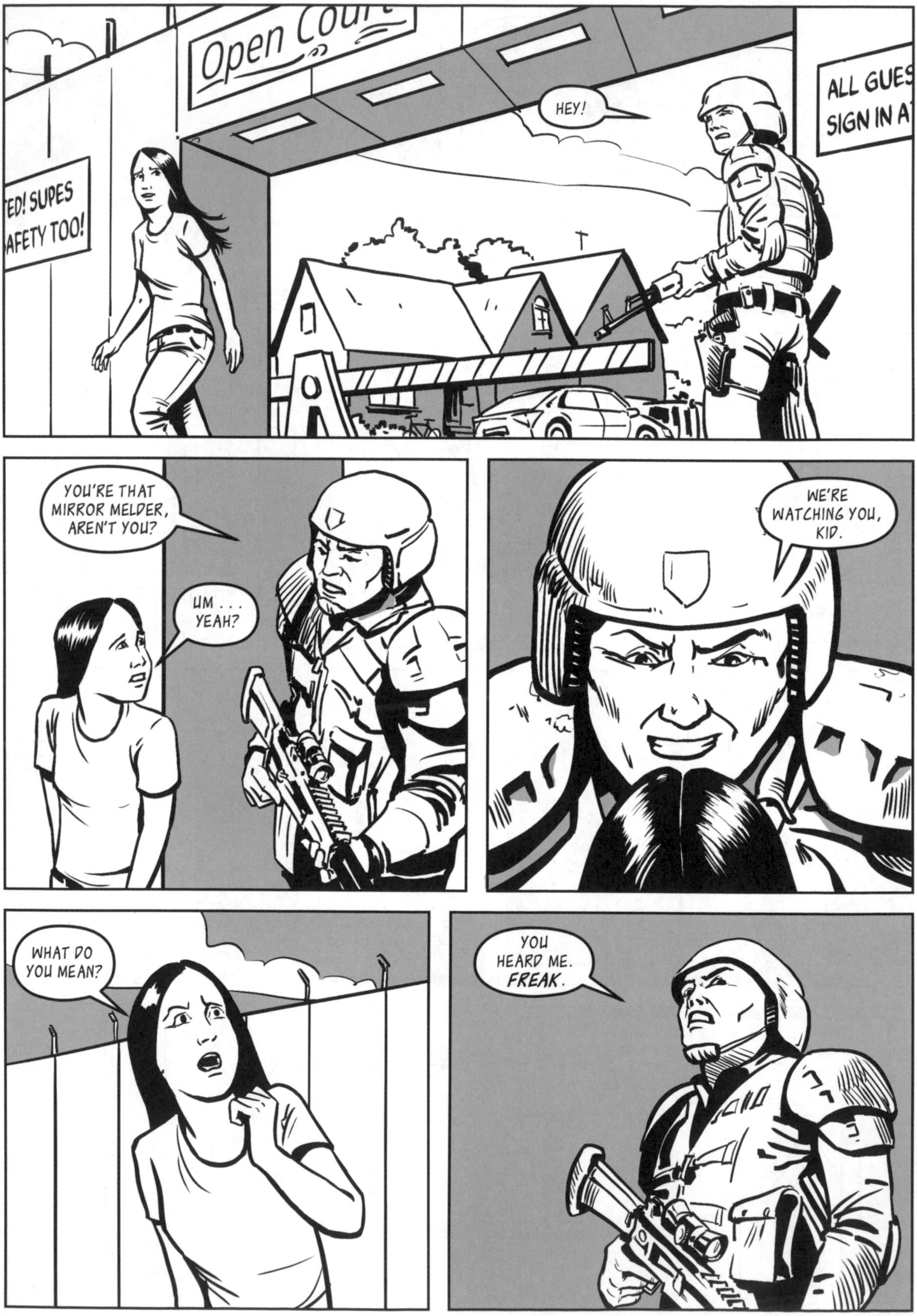
Open Court
ALL GUES
SIGN IN A
TED! SUPES
AFETY TOO!
HEY!
YOU'RE THAT MIRROR MELDER, AREN'T YOU?
UM . . . YEAH?
WE'RE WATCHING YOU, KID.
WHAT DO YOU MEAN?
YOU HEARD ME. *FREAK*.

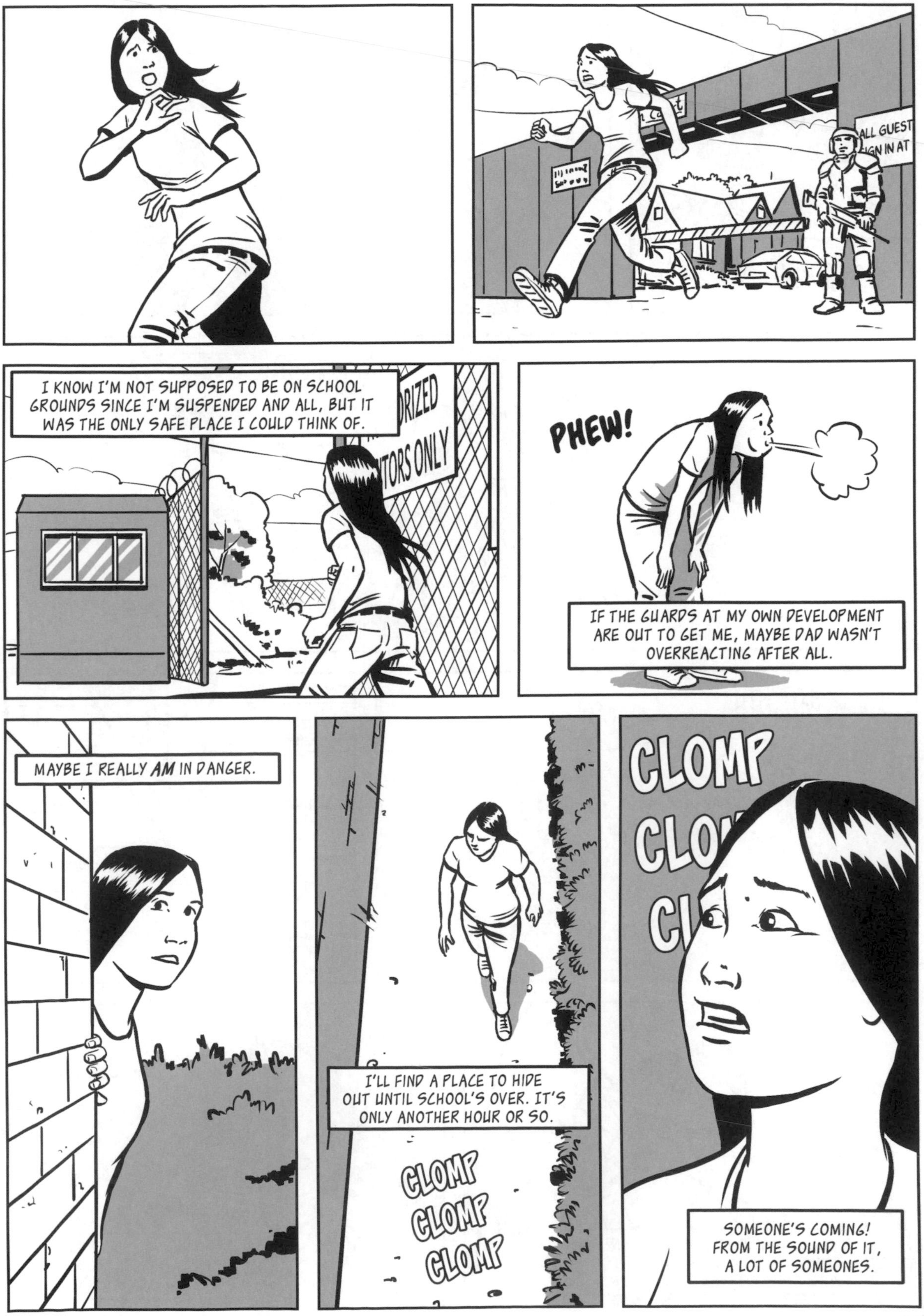
ALL GUEST
I KNOW I'M NOT SUPPOSED TO BE ON SCHOOL GROUNDS SINCE I'M SUSPENDED AND ALL, BUT IT WAS THE ONLY SAFE PLACE I COULD THINK OF.
PHEW!
IF THE GUARDS AT MY OWN DEVELOPMENT ARE OUT TO GET ME, MAYBE DAD WASN'T OVERREACTING AFTER ALL.
MAYBE I REALLY *AM* IN DANGER.
I'LL FIND A PLACE TO HIDE OUT UNTIL SCHOOL'S OVER. IT'S ONLY ANOTHER HOUR OR SO.
CLOMP
CLOMP
CLOMP
CLOMP
SOMEONE'S COMING! FROM THE SOUND OF IT, A LOT OF SOMEONES.

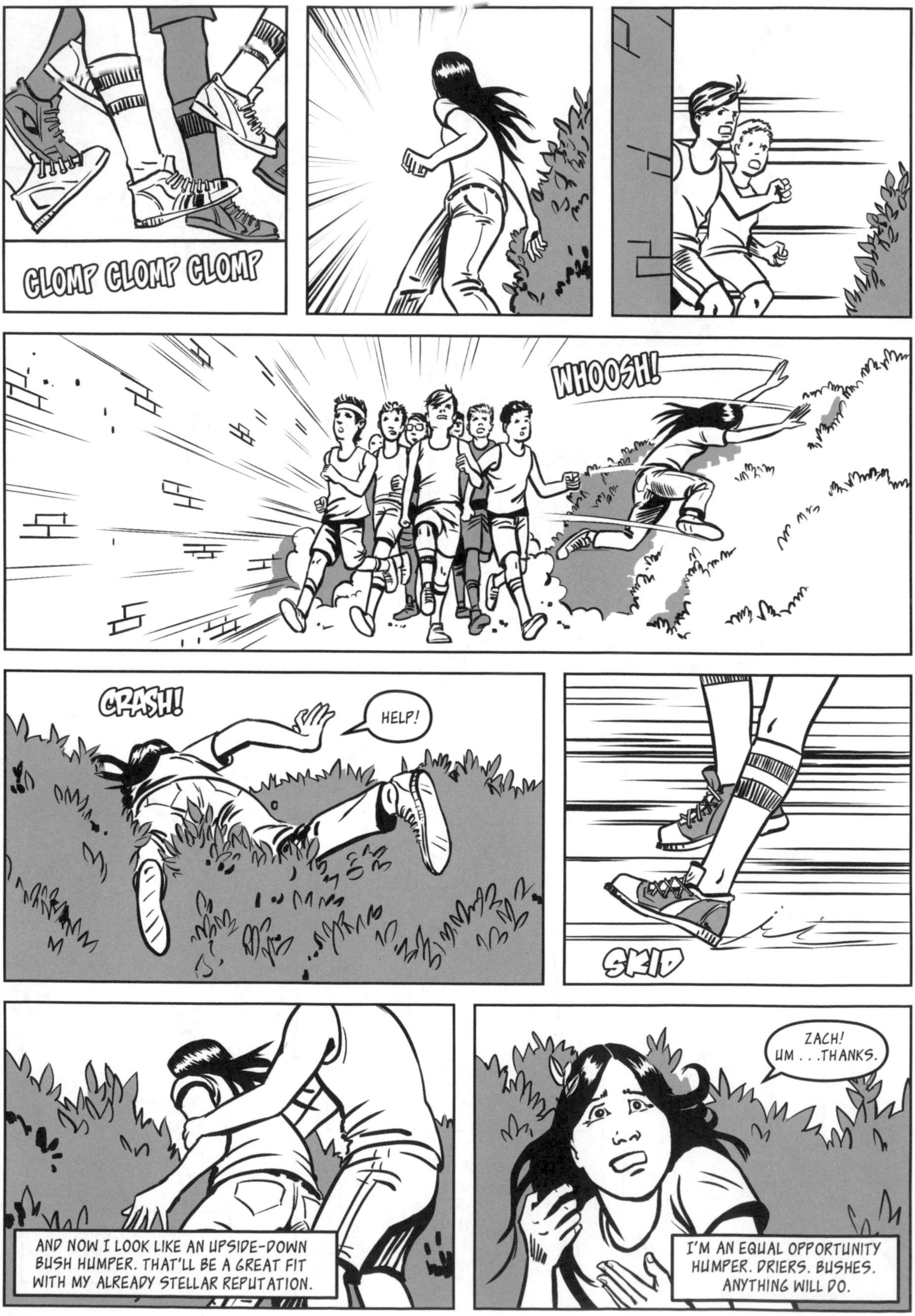

CLOMP CLOMP CLOMP
WHOOSH!
CRASH!
HELP!
SKID
AND NOW I LOOK LIKE AN UPSIDE-DOWN BUSH HUMPER. THAT'LL BE A GREAT FIT WITH MY ALREADY STELLAR REPUTATION.
ZACH! UM . . . THANKS.
I'M AN EQUAL OPPORTUNITY HUMPER. DRIERS. BUSHES. ANYTHING WILL DO.

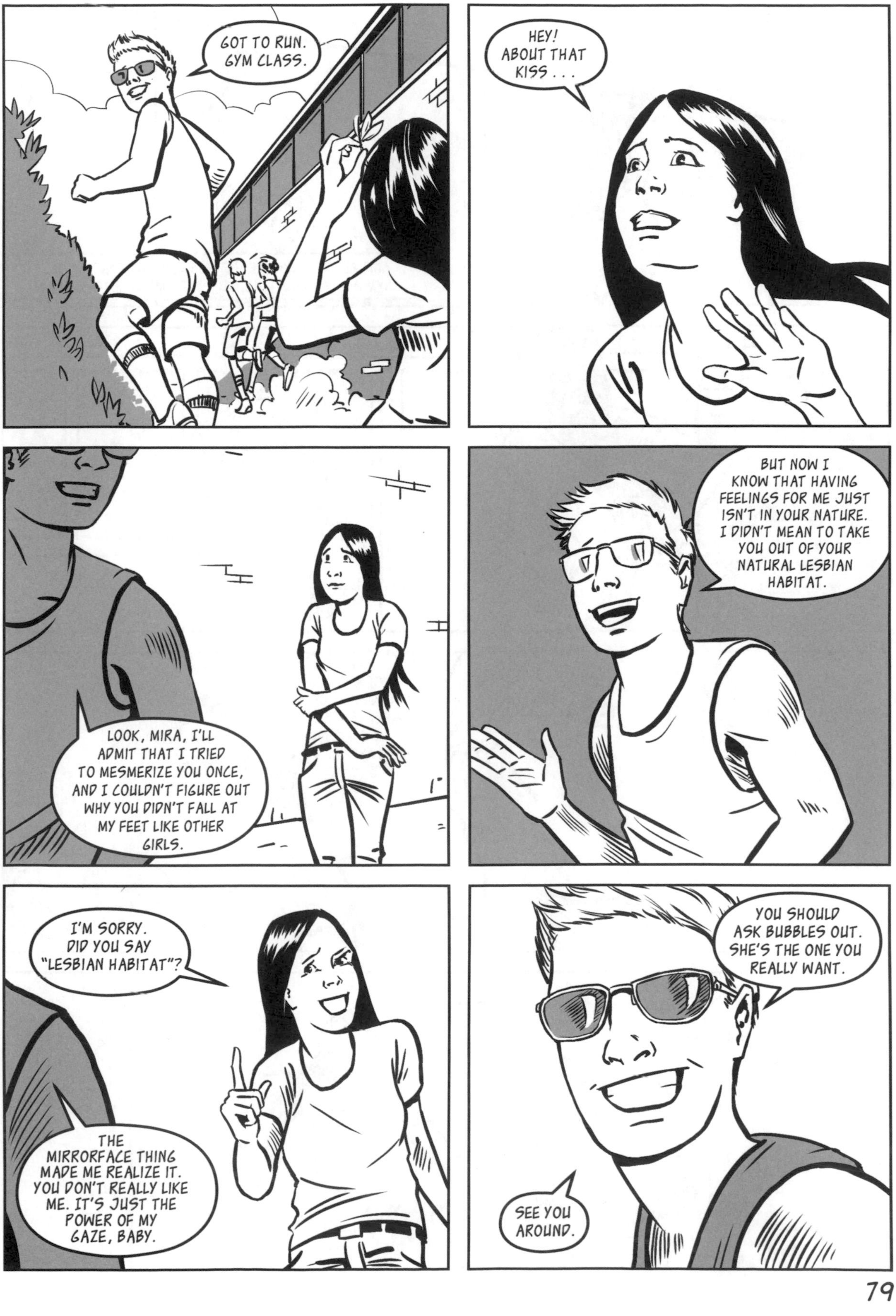
GOT TO RUN. GYM CLASS.
HEY! ABOUT THAT KISS . . .
LOOK, MIRA, I'LL ADMIT THAT I TRIED TO MESMERIZE YOU ONCE, AND I COULDN'T FIGURE OUT WHY YOU DIDN'T FALL AT MY FEET LIKE OTHER GIRLS.
BUT NOW I KNOW THAT HAVING FEELINGS FOR ME JUST ISN'T IN YOUR NATURE. I DIDN'T MEAN TO TAKE YOU OUT OF YOUR NATURAL LESBIAN HABITAT.
I'M SORRY. DID YOU SAY "LESBIAN HABITAT"?
THE MIRRORFACE THING MADE ME REALIZE IT. YOU DON'T REALLY LIKE ME. IT'S JUST THE POWER OF MY GAZE, BABY.
YOU SHOULD ASK BUBBLES OUT. SHE'S THE ONE YOU REALLY WANT.
SEE YOU AROUND.

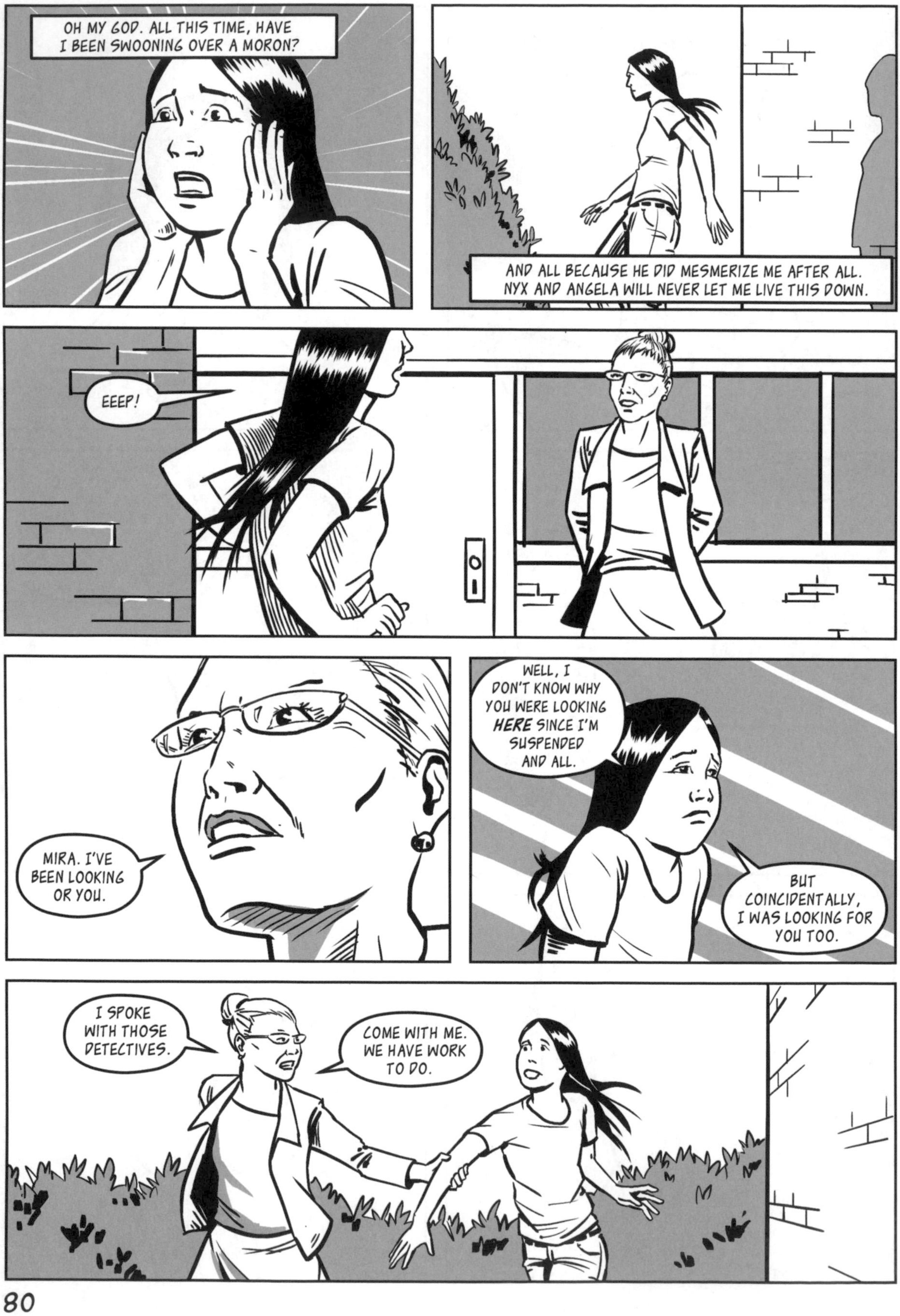
OH MY GOD. ALL THIS TIME, HAVE I BEEN SWOONING OVER A MORON?
AND ALL BECAUSE HE DID MESMERIZE ME AFTER ALL. NYX AND ANGELA WILL NEVER LET ME LIVE THIS DOWN.
EEEP!
MIRA. I'VE BEEN LOOKING OR YOU.
WELL, I DON'T KNOW WHY YOU WERE LOOKING **HERE** SINCE I'M SUSPENDED AND ALL.
BUT COINCIDENTALLY, I WAS LOOKING FOR YOU TOO.
I SPOKE WITH THOSE DETECTIVES.
COME WITH ME. WE HAVE WORK TO DO.

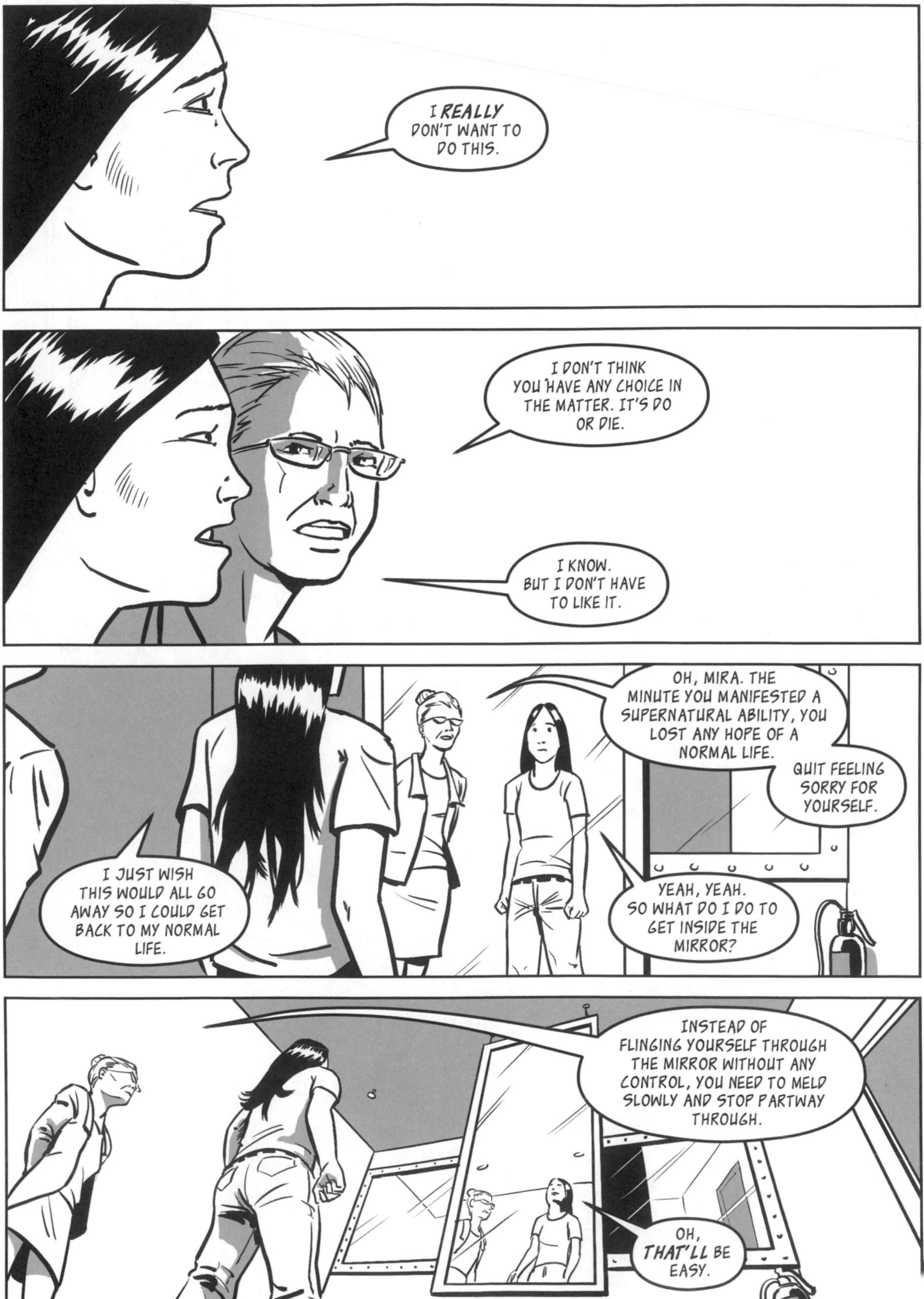
I REALLY DON'T WANT TO DO THIS.
I DON'T THINK YOU HAVE ANY CHOICE IN THE MATTER. IT'S DO OR DIE.
I KNOW. BUT I DON'T HAVE TO LIKE IT.
I JUST WISH THIS WOULD ALL GO AWAY SO I COULD GET BACK TO MY NORMAL LIFE.
OH, MIRA. THE MINUTE YOU MANIFESTED A SUPERNATURAL ABILITY, YOU LOST ANY HOPE OF A NORMAL LIFE.
QUIT FEELING SORRY FOR YOURSELF.
YEAH, YEAH. SO WHAT DO I DO TO GET INSIDE THE MIRROR?
INSTEAD OF FLINGING YOURSELF THROUGH THE MIRROR WITHOUT ANY CONTROL, YOU NEED TO MELD SLOWLY AND STOP PARTWAY THROUGH.
OH, THAT'LL BE EASY.

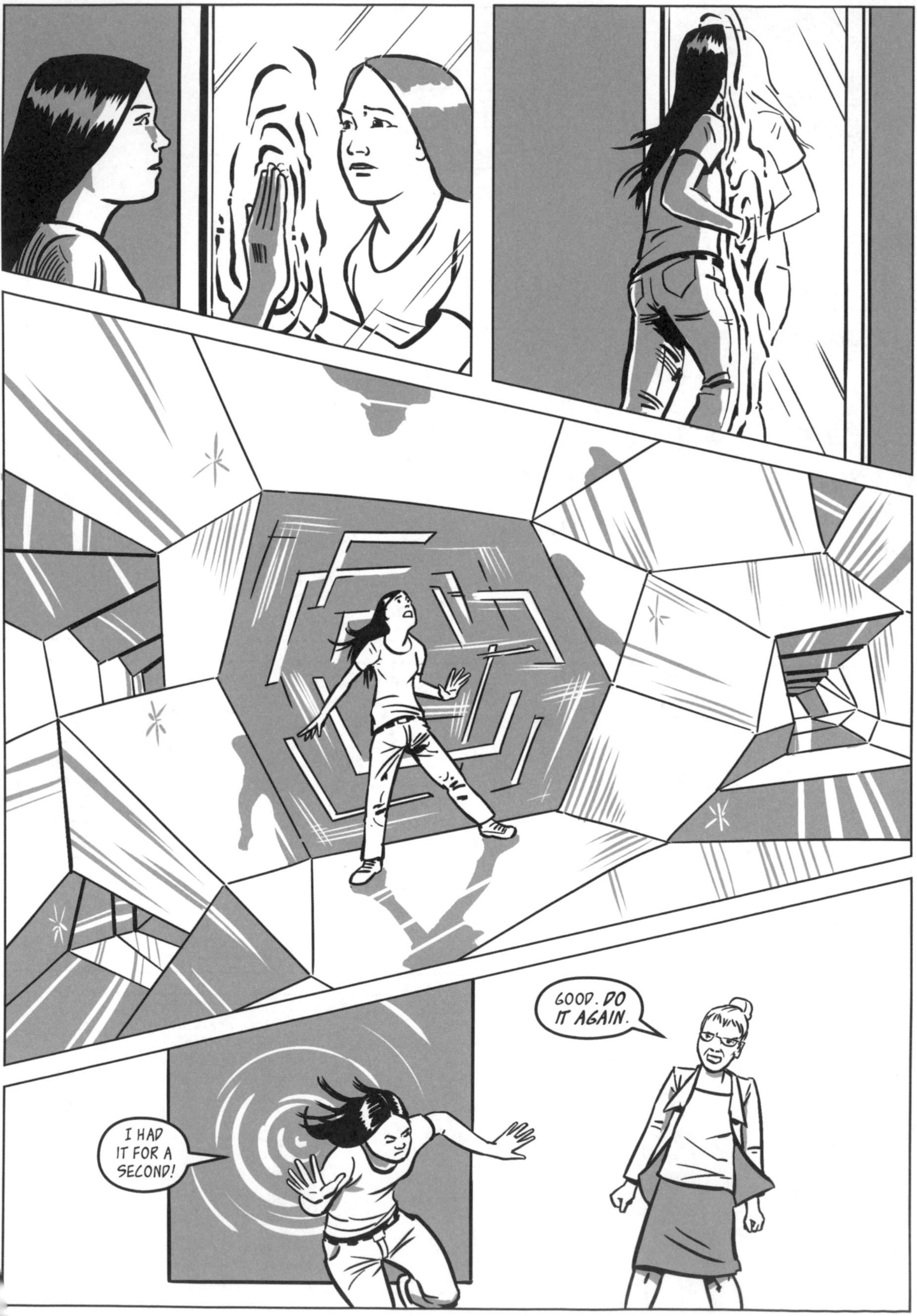
GOOD. DO IT AGAIN.
I HAD IT FOR A SECOND!

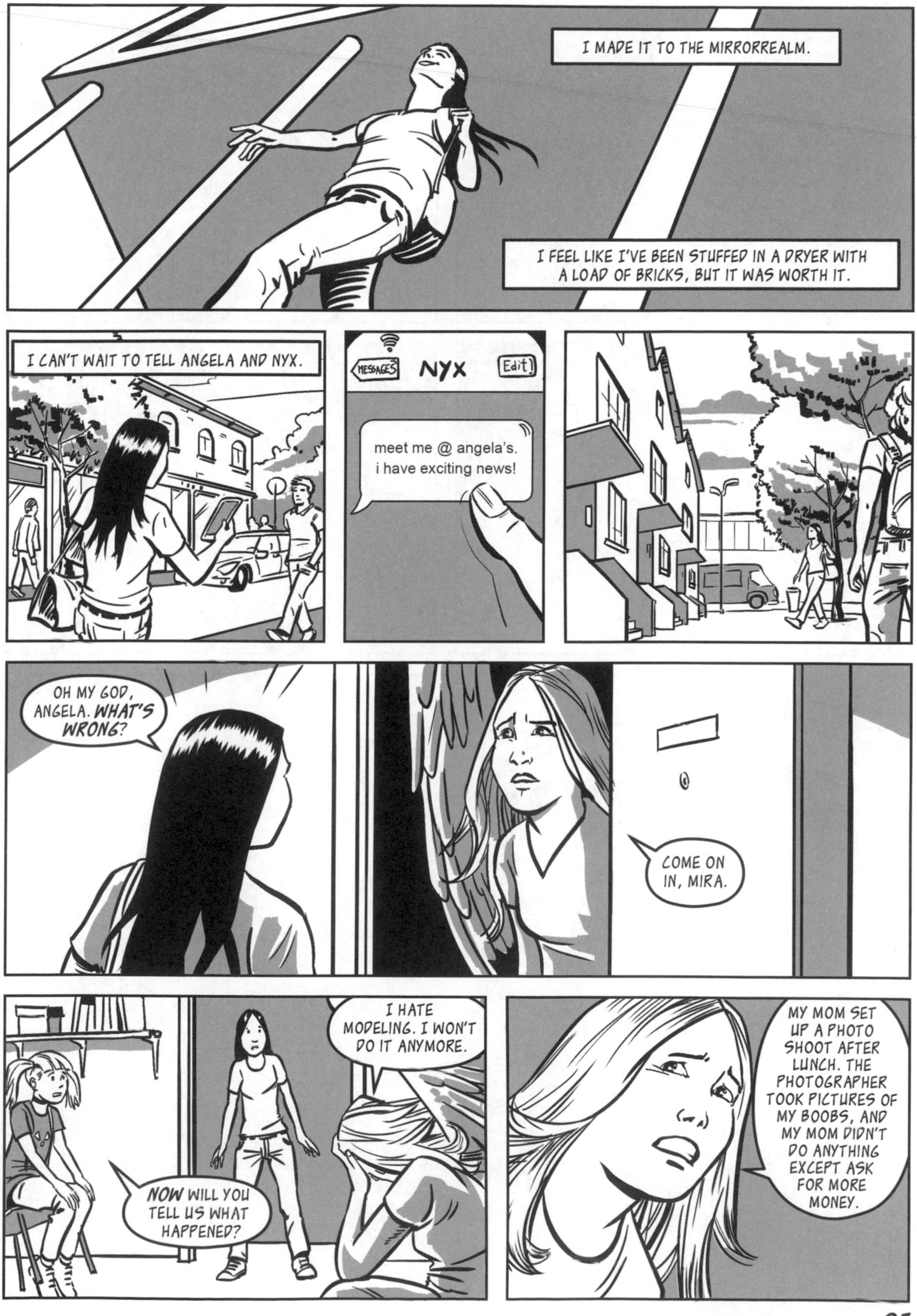
I MADE IT TO THE MIRRORREALM.
I FEEL LIKE I'VE BEEN STUFFED IN A DRYER WITH A LOAD OF BRICKS, BUT IT WAS WORTH IT.
I CAN'T WAIT TO TELL ANGELA AND NYX.
MESSAGES
NYX
Edit
meet me @ angela's. i have exciting news!
OH MY GOD, ANGELA. WHAT'S WRONG?
COME ON IN, MIRA.
I HATE MODELING. I WON'T DO IT ANYMORE.
NOW WILL YOU TELL US WHAT HAPPENED?
MY MOM SET UP A PHOTO SHOOT AFTER LUNCH. THE PHOTOGRAPHER TOOK PICTURES OF MY BOOBS, AND MY MOM DIDN'T DO ANYTHING EXCEPT ASK FOR MORE MONEY.

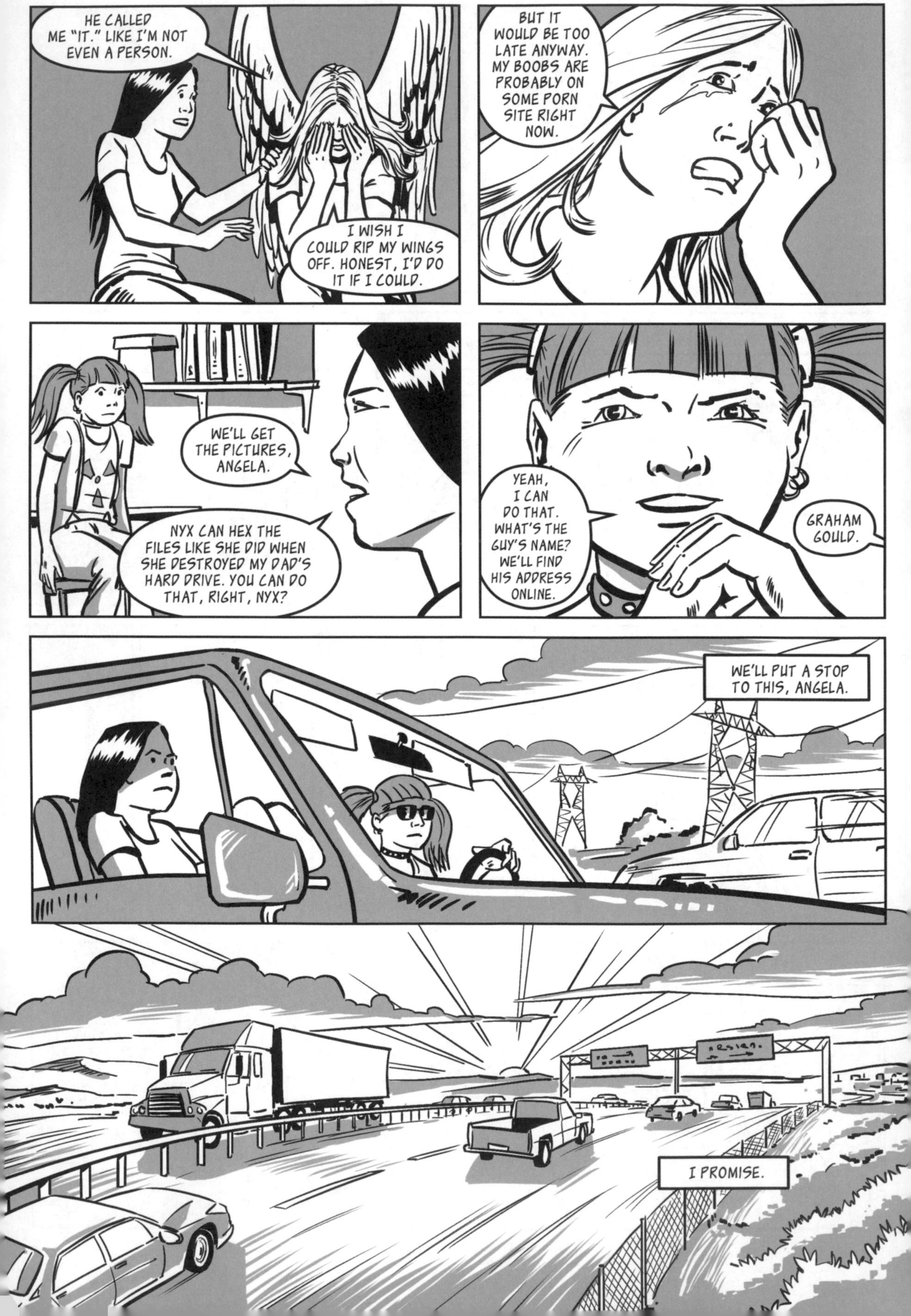
HE CALLED ME "IT." LIKE I'M NOT EVEN A PERSON.
I WISH I COULD RIP MY WINGS OFF. HONEST, I'D DO IT IF I COULD.
BUT IT WOULD BE TOO LATE ANYWAY. MY BOOBS ARE PROBABLY ON SOME PORN SITE RIGHT NOW.
WE'LL GET THE PICTURES, ANGELA.
NYX CAN HEX THE FILES LIKE SHE DID WHEN SHE DESTROYED MY DAD'S HARD DRIVE. YOU CAN DO THAT, RIGHT, NYX?
YEAH, I CAN DO THAT. WHAT'S THE GUY'S NAME? WE'LL FIND HIS ADDRESS ONLINE.
GRAHAM GOULD.
WE'LL PUT A STOP TO THIS, ANGELA.
I PROMISE.

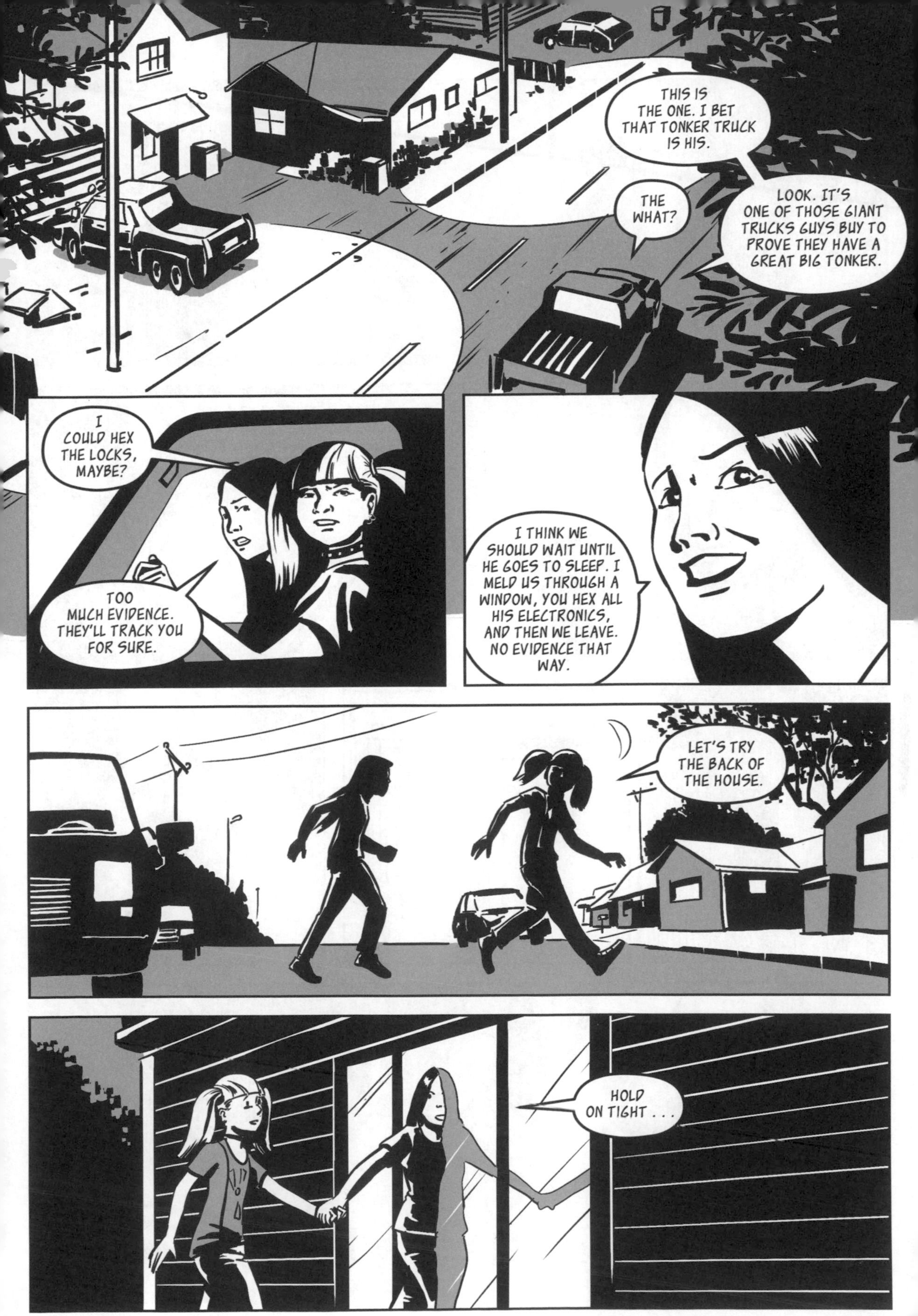
THIS IS THE ONE. I BET THAT TONKER TRUCK IS HIS.
THE WHAT?
LOOK. IT'S ONE OF THOSE GIANT TRUCKS GUYS BUY TO PROVE THEY HAVE A GREAT BIG TONKER.
I COULD HEX THE LOCKS, MAYBE?
TOO MUCH EVIDENCE. THEY'LL TRACK YOU FOR SURE.
I THINK WE SHOULD WAIT UNTIL HE GOES TO SLEEP. I MELD US THROUGH A WINDOW, YOU HEX ALL HIS ELECTRONICS, AND THEN WE LEAVE. NO EVIDENCE THAT WAY.
LET'S TRY THE BACK OF THE HOUSE.
HOLD ON TIGHT . . .

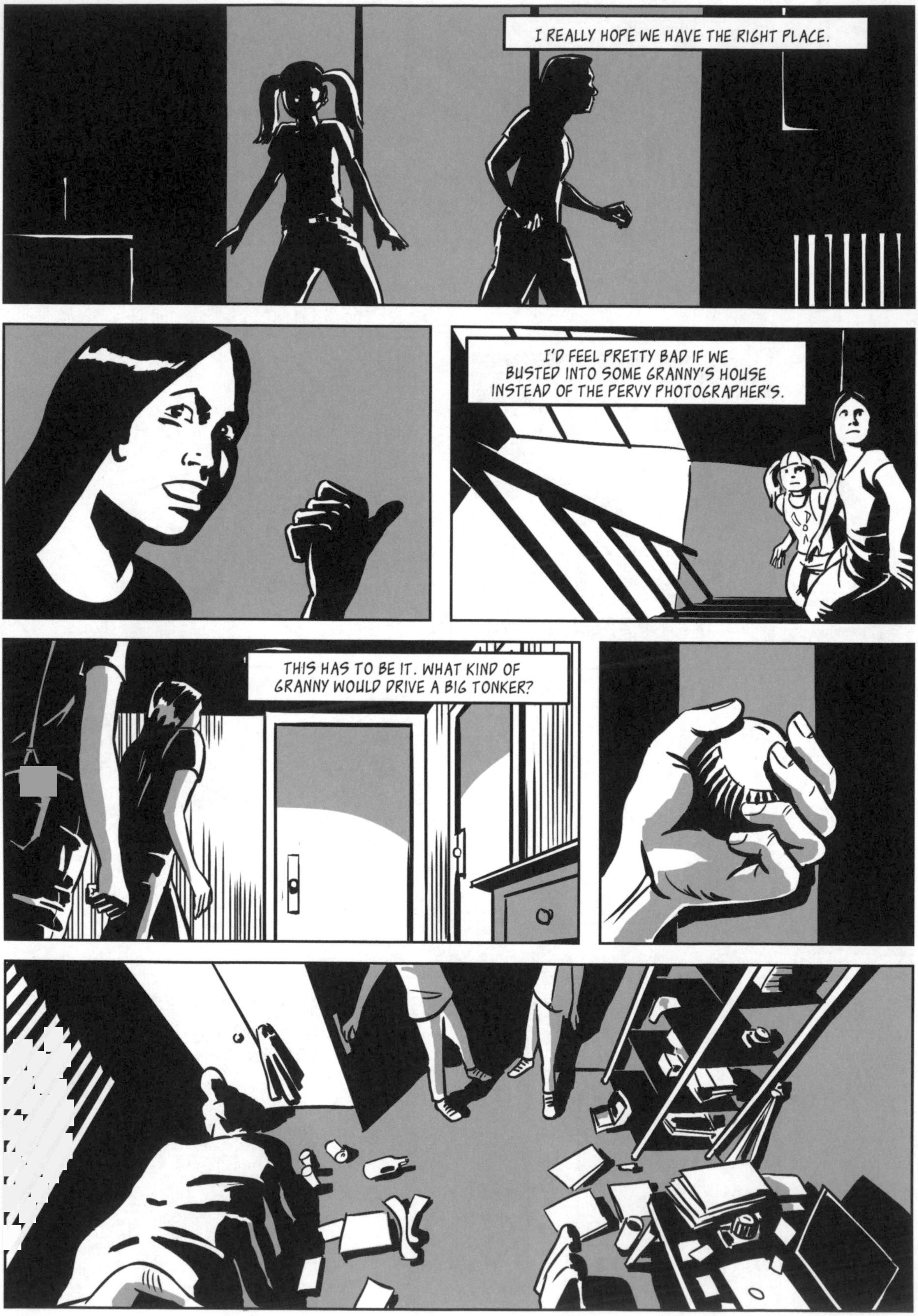
I REALLY HOPE WE HAVE THE RIGHT PLACE.
I'D FEEL PRETTY BAD IF WE BUSTED INTO SOME GRANNY'S HOUSE INSTEAD OF THE PERVY PHOTOGRAPHER'S.
THIS HAS TO BE IT. WHAT KIND OF GRANNY WOULD DRIVE A BIG TONKER?

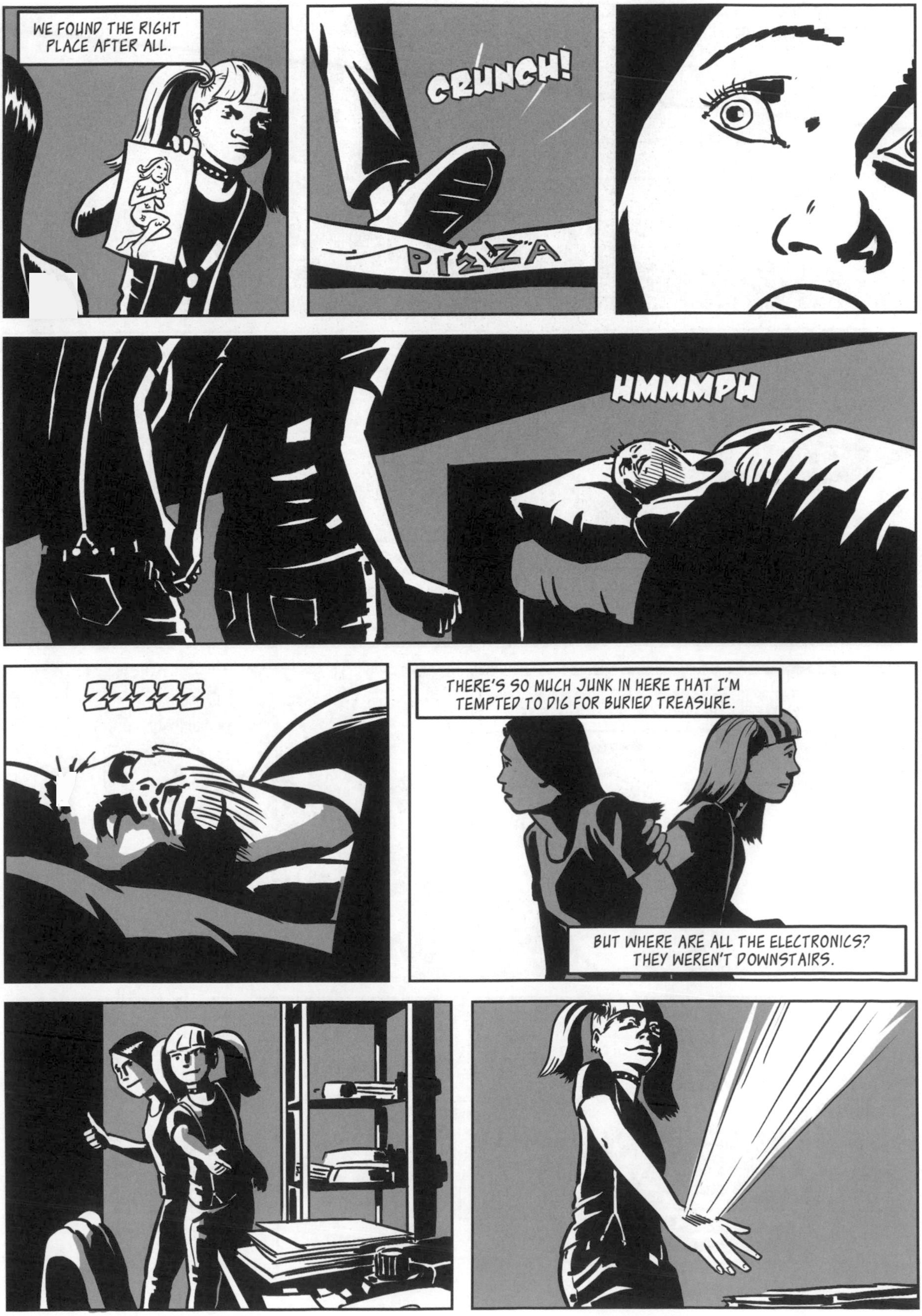
WE FOUND THE RIGHT PLACE AFTER ALL.
CRUNCH!
PIZZA
HMMMPH
ZZZZZ
THERE'S SO MUCH JUNK IN HERE THAT I'M TEMPTED TO DIG FOR BURIED TREASURE.
BUT WHERE ARE ALL THE ELECTRONICS? THEY WEREN'T DOWNSTAIRS.

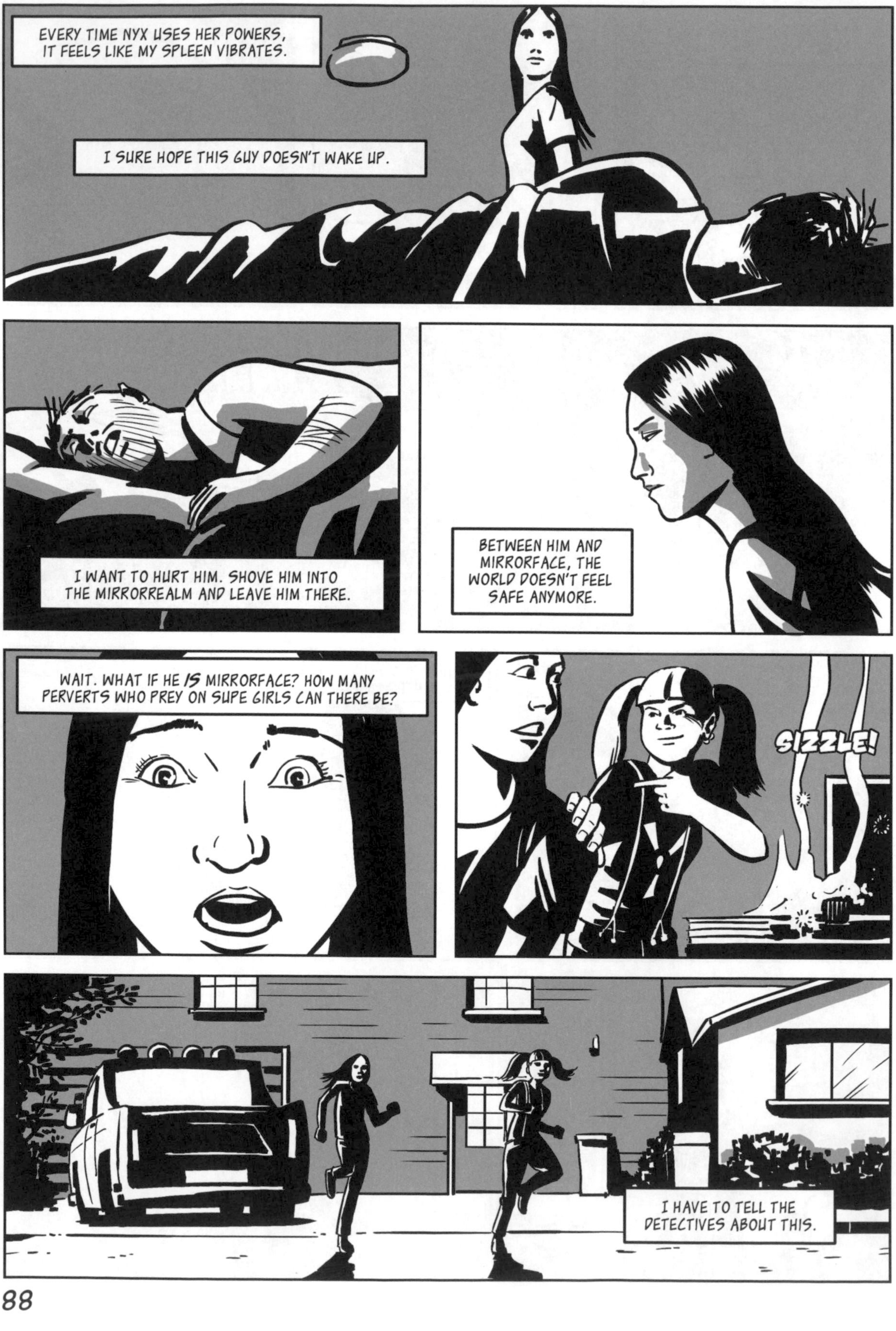
EVERY TIME NYX USES HER POWERS, IT FEELS LIKE MY SPLEEN VIBRATES.
I SURE HOPE THIS GUY DOESN'T WAKE UP.
I WANT TO HURT HIM. SHOVE HIM INTO THE MIRRORREALM AND LEAVE HIM THERE.
BETWEEN HIM AND MIRRORFACE, THE WORLD DOESN'T FEEL SAFE ANYMORE.
WAIT. WHAT IF HE *IS* MIRRORFACE? HOW MANY PERVERTS WHO PREY ON SUPE GIRLS CAN THERE BE?
SIZZLE!
I HAVE TO TELL THE DETECTIVES ABOUT THIS.

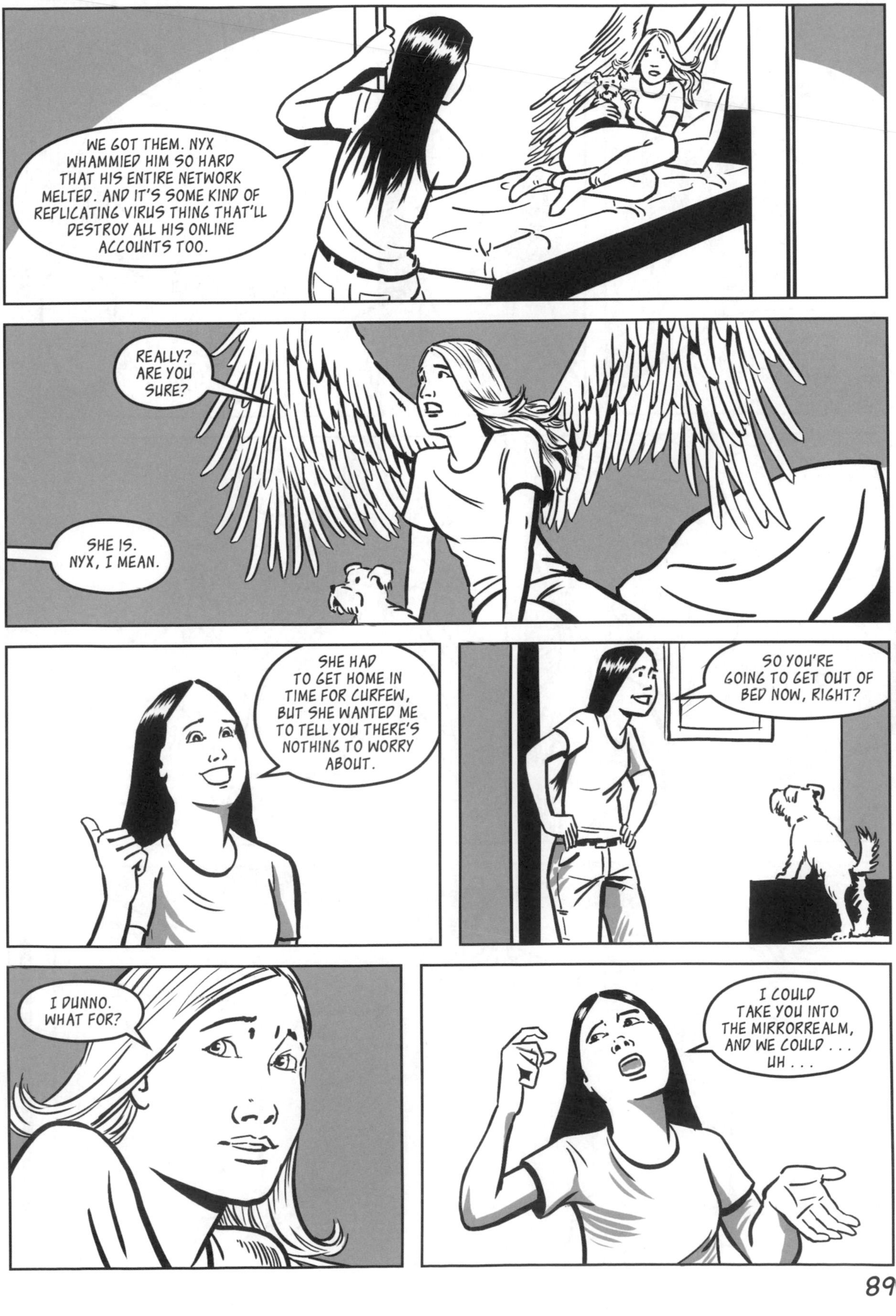
WE GOT THEM. NYX WHAMMIED HIM SO HARD THAT HIS ENTIRE NETWORK MELTED. AND IT'S SOME KIND OF REPLICATING VIRUS THING THAT'LL DESTROY ALL HIS ONLINE ACCOUNTS TOO.
REALLY? ARE YOU SURE?
SHE IS. NYX, I MEAN.
SHE HAD TO GET HOME IN TIME FOR CURFEW, BUT SHE WANTED ME TO TELL YOU THERE'S NOTHING TO WORRY ABOUT.
SO YOU'RE GOING TO GET OUT OF BED NOW, RIGHT?
I DUNNO. WHAT FOR?
I COULD TAKE YOU INTO THE MIRRORREALM, AND WE COULD . . . UH . . .

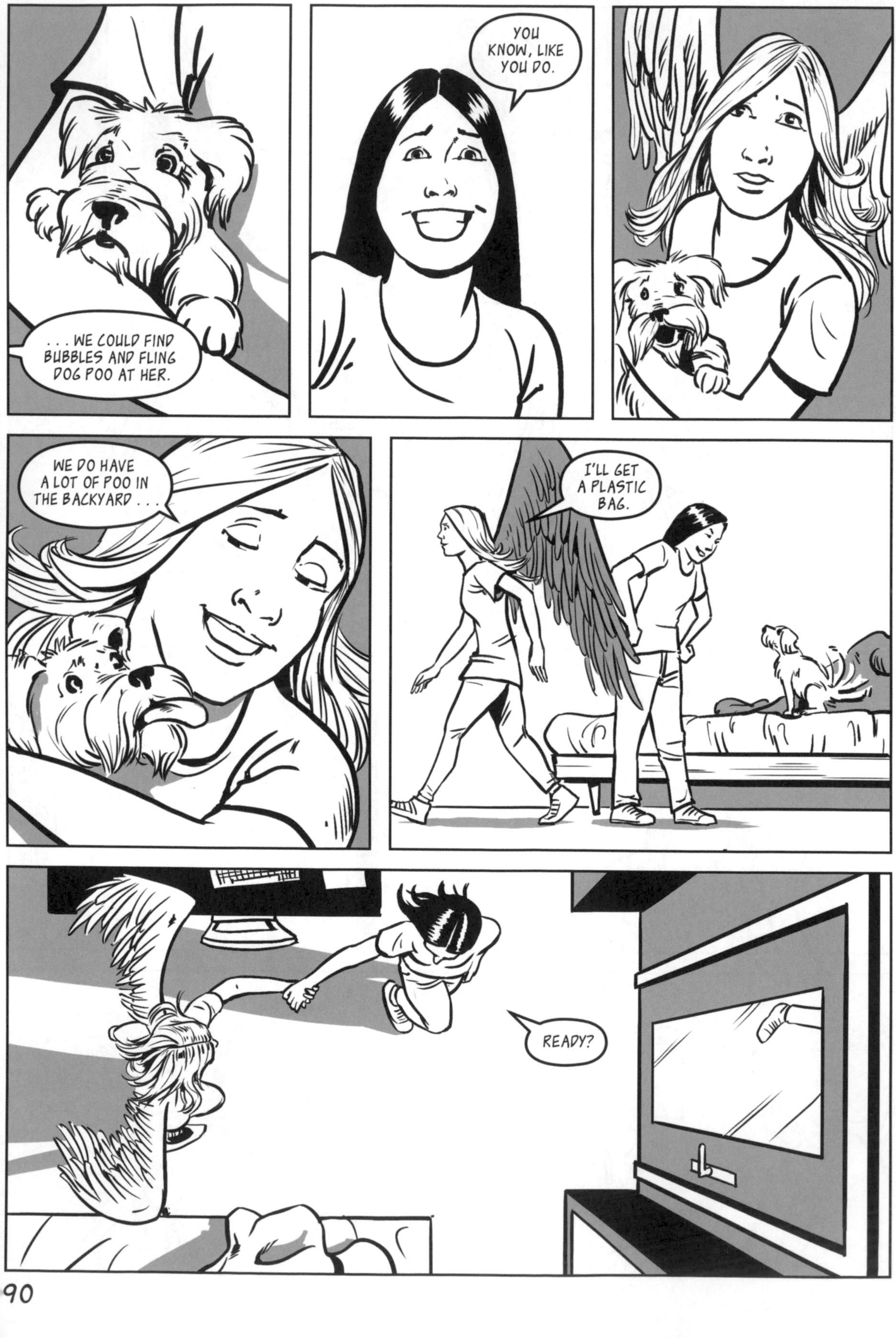
. . . WE COULD FIND BUBBLES AND FLING DOG POO AT HER.
YOU KNOW, LIKE YOU DO.
WE DO HAVE A LOT OF POO IN THE BACKYARD . . .
I'LL GET A PLASTIC BAG.
READY?

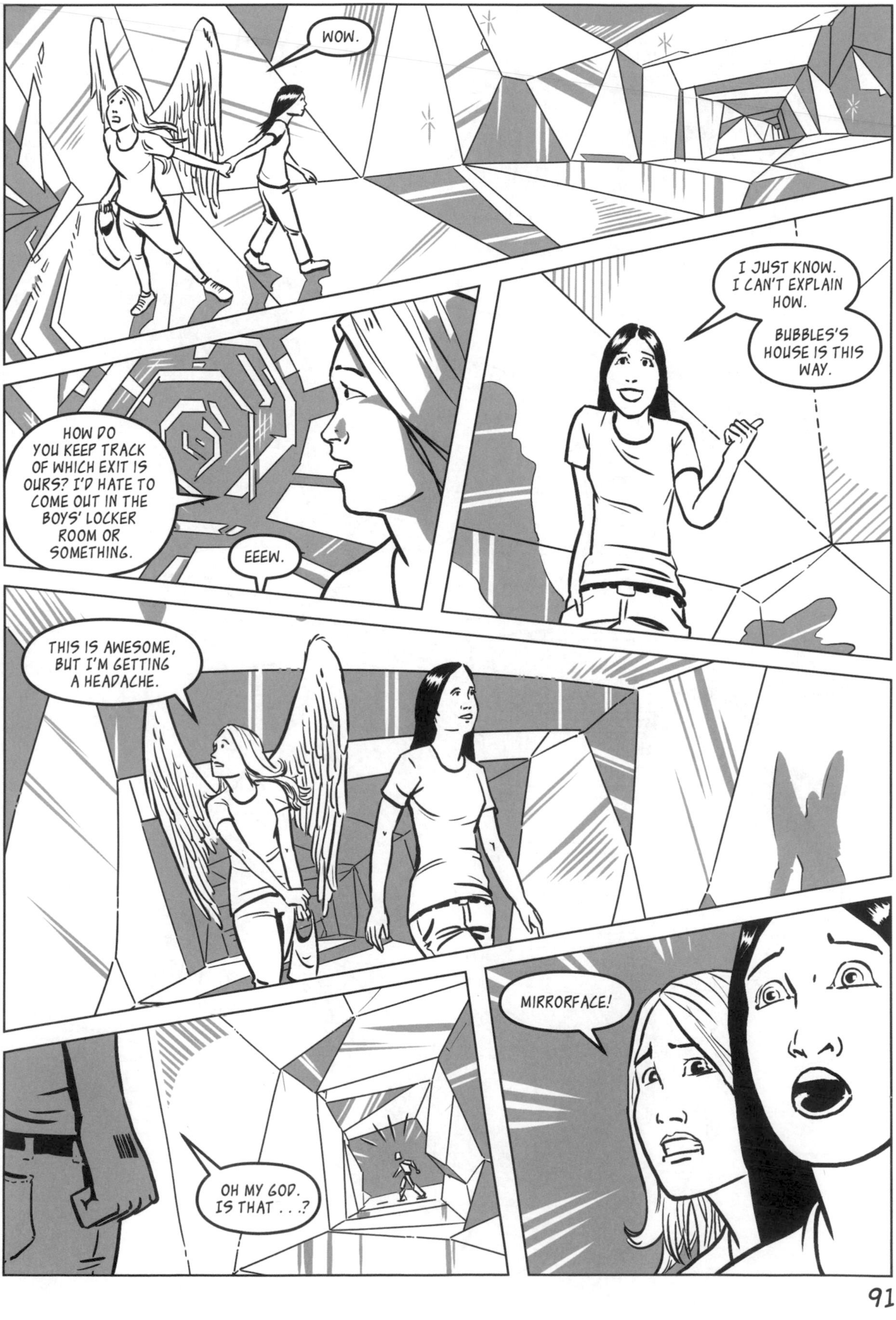
WOW.
HOW DO YOU KEEP TRACK OF WHICH EXIT IS OURS? I'D HATE TO COME OUT IN THE BOYS' LOCKER ROOM OR SOMETHING.
EEEW.
I JUST KNOW. I CAN'T EXPLAIN HOW.
BUBBLES'S HOUSE IS THIS WAY.
THIS IS AWESOME, BUT I'M GETTING A HEADACHE.
OH MY GOD. IS THAT . . .?
MIRRORFACE!

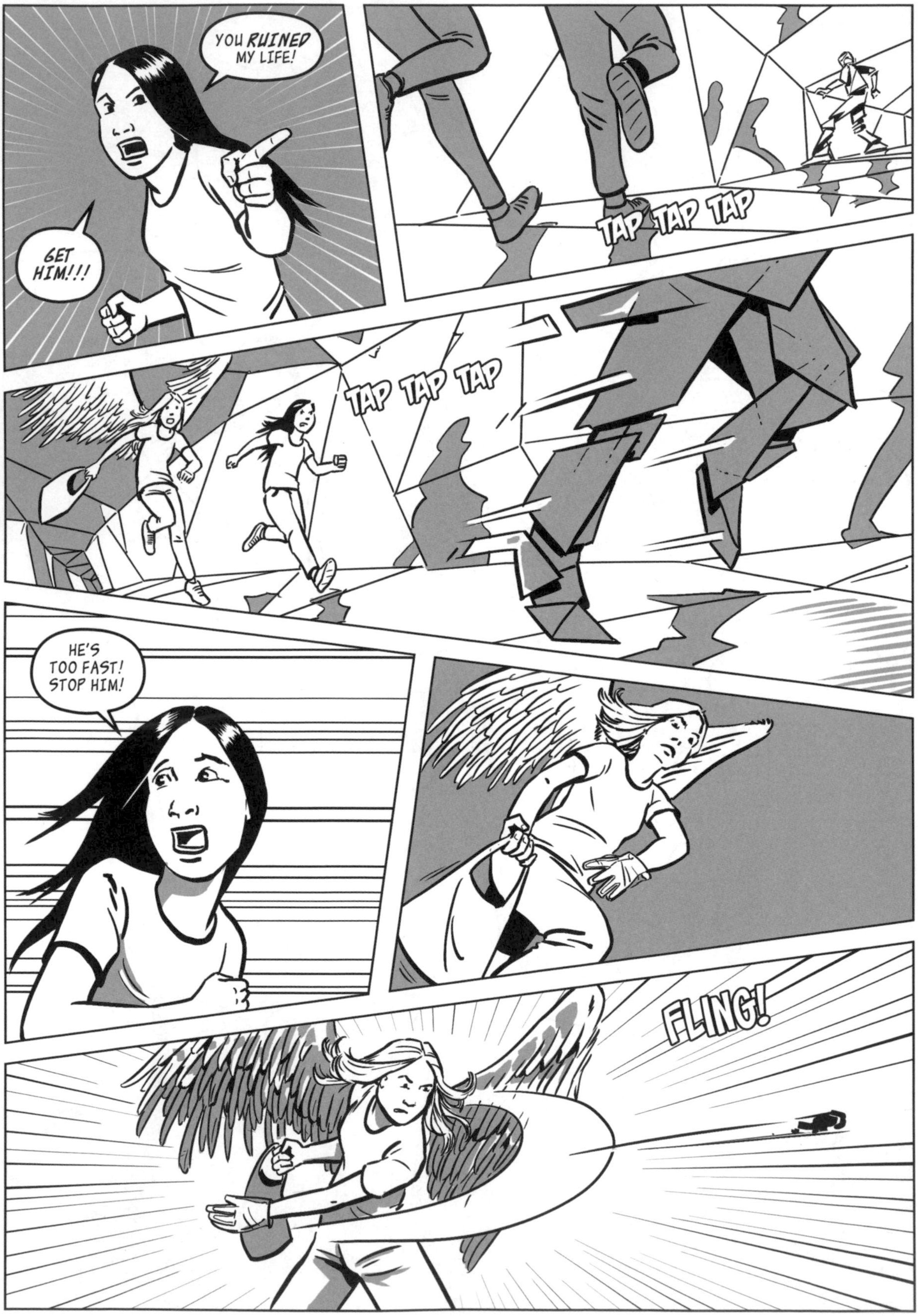
YOU RUINED MY LIFE!
GET HIM!!!
TAP TAP TAP
TAP TAP TAP
HE'S TOO FAST! STOP HIM!
FLING!

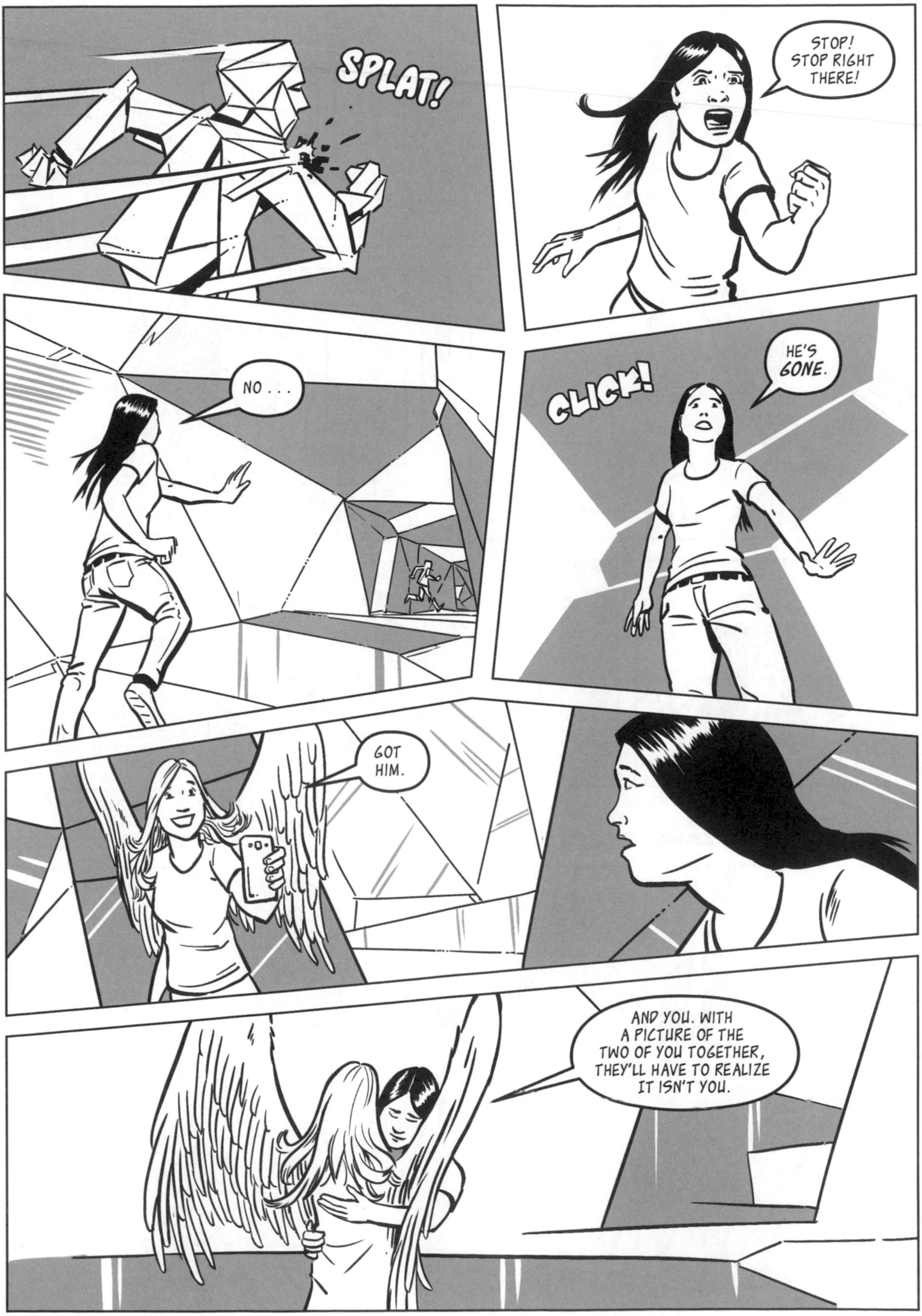
SPLAT!
STOP! STOP RIGHT THERE!
NO . . .
CLICK!
HE'S GONE.
GOT HIM.
AND YOU. WITH A PICTURE OF THE TWO OF YOU TOGETHER, THEY'LL HAVE TO REALIZE IT ISN'T YOU.

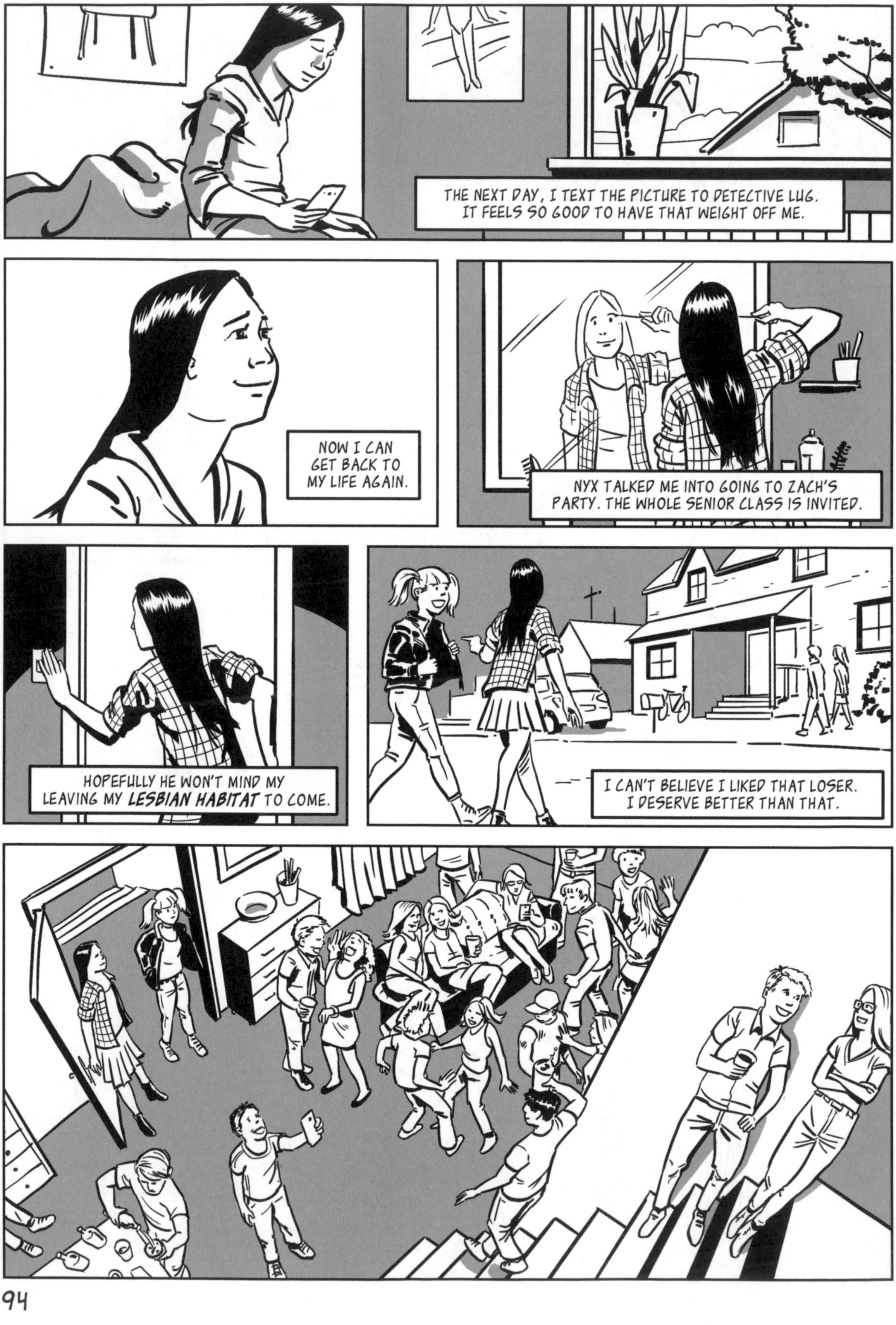
THE NEXT DAY, I TEXT THE PICTURE TO DETECTIVE LUG. IT FEELS SO GOOD TO HAVE THAT WEIGHT OFF ME.
NOW I CAN GET BACK TO MY LIFE AGAIN.
NYX TALKED ME INTO GOING TO ZACH'S PARTY. THE WHOLE SENIOR CLASS IS INVITED.
HOPEFULLY HE WON'T MIND MY LEAVING MY ***LESBIAN HABITAT*** TO COME.
I CAN'T BELIEVE I LIKED THAT LOSER. I DESERVE BETTER THAN THAT.

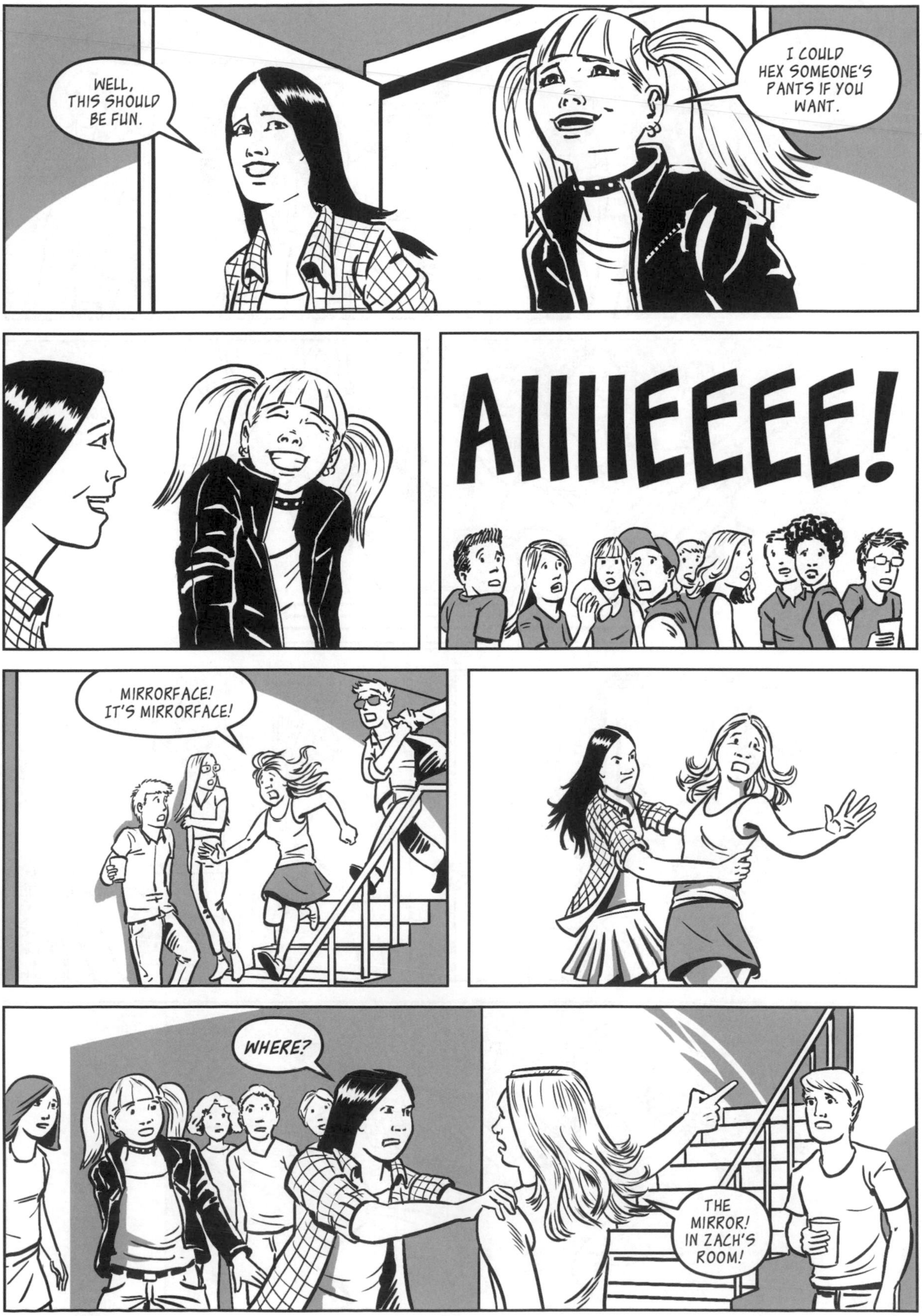
WELL, THIS SHOULD BE FUN.
I COULD HEX SOMEONE'S PANTS IF YOU WANT.
AIIIEEEE!
MIRRORFACE! IT'S MIRRORFACE!
WHERE?
THE MIRROR! IN ZACH'S ROOM!

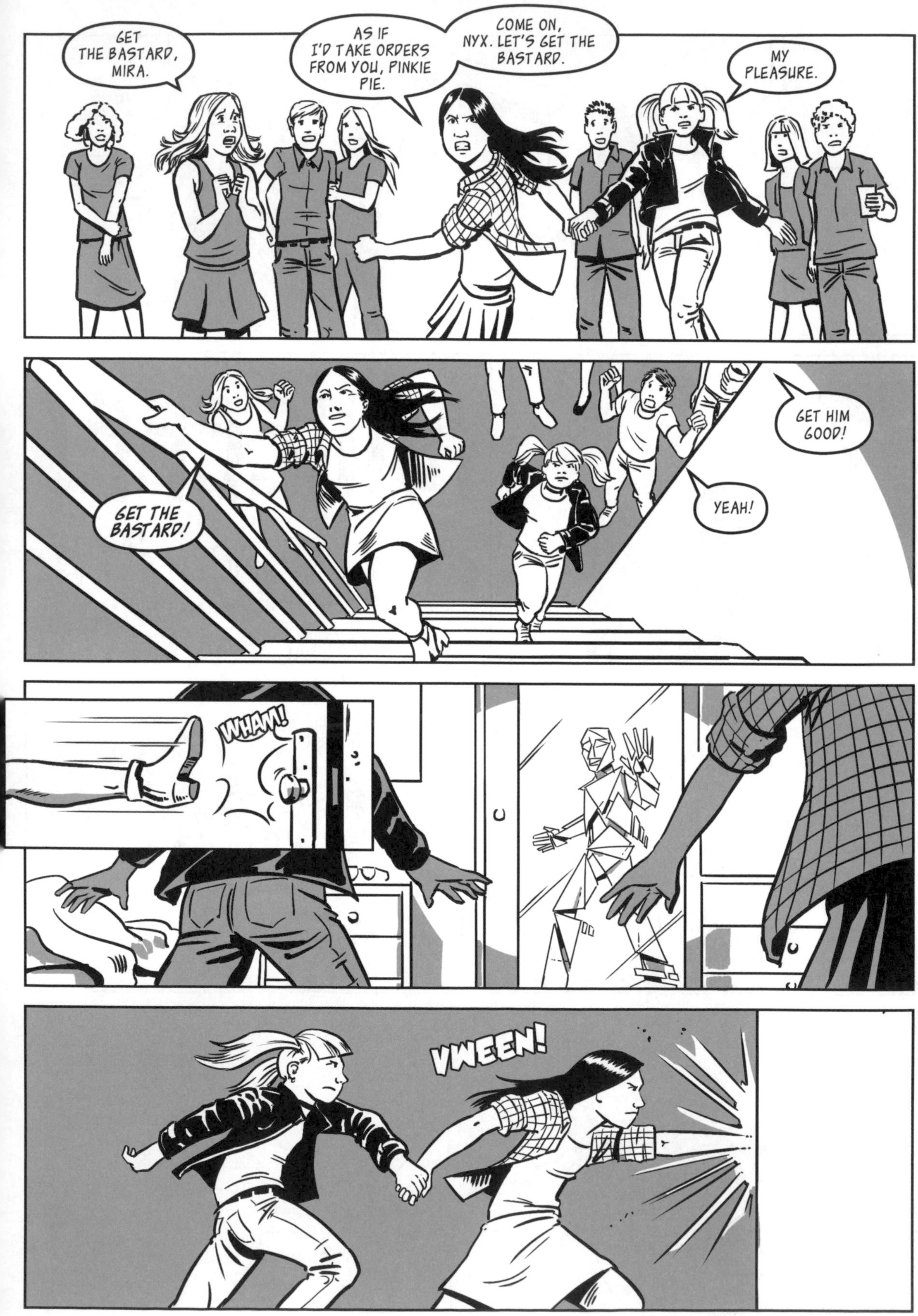
GET THE BASTARD, MIRA.
AS IF I'D TAKE ORDERS FROM YOU, PINKIE PIE.
COME ON, NYX. LET'S GET THE BASTARD.
MY PLEASURE.
GET THE BASTARD!
GET HIM GOOD!
YEAH!
WHAM!
VWEEN!

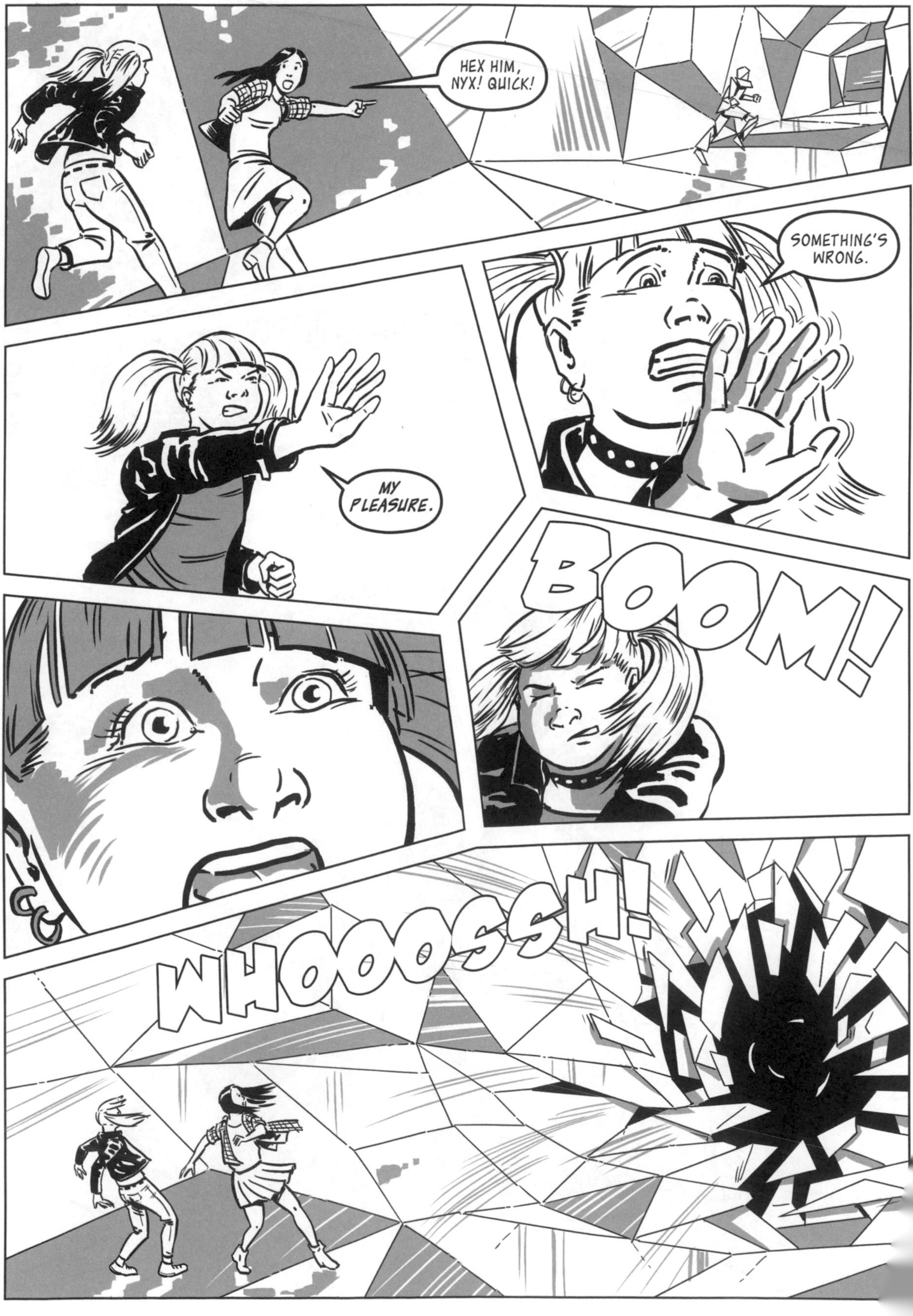
HEX HIM, NYX! QUICK!
SOMETHING'S WRONG.
MY PLEASURE.
BOOM!
WHOOOOSSH!

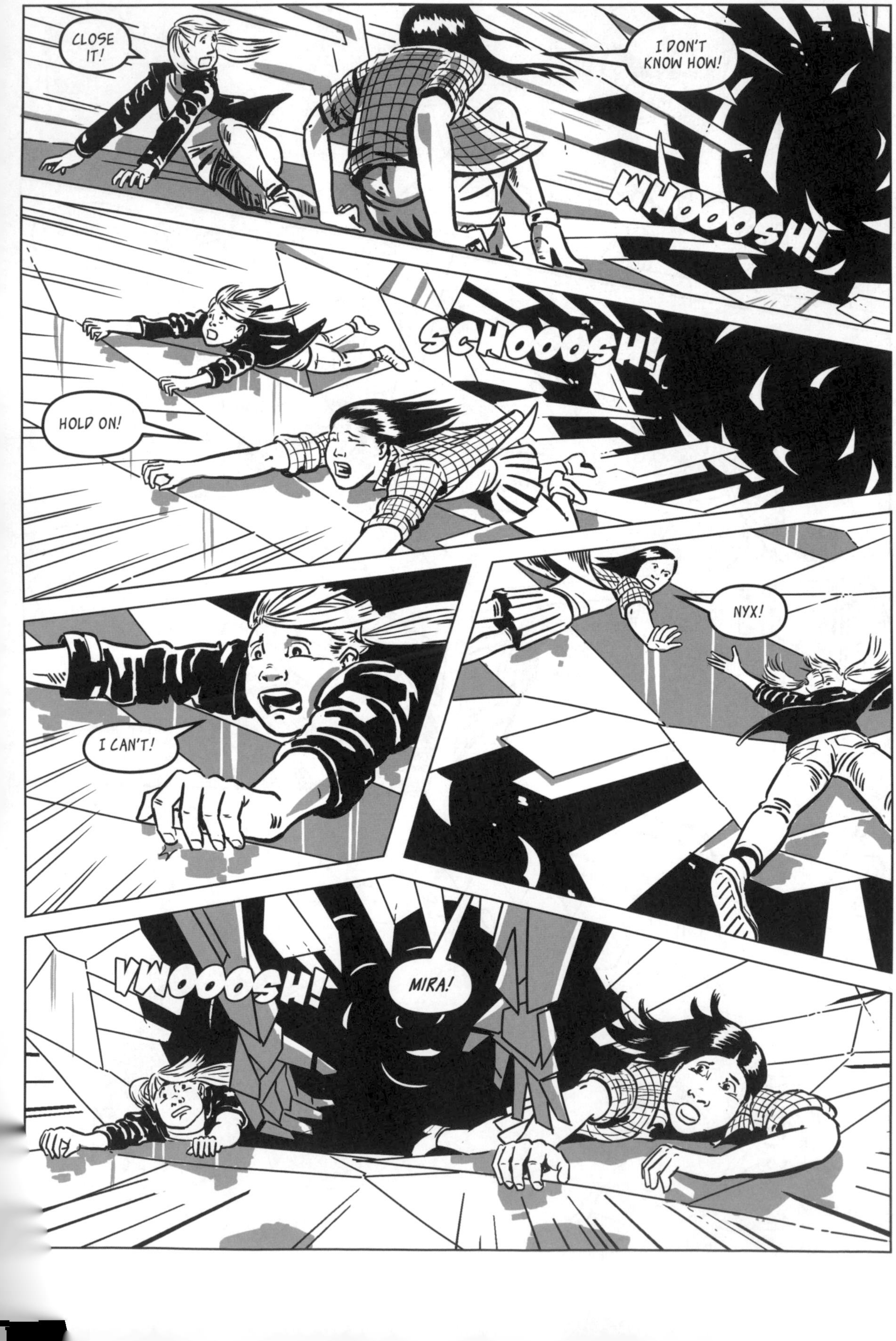
CLOSE IT!
I DON'T KNOW HOW!
WHOOOOSH!
SCHOOOOSH!
HOLD ON!
I CAN'T!
NYX!
VWOOOSH!
MIRA!

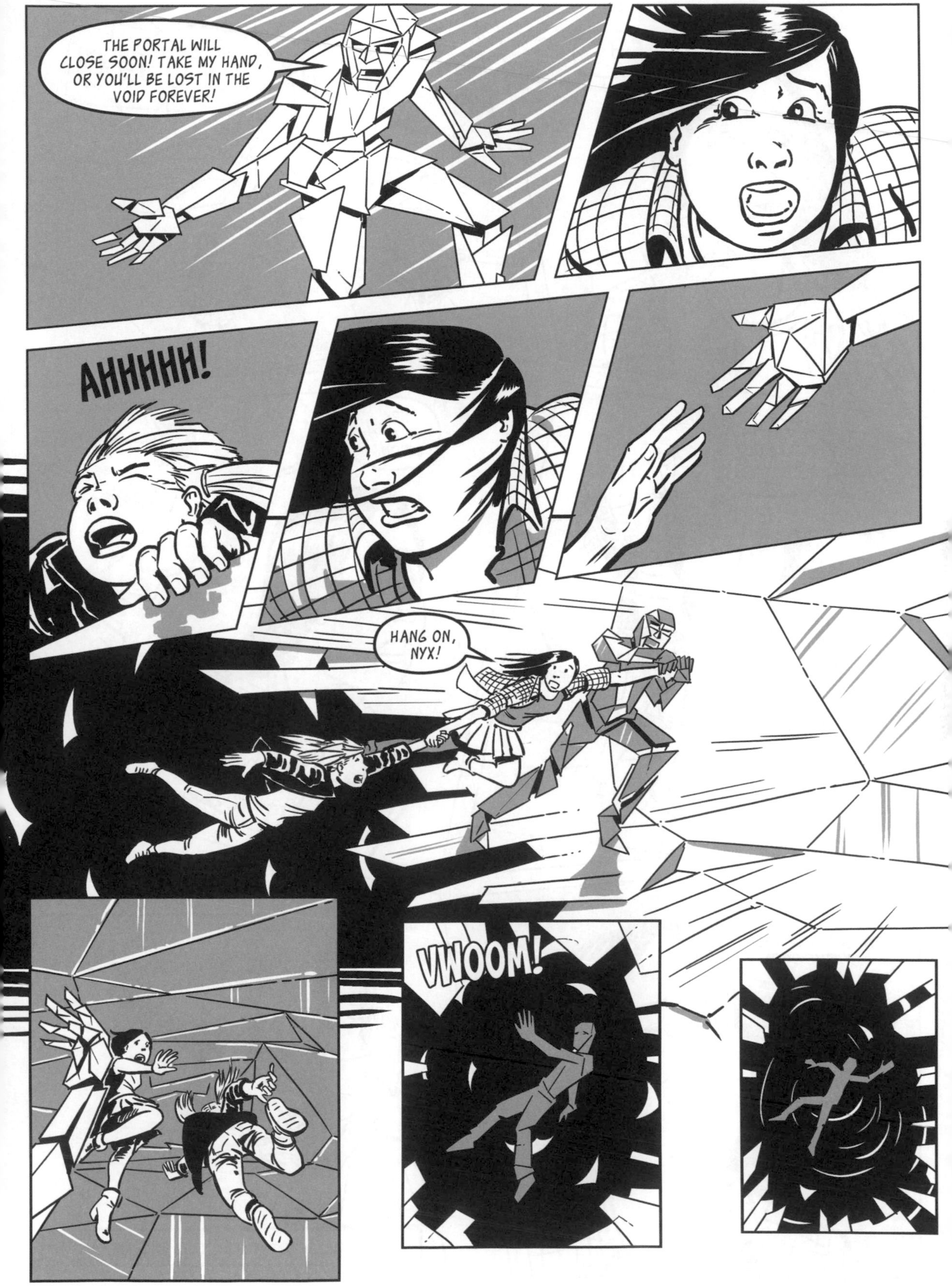
THE PORTAL WILL CLOSE SOON! TAKE MY HAND, OR YOU'LL BE LOST IN THE VOID FOREVER!
AHHHHH!
HANG ON, NYX!
VWOOM!

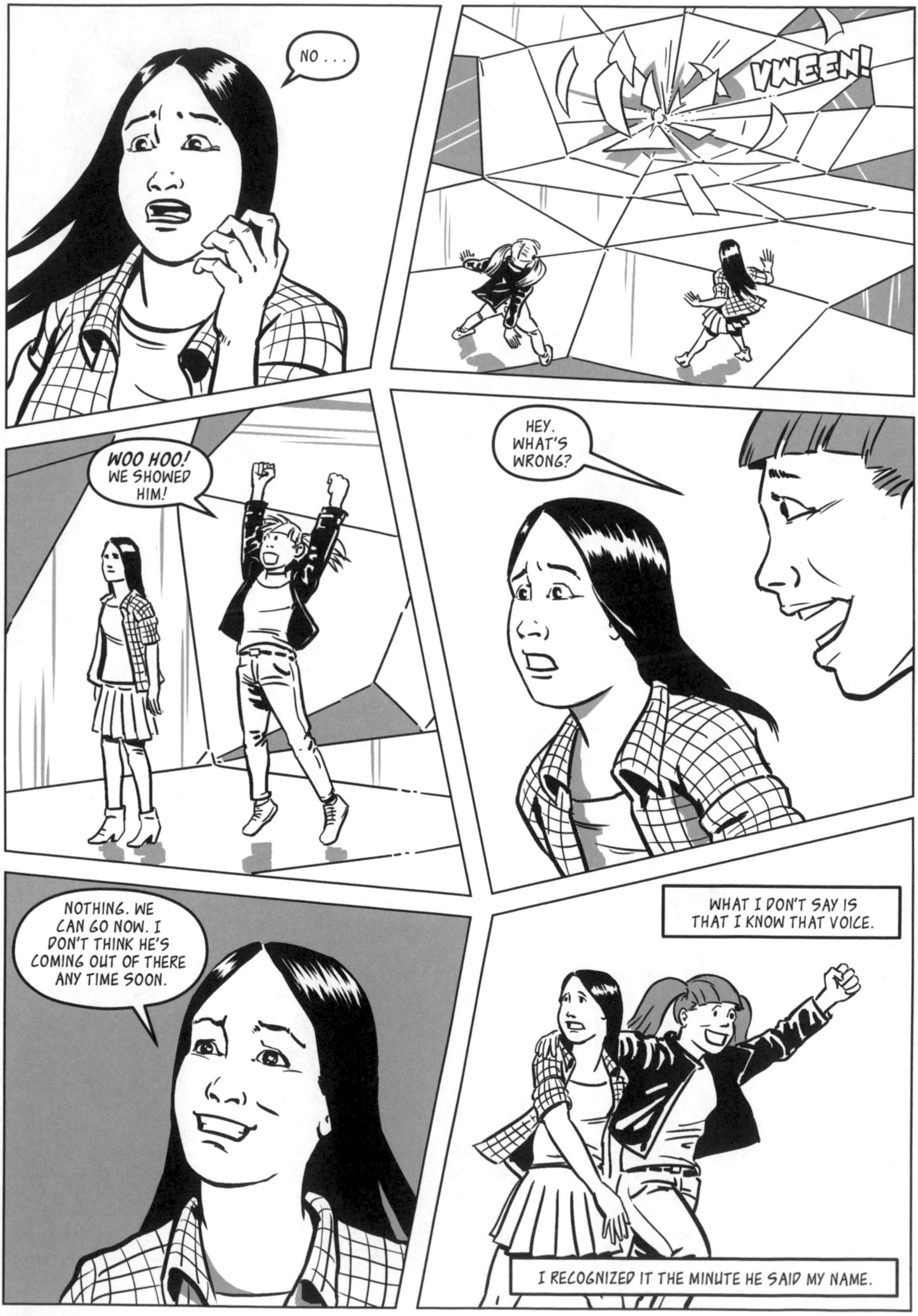
NO . . .
VWEEN!
WOO HOO! WE SHOWED HIM!
HEY. WHAT'S WRONG?
NOTHING. WE CAN GO NOW. I DON'T THINK HE'S COMING OUT OF THERE ANY TIME SOON.
WHAT I DON'T SAY IS THAT I KNOW THAT VOICE.
I RECOGNIZED IT THE MINUTE HE SAID MY NAME.

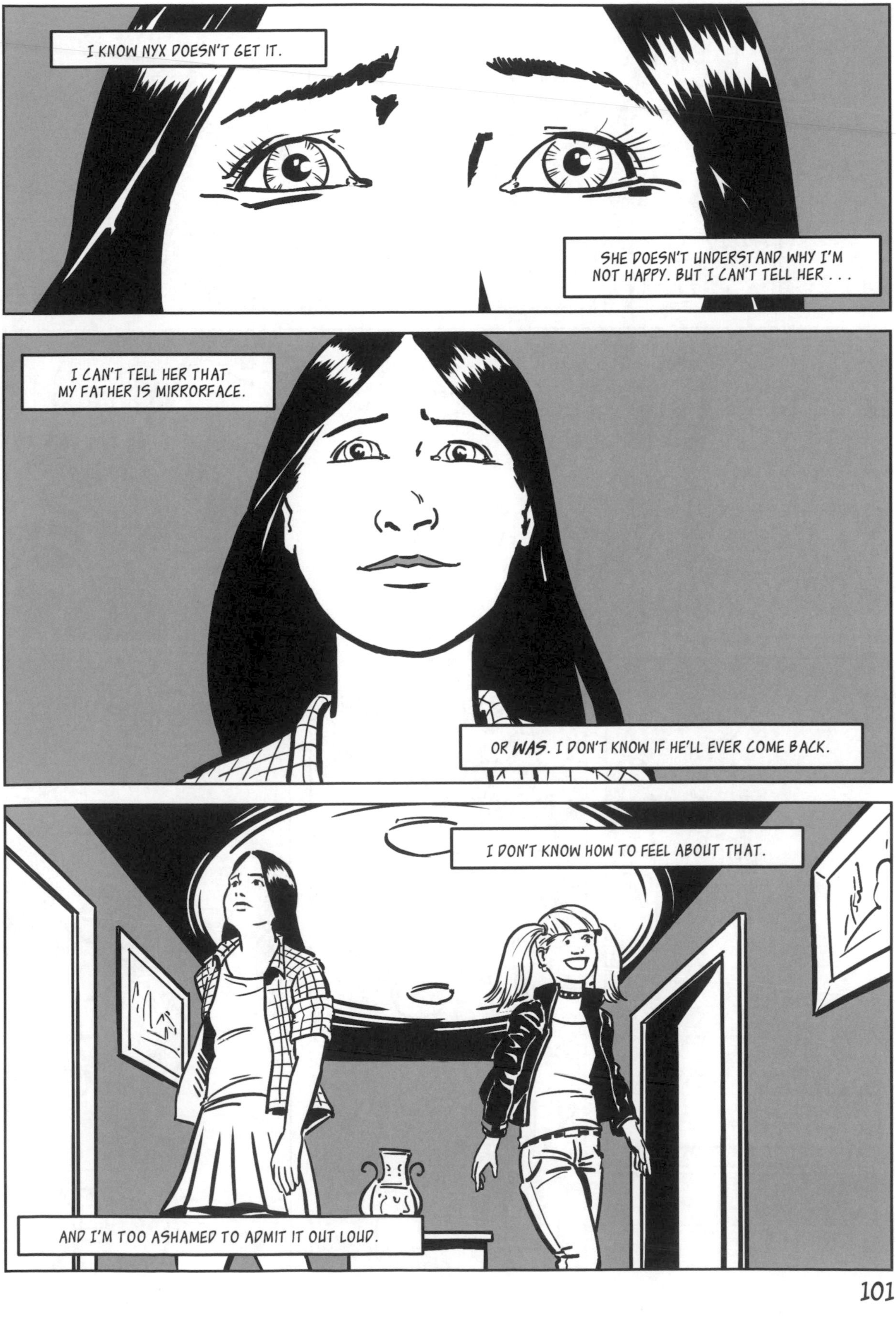
I KNOW NYX DOESN'T GET IT.
SHE DOESN'T UNDERSTAND WHY I'M NOT HAPPY. BUT I CAN'T TELL HER . . .
I CAN'T TELL HER THAT MY FATHER IS MIRRORFACE.
OR **WAS**. I DON'T KNOW IF HE'LL EVER COME BACK.
I DON'T KNOW HOW TO FEEL ABOUT THAT.
AND I'M TOO ASHAMED TO ADMIT IT OUT LOUD.

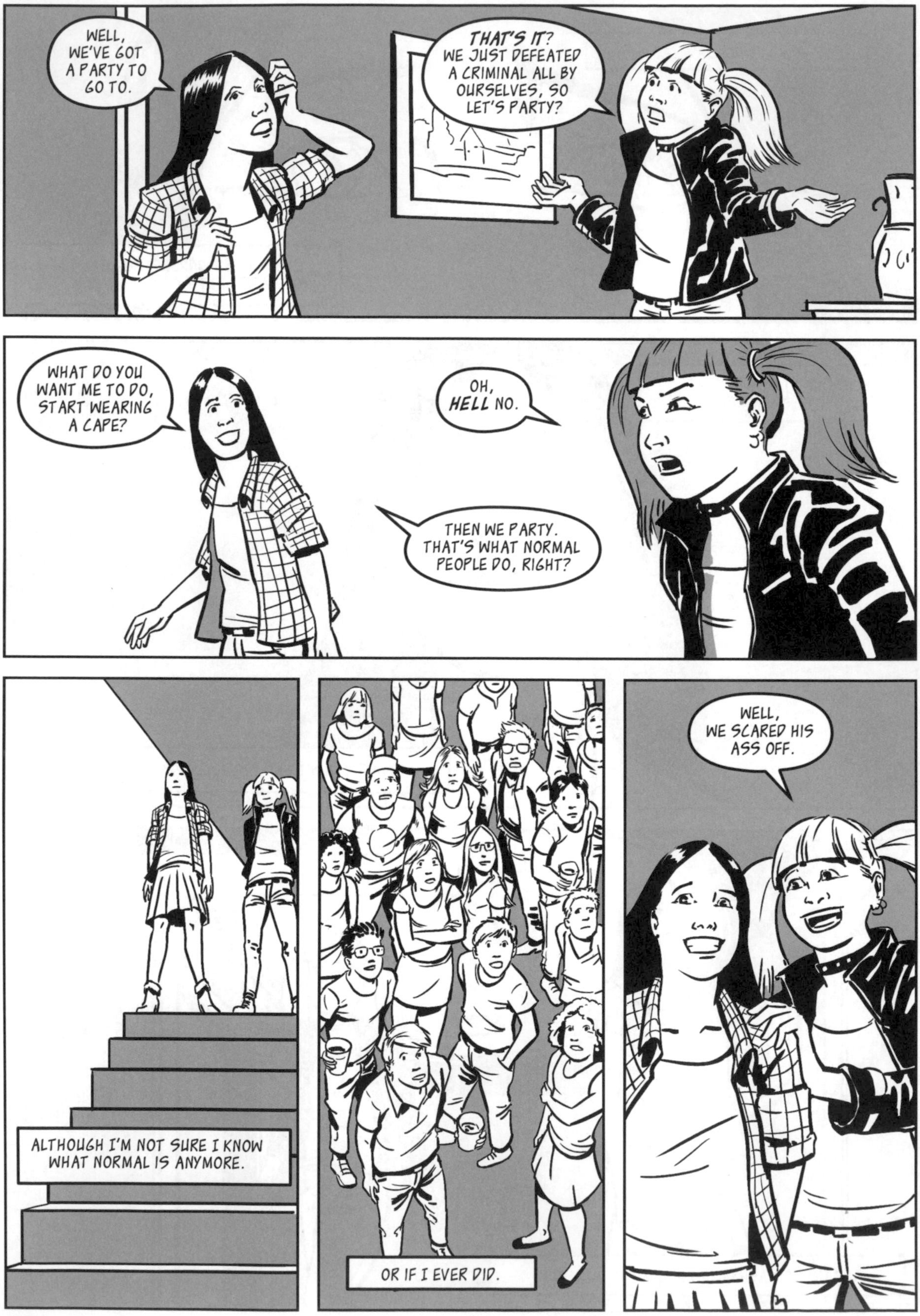
WELL, WE'VE GOT A PARTY TO GO TO.
THAT'S IT? WE JUST DEFEATED A CRIMINAL ALL BY OURSELVES, SO LET'S PARTY?
WHAT DO YOU WANT ME TO DO, START WEARING A CAPE?
OH, HELL NO.
THEN WE PARTY. THAT'S WHAT NORMAL PEOPLE DO, RIGHT?
ALTHOUGH I'M NOT SURE I KNOW WHAT NORMAL IS ANYMORE.
OR IF I EVER DID.
WELL, WE SCARED HIS ASS OFF.

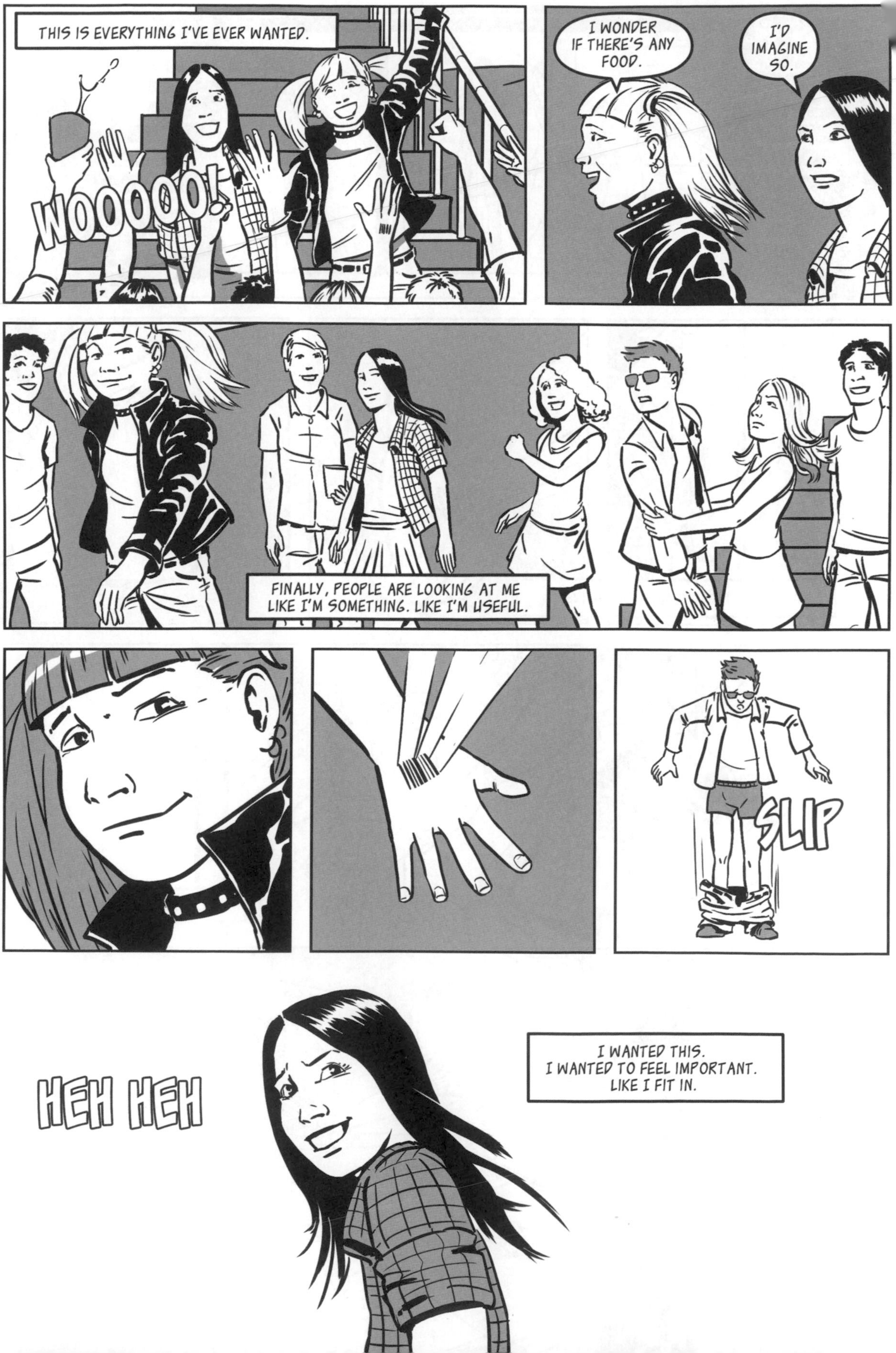
THIS IS EVERYTHING I'VE EVER WANTED.
WOOOOO!
I WONDER IF THERE'S ANY FOOD.
I'D IMAGINE SO.
FINALLY, PEOPLE ARE LOOKING AT ME LIKE I'M SOMETHING. LIKE I'M USEFUL.
SLIP
HEH HEH
I WANTED THIS.
I WANTED TO FEEL IMPORTANT.
LIKE I FIT IN.

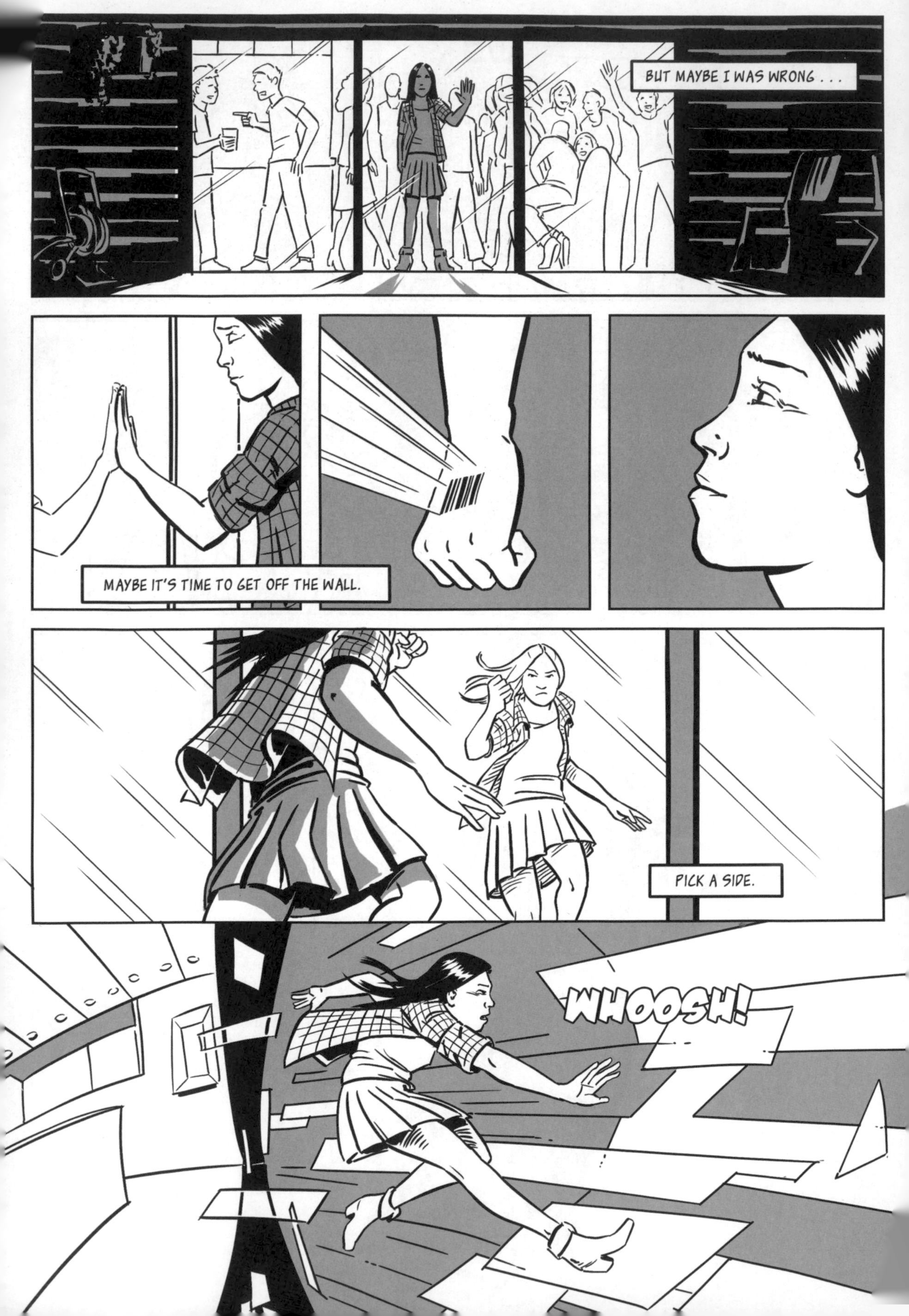
BUT MAYBE I WAS WRONG . . .
MAYBE IT'S TIME TO GET OFF THE WALL.
PICK A SIDE.
WHOOSH!